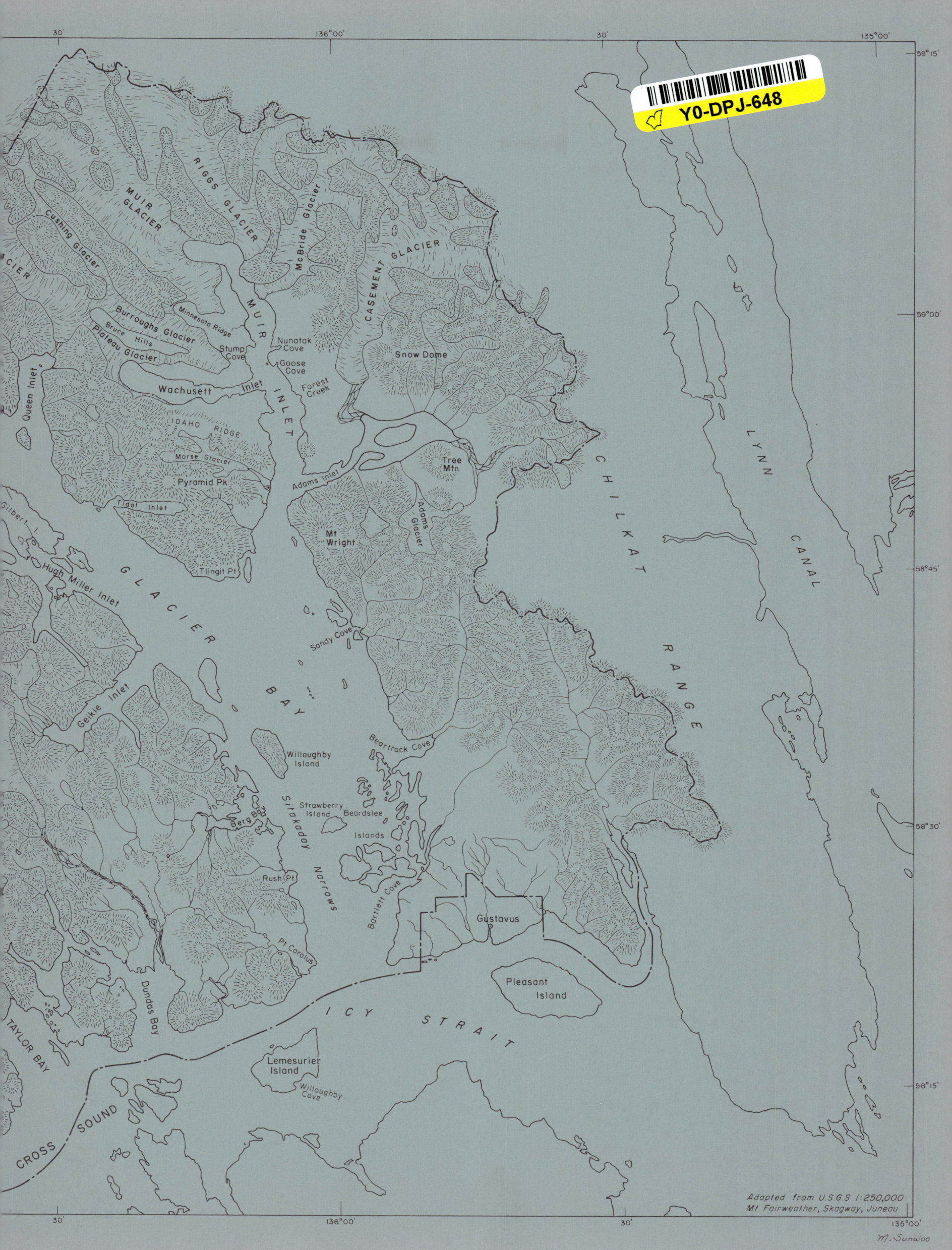

SIERRA CLUB EXHIBIT FORMAT SERIES

Winner of the Carey-Thomas Award in 1964
  for the best achievement in creative publishing in the United States

EDITED BY DAVID BROWER

1. *This Is the American Earth,* by Ansel Adams and Nancy Newhall
2. *Words of the Earth,* by Cedric Wright
3. *These We Inherit: The Parklands of America,* by Ansel Adams
4. *"In Wildness Is the Preservation of the World,"* by Eliot Porter
5. *The Place No One Knew: Glen Canyon on the Colorado,* by Eliot Porter
6. *The Last Redwoods: Photographs and Story of a Vanishing Scenic Resource,* by Philip Hyde and François Leydet
7. *Ansel Adams: A Biography. Volume I: The Eloquent Light,* by Nancy Newhall
8. *Time and the River Flowing: Grand Canyon,* by François Leydet
9. *Gentle Wilderness: The Sierra Nevada,* text from John Muir, photographs by Richard Kauffman
10. *Not Man Apart: Photographs of the Big Sur Coast,* with lines from Robinson Jeffers
11. *The Wild Cascades: Forgotten Parkland,* by Harvey Manning. with lines from Theodore Roethke
12. *Everest: The West Ridge,* by Thomas F. Hornbein, with photographs from the American Mount Everest Expedition
13. *Summer Island: Penobscot Country,* by Eliot Porter
14. *Navajo Wildlands: As Long as the Rivers Shall Run,* by Philip Hyde
15. *Kauai and the Park Country of Hawaii,* by Robert Wenkam Edited by Kenneth Brower
16. *Glacier Bay: The Land and the Silence,* by Dave Bohn

The end paper map is contributed by
Moonok Sunwoo, field companion of 1965.

The termini-positions map on page 109 is contributed by
the American Geographical Society of New York, with special
acknowledgment to William O. Field for surveying
efforts in Glacier Bay spanning forty years.

Wm R Patterson

GLACIER BAY

But the sound lingers on when one has heard. Down the centuries the booming primeval thunder.

Reid Glacier. 1965

No significant preserving of nature can be done with slight sacrifice. The true test will come when great sacrifices are needed, when it becomes necessary to fight the indifference of most of the world and the active opposition of much of it, to surmount man's ingrained determination to put the far future out of his mind in matters of current profit.

Besides the inherent technical difficulties of wilderness conservation, the effort to save original nature faces a whole constellation of other kinds of problems. The easiest obstacle to recognize is the opposition by people who oppose the keeping of wilderness for material reasons. These people would shape the world into an ant hill; they are clearly mad. It is unthinkable that they will much longer control the destiny of the race. There is another block of humanity that simply does not care; and an unsorted lot who think of themselves as conservationists, and who in one way or another are, but who are not facing the really tough obligation at all. I refer to all people who think of saving nature for meat, water, timber or picnic grounds for the future; and to the hunters who hope their grandsons will get red blood by shooting things, and to the reverence-for-life cultists who are foredoomed to inconsistency, and to the biologists who resist the loss of material for study, and to keepers of zoological gardens who preserve nature in cages. Putting this mixture of motives and aspirations together under the label conservation has made, in some cases, a temporarily stronger front. But it has muddied the real issue, hidden the dimensions of the long job and kept everybody from articulating the awful certainty that the hard saving has got to be done for the sake of abstract values.

Archie Carr

Below us was the great land. Indeed, all Glacier Bay is the great land, unique, wild, and magnificent. It should exist intact solely for its own sake. No justification, rationale, or excuse is needed. For its own sake and no other reason.

Mount Fairweather (left) from Lituya Bay. 1965. Cenotaph Island (center), and spur (right) stripped to 1740 feet by great wave of 1958.

Make no mistake about it, an enormous amount of personality was invested in that tiny plot of land in the wilderness...

Cabin group, Reid Inlet. 1966.
Watercolor by Carol Janda.

*Reid Glacier and Tarr Inlet
from peak 4710. 1965*

GLACIER BAY

The Land and the Silence

Photographs and Text by DAVE BOHN

Edited by DAVID BROWER

SIERRA CLUB · SAN FRANCISCO

The Sierra Club, founded in 1892 by John Muir, has devoted itself to the study and protection of national scenic resources, particularly those of mountain regions. All Sierra Club publications are part of the nonprofit effort the club carries on as a public trust. The club is affiliated with the International Union for Conservation, the Natural Resources Council of America, and the Federation of Western Outdoor Clubs. There are chapters in California, the Pacific Northwest, the Great Basin, the Southwest, the Great Lakes region, and on the Atlantic seaboard. Participation is invited in the program to enjoy and preserve wilderness, wildlife, forests, and streams. Main office: Mills Tower, San Francisco. Other offices: The Biltmore, New York; 705 Dupont Circle Building, Washington, D.C.; Auditorium Building, Los Angeles.

Acknowledgment is made to the following publishers: Houghton Mifflin Company, Boston, for permission to reprint material from John Muir's *Travels in Alaska* and W. F. Badè's *The Life and Letters of John Muir;* Time Inc., New York, for permission to reprint material from *The Reptiles*, by Archie Carr and The Editors of Life, copyright Time Inc., 1963; The Curtis Publishing Company, New York, for the editorial *Why Have Any Principles?*, reprinted with permission of *The Saturday Evening Post*, copyright 1936, The Curtis Publishing Company.

Publisher's Note: The book is set in Centaur and Arrighi by Mackenzie & Harris, Inc., San Francisco. It was printed on Warren's Cameo Brilliant Dull and Champion's Kromekote cast coated by H. S. Crocker Co., Inc., San Bruno. The black and white photographs are reproduced by double impression, two-color offset lithography, the color photographs by four-color process lithography. Offset plates, including color, were produced by H. S. Crocker Co., Inc., San Bruno. The book is double-spread collated and bound in Columbia Mills' Sampson linen by Russell-Rutter Co., Inc., New York City. The design is by David Brower. Layout is by Dave Bohn.

PUBLICATIONS COMMITTEE 1966-1967

AUGUST FRUGÉ, *Chairman*, CHARLES B. HUESTIS, MARTIN LITTON
GEORGE MARSHALL (*ex officio, President of the Club*)
WILLIAM E. SIRI, CLIFFORD J. RUDDEN, *Controller*
DAVID BROWER, *Executive Director*, HUGH NASH, *Secretary*

Copyright 1967 by the Sierra Club, Library of Congress Catalog Card No. 67-20028
Manufactured in the United States of America

*To my mother and father
who put up with me then
and Diana
who puts up with me now*

Baby seal, Johns Hopkins Inlet. 1966

Preface

EVERY NOW and then a man steps onto a landscape and stubs his toe, violently, on the wonder of it all. Not all people can share such wonder or will want to. But Dave Bohn fortunately wanted to and could, and has brought back alive the awesome landscape that Glacier Bay National Monument is. His is an extraordinary one-man show, in which the photographer also selects the cast and directs the play. He has mastered the history and brought on stage the men and women whose imaginations were stimulated by elemental ruggedness: Tchirikov—two hundred forty years ago—and Lapérouse and Vancouver, Muir and Burroughs and Scidmore, Huscroft and the Ibachs, Cooper and Field. They are all here moving across the great landscape.

The photographs—five years of them, from a tent, in the snow and the gales and the floating ice, that meant numb feet, frigid hands, sometimes-wet cameras—were not made to illustrate the text, they were taken for themselves. Nor was the text written for the photographs. But when the elements are brought together, the Glacier Bay country comes through—a combination of man, camera, notebook, and empathy that is not going to happen again soon.

At this moment in time Alaska has the opportunity to be unique among states, the opportunity to treat with respect much of its remarkable wilderness, to prevent the ruinous economic rationalizations which have stripped away so much of the landscape in so many other places. As to the philosophy of the continued existence of land for what is there, this book speaks eloquently to Alaskans, and to all others who believe that untrammeled space —again for its own sake—should remain available on this planet.

Berkeley, California
February 1967

DAVID BROWER
Executive Director, Sierra Club

Foreword

IN ALASKA, where spectacular natural scenes are commonplace, Glacier Bay and the surrounding land features are perhaps the most awe-inspiring of them all. It is appropriate that this beautiful area has been preserved as a unit of our National Park System.

The future will bring increasing demands upon Alaska's now immense store of natural resources. Such demands will intensify management to produce more fish, forests and minerals to feed, clothe and house our growing population. These resources are a part of our heritage and wealth, and our nation is strong in great measure because we have them. No nation is so wealthy, however, that it can afford not to save a few islands of primitive earth, so that children of new generations can know and appreciate its natural history and culture. We can be thankful for those whose foresight and wisdom made such possible.

It was my great privilege to serve as Superintendent of this fine National Monument for eight years, and during that time I had the opportunity to know the author. Seldom does one find a person whose ideals are so high, who loves and appreciates wilderness so much, yet who has the perception and skill required to impart to others his feeling for that wilderness. Although he is knowledgeable and articulate, his great forte is interpretation through the lens of the camera.

To this end Dave Bohn has found success through the collection of photographs in this book. His camera has seen the beauty of cloud draped peaks, windswept waters and rain drenched forests, as well as sculptured ice, and placid lakes in brilliant sunshine.

This book will be of much value to those who have been there, and to those who would go. It is a tribute of a fine artist to a superb wilderness park.

Juneau, January 1966   L. J. MITCHELL

IAPPRECIATE the opportunity to express a few thoughts here, although I find myself yet unable to comprehend the geographic magnitude of Glacier Bay National Monument, and even more am I awed by the dramatic story of time and land that is this magnificent area.

One cannot help but be impressed with the opportunities; the chance to learn more of our land and its formation through scientific studies; the reality of telling a story, dramatically and graphically illustrated to encourage an ecological conscience as our visitors see tomorrow and yesterday; the privilege of aiding visitors to enjoy this vast scenic area of almost limitless wilderness; and finally having an opportunity to be a part of the planning and management necessary to insure that these many experiences remain possible for generations to come.

"It is crucial that proposals for development be viewed with the greatest caution and skepticism and undertaken, when absolutely necessary, with great circumspection," said Dr. Stanley A. Cain, Assistant Secretary of the Interior at the ceremony in Yellowstone National Park commemorating the 50th Anniversary of the National Park Service. He was referring to the preservation of the great National Parks. I think the advice is sound, and that both you and Dr. Cain will agree that Glacier Bay National Monument is such a place.

I would hope that Glacier Bay, this great northland fjord, is our road, with its inlets the spurs furnishing all necessary access; that developments will be limited and compact; that remoteness will continue to be its primary protection; and that the services of our personnel will be geared to safety of the visitor and protection of the area through personal contact and interpretation.

Think of these things as you turn back the pages of time.

Juneau, October 1966

ROBERT HOWE
Superintendent, Glacier Bay
National Monument

Heather Nunatak from summit of 4710. 1965

Acknowledgments

I TRUST those who appear on this page recognize my awareness of the inadequacy of one or two sentences proposing to thank them for hours, days, or weeks of their time. I can only hope some sort of vested interest in the final product will serve as the real expression of gratitude to those who made possible that product.

William S. Cooper, Boulder, Colorado, for making sure, forty years ago, that there would be such a piece of land to write about. And for granting me permission to continue to trespass on his domain.

David Brower, Executive Director, Sierra Club, for his faith in this project when first presented, and thereafter. From faith to the other end of the presses is a long, long pull.

William J. Schwarz, Berkeley, for his lengthy critical commentary on the manuscript, over a period of five months, during which time I think he came to know more about the book than I do.

The Preparatory Department staff at H. S. Crocker Co., Inc., San Bruno, who labored for so many months over the offset reproductions on Kromekote, for putting up with me as we split hairs, then split them again: Tom Peterson, Preparatory Supervisor; Bert Buzzell, Foreman, Art Department; Bob Nielsen, Assistant Foreman, Art Department; Gunther Hufnagel, Foreman, Camera Department; George Poeschel, Master cameraman; Fred Ulfelder, proofing press operator.

Richard N. Kauffman, President, H. S. Crocker Co., Inc., for his willingness to take on such a sticky project, and James Curtis, Manager of Estimating, for staying with me during my misunderstandings of collation.

My wife, Diana, who did *not* do any of the typing on the manuscript, mainly because I'll be damned if I know why female spouses usually end up with that chore, for her ability to take in stride weeks of cooking on a Svea, and in general her ability to survive a five-year book, even though I was reasonably cool about the whole mess.

Dick Davis, Alaska Sleeping Bag Co., Portland, Oregon, and Allen Steck, The Ski Hut, Berkeley, who, in the first two years of the project helped so much with expedition equipment.

E. D. Bohn, posthumously, for continuing aid in the chosen field.

Matilda Dring, Curator of Photography, San Francisco Maritime Museum, and Mrs. Anna M. Ibbotson, Acting Librarian, Washington State Historical Museum Library, Tacoma, for their aid in finding some of the historical photographs.

Alexander Dolgapolov, South Laguna, California, for his generosity with his library, and for leading me to the Shelekhoff manuscript.

John Barr Tompkins, Head of Public Services, Bancroft Library, for his patience with me as I lived in the Bancroft (with pencil only) during the initial months of the bibliography.

Mrs. Leon S. Vincent, Seattle, for the hospitality when we gathered to look over some of the contemporary historical slides.

Calvin J. Heusser, Research Associate, American Geographical Society, New York, and Richard P. Goldthwait, Chairman, Department of Geology, Ohio State University, for their critical comments on the botanical and geological aspects of the manuscript.

Bradford Washburn, Director, Museum of Science, Boston, for his immediate cooperation in making available to me some of his early photographs in the Monument.

Robert Bates, Exeter, New Hampshire, for the affectionate piece on that important character—Huscroft of Lituya Bay.

Donna Abolin, Oakland, friend of long standing, who performed prodigious feats of marathon typing as the wire approached.

Mrs. George Dalton, Hoonah, Alaska, for her willingness to give me some insight into the living legend of Kooshta-kah, the land otter man.

Don Gallagher of the *Forester*, for his gallant hospitality aboard, as we rode lumpy waters during the wild rains of September 1966, discussing Joe and Muz Ibach.

Luella Smith, The Photo Shop Studio, Sitka, Alaska, for the opportunity to see the remarkable large-negative work of her Father, James H. Gilpatrick, in Glacier Bay 1928.

Arthur G. Maki, Washington, D.C., who shared three field seasons with me during the project, for his patience while I fiddled with cameras and often shouted and swore at the weather.

Moonok Sunwoo, field companion of 1965, for the fine end paper map and the gourmet Korean meals served at the little red cabin, Reid Inlet.

George Haselton, Institute of Polar Studies, Ohio State University, for giving us the extra gasoline needed for the run to Sandy Cove in our twelve-foot rowboat, 1964.

Forrest Tregea, Executive Director, Associated Students, University of California, Berkeley, for his uncanny knowledge that, when it was time for me to photograph an iceberg, it was time.

The staff and students at the ASUC Studio, Berkeley, for providing the atmosphere—either consciously or unconsciously—conducive to a sustained project of this nature.

William O. Field, Chairman, Department of Exploration and Field Research, American Geographical Society, New York, for aid in unearthing some of the classic historical photographs, for continuing interest and aid in a venture which was really his domain, and for the opportunity to spend the final days of the project with him on his fortieth anniversary in Glacier Bay.

L. J. Mitchell, former Superintendent of Glacier Bay and Sitka National Monuments (1958-1966), who sat in on the early stages of this book and initiated the magnificent logistical support provided by the National Park Service, and for his written contribution to the book.

David Butts, Chief Ranger, Bartlett Cove, 1964, and Theodore Sullivan, Chief Ranger 1965 and 1966, for logistical support and cooperation far beyond the call of duty.

James Sanders, captain, USNPS *Nunatak*, for hospitality aboard and logistical support, including the gathering of groceries at Juneau.

Robert Howe, Superintendent, Glacier Bay and Sitka National Monuments, for his enthusiasm in the continuance of National Park Service logistical support for this project, for his written contribution to the book, and for his exciting company during my last twelve days in the Monument, aboard USNPS *Nunatak*.

Kenwood Youmans, USNPS, Bartlett Cove, for unlimited hospitality at Bartlett Cove in 1965 and 1966, and for the early discussions which laid the basis for all the historical research that followed.

Charles V. Janda, USNPS, and wife Carol, Bartlett Cove, for unlimited hospitality during the field seasons of 1965 and 1966, for the recurring discussions on Park Service philosophy—and the philosophy of land and space, for their own feelings about the land they are charged with administering, and to Chuck Janda specifically for his photographic contributions to the book.

All National Park Service personnel, Juneau and Bartlett Cove, Alaska, collectively, for aid without which this book could not have been completed. I am indebted beyond measure.

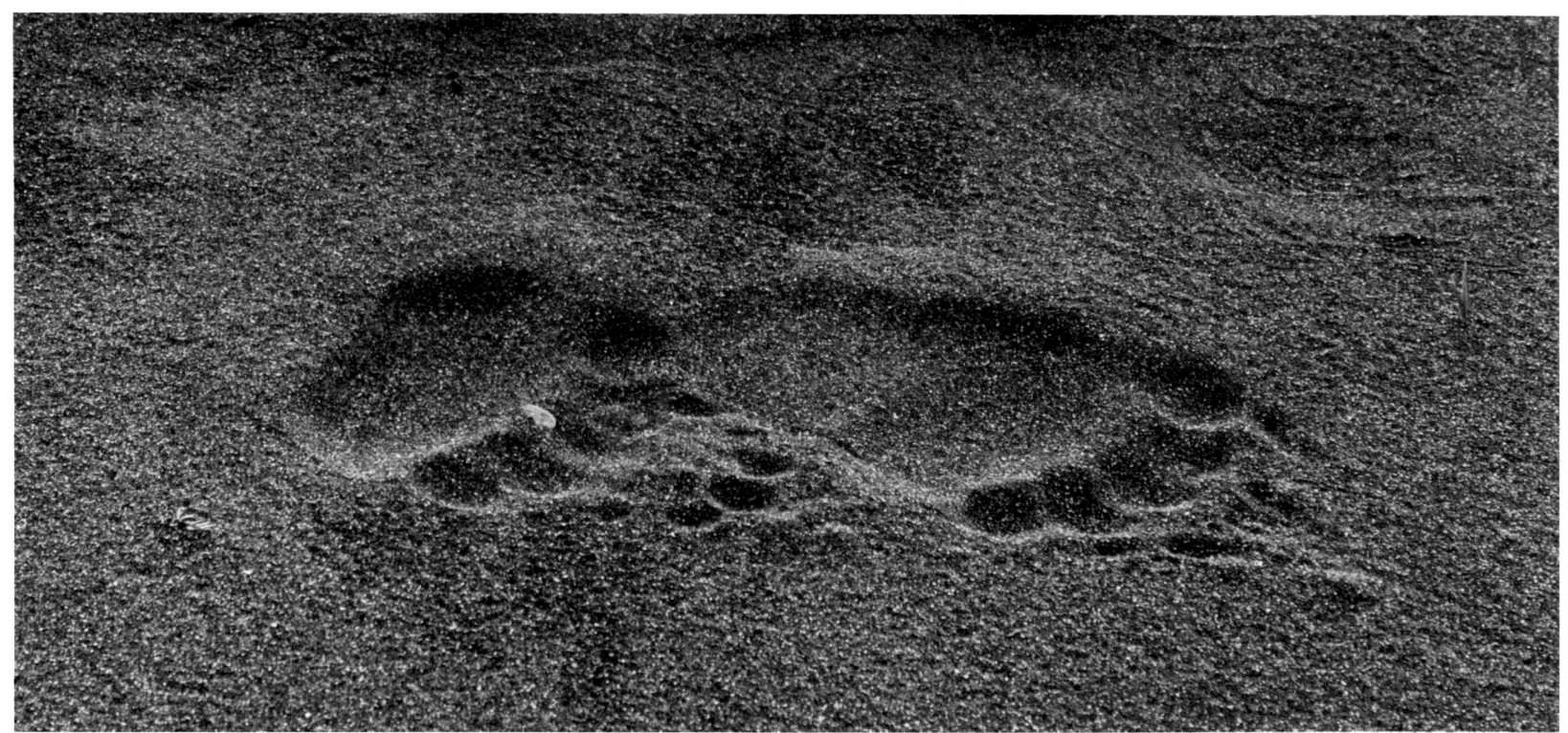

Brown bear tracks, Lituya Bay. 1966

"Midnight Sun on the Fairweather Range, Alaska." 1898.
Oil on metal by J. E. Stuart (collection of the author).

Contents

   Introduction 23
I The Lake Within the Point 25
II Bay of Great Glaciers 38
III The Wondrous Scene 57
IV A Lone Prospector 80
V Democracy at Work 94
VI Home at Glacier Bay 111
Place Names 156
Bibliography 159
Index 164

Introduction

IN LATE APRIL 1962, I stood on a wild desolate beach in southeastern Alaska. The sun was low in the northwest, there was a high wind, the surf was enormous. This was Cape Fairweather and it was a beginning. I knew very little about the peaks rising above the clouds, of the fjord country beyond the mountains I had heard vaguely; and I was scarcely aware that the Fairweather Range was part of something called Glacier Bay National Monument.

From the summit of Lituya Mountain five weeks later, I first saw those fjords, barely. But as the expedition of 1962 ended, I flew east with Layton Bennett in a ski-wheel Piper Cub—east under a great storm sky and low ceiling over northern Glacier Bay. Below us was ice and rock and water, and a hint of green. Bennett screamed something about strange land, and I screamed back, but I don't remember what I said. I do remember a certain uneasiness as I looked down. Strange country? No, but a foreshadowing of primitive land, floating ice, and great wilderness. We flew on to the east, out from under the storm sky into brilliance at six in the morning, east over hundreds of square miles of glaciers and nunataks and space.

The beginning, at Cape Fairweather in 1962, seems long ago, and I cannot explain what I have learned about this land, though *Glacier Bay* makes some suggestions with words and photographs. But if you prefer the flower by the trailside, remember there are no trails except brown bear paths and hundreds of miles of waterways. No trails in the usual sense, but why should there be? There are beaches, moraines, snowfields, forests, coves, inlets. With two legs and a million years of experience behind us, what more is needed? Two legs, and stay clear of the alder.

Nevertheless, this is not easy country you are about to wander through. It is huge. Forty-four hundred square miles. There are giant waves, avalanches, thundering glaciers, savage streams, violent winds, monumental rains, and earthquakes. It is land still emerging from the Little Ice Age. New-born land, where there actually are small, dainty things to look at, but where the mood is essentially sombre, bold, austere, brooding. It is harsh land, where errors in judgment are rarely forgiven. But as always, harsh land can yield great rewards in many ways, after a time.

* * *

Below us was the great land. Indeed, all Glacier Bay is the great land, unique, wild, and magnificent. It should exist intact solely for its own sake. No justification, rationale, or excuse is needed. *For its own sake* and no other reason.

Berkeley, California
December 1966

DAVE BOHN

I *The Lake Within the Point*[1]

OFF THE fog-shrouded coast of southeastern Alaska, July 15, 1741—latitude 55°36'3"—stood the Russian packet boat *St. Paul*, Alexis Tchirikov commanding: "At two in the morning we distinguished some very high mountains and, as the light at the time was not very good, we brought to. An hour later the land stood out much better and we could make out trees. This must be America, judging by the latitude and the longitude, for we were at that hour in latitude 55°21' N and longitude from Vaua 61°55'."[2]

* * *

It *was* America, and Tchirikov had sighted land just one day before Vitus Bering broke out of the same fog two hundred miles to the northwest and named Mount St. Elias. But Bering and Tchirikov had been separated for twenty-six days, and would never see each other again. Tchirikov's *St. Paul*, in the meantime, moved north and somewhat west, and on July 18 the journal records the following: "At 3:30 in the afternoon we went as close to the shore as we dared. We sent the boat ashore in charge of Fleet Master Dementiev who had with him ten armed men. He took with him a hand compass, a small lead, two empty water casks, a grapnel, and a cable. He had written orders; and among other things he was told to make for the opening [Lisianski Strait] which seemed to us a bay and to take its bearings. The position of the bay and other details relating to it are recorded in their places so that it can be more easily identified. At the end of the day we saw high snow-covered mountains extending to the northward and ending in NW by N."[3]

Those snow-covered peaks extending north into the unknown were the Fairweather Range, and with Tchirikov's entry the human history of what is now Glacier Bay National Monument opens. At least, human history as we know it. The Tlingits had been on the coast for generations, but Tchirikov was no ethnologist and in fact had no chance to be. The boat sent into Lisianski Strait on 18 July 1741 did not return to the ship. The *St. Paul* hovered near the coast in good weather, and on 23 July sighted fire on the beach, but still no boat. On 24 July four men in a second boat were sent ashore in fair weather and a calm sea. On 25 July two boats were sighted returning to the ship:

First hour. We noticed two boats rowing from the bay into which our boats had gone; one of them was large, and the other small. We naturally thought they were our boats, and we stood towards them. There was very little wind stirring, and I ordered that the sails be taken in and the shrouds tightened. When the small boat drew close to us we became aware that it was not our boat, for it had a sharp bow, and that those in it did not row with oars but paddled. The boat did not, however, come near enough so that we could see the faces of those in it. All that we did see was that it contained four persons, one at the stern and the others at the paddle. One of them had on clothes of red material. Being that far away they stood up and shouted twice "Agai, Agai," waved their hands, and turned back to shore. I commanded my men to wave white kerchiefs, and to invite those in the boat to come to our ship. Many of my men did that but it did no good; the boat proceeded on its way to shore. We could not pursue them because in the first place we had no wind, in the second place the small boat went very fast, and the large one had stopped a considerable distance from us. They continued to pull away and finally disappeared in the bay from which they had come. We then became convinced that some misfortune had happened to our men, for it was the eighth day since the Fleet Master had left; during that period there was plenty of fine weather for returning, and we had sailed quite close to the place, and yet he did not appear. Since the boat-

Fairweather Range from Bartlett Cove. 1964

swain had gone we had not been away from the place, the weather had been fair, and if a misfortune had not overtaken them they would have returned. The fact that the Americans did not dare to approach our ship leads us to believe that they have either killed or detained our men. We remained close to the place until evening, hoping that our boats would come out. Towards evening, however, we had to keep away from shore because of the danger.[4]

There were no more small boats to send ashore, and the *St. Paul*, after waiting two more days, began the long trip home to Avacha Bay in eastern Kamchatka. As for Tchirikov's lost men, not even Tlingit legend[5] has anything to say of them. The fog shuts down.

The American northwest coast at last. But it would be forty-five years before the next *recorded* landing was made by a white man anywhere on one of the wildest coastlines in the world, latitude 58°10'N to 58°50'N, Cross Sound to Cape Fairweather. Fog and rain and snow, the mountains often obscured for weeks, sea otter, brown bear, Tlingit summer villages, the Northwest Passage, the mists of legend, of superstition, of misinformation. But the imperial powers were closing in on this coastline and in 1778, sailing for England on a voyage of discovery to the Pacific Ocean, Captain James Cook aboard His Majesty's Sloop *Resolution* reached Prince William Sound in 61°N latitude. Remarkably enough, also aboard were Midshipman George Vancouver and a certain Master William Bligh. Captain Cook did not say much about the coastline, but the fog lifted just long enough for him to see an entire range of great mountains; thus on the 3rd of May, 1778:

> I continued to steer North North West, half West, and North West by West, as the coast trended, with a fine gale at North East, and clear weather. At half an hour past four in the morning, on the three, Mount Edgcumbe bore South 54° East, a large inlet, North 50° East, distant six leagues, and the most advanced point of the land, to the North West lying under a very high peaked mountain, which obtained the name of Mount Fair Weather, bore 32° West. The inlet was named Cross Sound as being first seen on that day, so marked in our calendar. It appeared to branch in several arms, the largest of which turned to the Northward. The South East point of this sound is a high promontory, which obtained the name of Cross Cape. It lies in the latitude of 56°57', and its longitude is 223°21'. At noon it bore South East; and the point, under the peaked mountain, which was called Cape Fair Weather, North by West a quarter West, distant thirteen leagues.[6]

Cook was fortunate to see those peaks on such short notice, and he certainly could not have produced a more deceptive name for the huge mountain. Indeed, climbers who have had experience on or near Mount Fairweather are inclined to feel at times that Cook was the last person to see the peak.

During the decade following Cook, there were probably scattered Russian-Aleut landings to hunt sea otter, but nothing recorded. In 1786, however, the mist begins to clear, for there is a Tlingit tradition which tells of the coming of Yeahlth[7] to Lituya Bay, Yeahlth who came from the western horizon and whose great white wings turned as he moved across the water in an enormous ship. This is the way the Tlingits tell it:

No clouds were in the sky that day. The water lay smooth under a gentle western breeze, and young boys and girls were playing on the beach, while the men hunted and fished, and the old women prepared clams, wild game and berries for the winter, and dried salmon on the smoking racks. Yeahlth-kan the wise man, carved dishes and spoons as he sat in front of his log house. The dishes were birch, and the spoons were made from the horns of the mountain goat. The whole village was peaceful and quiet. Then suddenly the wolf-cry came— the sign of great news—and one of the hunters came running toward the camp as if he were very much frightened. As he came nearer folks heard him cry, faintly at first, and then louder and louder, "Yeahlth is coming; Yeahlth is coming; He comes from the western horizon. He is all white. His wings turn this way and that way as he moves across the water." And the messenger rushed to his wife and children and gathered them in his arms while the tribe surrounded him with excited questions. Then many of them went down to the point of land from which this strange sight had been seen; some of them remembered that the bright rays from Yeahlth would blind those who looked straight at him, and they took hollow kelp stocks and looked through them. Those with guilty consciences drove knives of bone horn or copper through the flesh over their breasts and held their faces and bodies in a rigid posture, expecting to be turned into stone. Others who did not fear the coming so much decorated their faces with paint and prepared to receive Yeahlth. Some thought of their children first, and these built fires of grasses and brushwood through the flames and smoke of which they drove their children in order to cleanse them of sin. And, as if attracted by the smoke, Yeahlth turned slightly from his course and headed directly across the water toward them.

When well within the harbor, Yeahlth's wings were folded; a harsh grating sound drove terror into the hearts of the wicked, but the good felt greater joy. And now more excitement than ever prevailed. At last Yeahlth-kan, the wise man, quieted their voices, and said: "My daughters, sons and grandchildren; I am old and have but little longer to live. My usefulness to you is nearly ended. Come what may, I will go out in my canoe and meet Yeahlth, and beg him to turn me into stone, that the others may be spared." Everyone agreed with this plan, and the young men brought the wise man's light hunting canoe to the water, where Yeahlth-kan entered it and paddled off to the great ship. When he approached the ship, the crew lowered ropes and hoisted him and his canoe on deck; to those who stayed ashore it seemed as if he had been caught up into the air and taken to the bosom of Yeahlth. When the canoe was swung in on deck, the ship's crew gathered about Yeahlth-kan, and he saw that their faces and their bare feet were white, while their eyes were grey and blue. They had strange clothing and their hair was brown, or auburn—some almost white, and often curly —not straight and black like his own. "Can this be Yeahlth?" the wise man wondered, and as he wondered a man appeared whose feet were covered, who wore clothing of a finer sort than that of the crew, and who seemed to be the chief. And to him, Yeahlth-kan prayed with arms outstretched; "E-shan, Oohan, Yeahlth—have mercy on us, Yeahlth!" The white chief spoke to a sailor standing near by and this one disappeared, to return with what folks now think must have been ship-biscuits, or pilot bread. It was offered to Yeahlth-kan but the wise man refused it, calling it a product of human skulls. Again the sailor disappeared and again returned. This time he had with him a bowl of what folks now think must have been freshly cooked rice. It was steaming hot, and when the grains came in contact with the cooler air on deck, they seemed to move slightly—Yeahlth-kan said: "Surely this is a dish of maggots they serve me," and he refused.

Then the white chief turned to his servant and spoke, and the man went away and brought back a glass filled with red liquor, which he handed to the wise man, who took it in his hand, thumb at bottom and forefinger at top of glass. "This is human blood," said Yeahlth-kan, "it will destroy the foundations of my people," and without touching it to his lips, he handed it back. At that moment a man came forward dressed entirely in white clothing. In his hand he carried and beat upon what the wise man called Ik-nadj-gau, a brass bell. The man stopped near him and he reached out and took hold of the bell. As he touched the bell, this man took the covering from his head—he was wearing a cap woven from strips of sea otter skins, with the fur left on. Now Yeahlth-kan had been taught and believed that every part of Yeahlth was alive. He tested the bell in his hand by biting it, but he could detect no life. And then the white chief made the universally known sign of a desire to trade, by crossing his hands twice in the air. Yeahlth-kan understood, and nodded his consent. All his hopes and fears in the presence of Yeahlth vanished—he was not in the presence of the god after all, but of human strangers—People-Who-Come-From-The-Horizon. In trade for his cap, the bell became his, and he exchanged his body garments of sea-otter skins for a strap of iron. Stark naked, with his bell and iron strap, he was lowered into the water and paddled ashore, where he related his experience to an excited crowd. Later in the day a boat was lowered from the ship. In it six men rowed about the bay, but did not approach the native village. This was the first time the tribe had seen oars used—for they always used paddles themselves. At sunrise the ship disappeared into the horizon from whence it had come, but the people of the village still talk about it, and some still talk of the second coming of Yeahlth.[8]

Jean François de Galaup, comte de Lapérouse had arrived in Lituya Bay, July 4, 1786. Lapérouse named the incomparable bay Port des Français, and was deeply impressed with what he had discovered. Unlike most of the early explorers, the French circumnavigator was intensely observant of what was going on around him, and at Port des Français he had ample time—twenty-six days—to watch the Tlingits. Here is what he wrote one hundred eighty years ago aboard the frigate *Boussole*, surrounded by gigantic wilderness and strange people:

At six in the morning we stood for the passage, to enter it with the end of the flood. The Astrolabe led, and we stationed a boat at each point as the preceding evening. The winds blew from the west and west-south-west; the direction of the entrance is north and south; so that every thing appeared in our favour: but at seven o'clock, when we were in the passage, the wind chopped about to the west-north-west and north-west by west, so that it was necessary to throw the ship up in the wind and lay all aback. Fortunately the flood carried the ships into the bay, though it drove us within half a pistol-shot of the rocks on the eastern point. During the thirty years that I have followed the sea I never saw two vessels so near being lost; and to have experienced such an event at the verge of the world would have enhanced our misfortune.

As soon as we arrived at our second anchorage, we erected our observatory on the island [Cenotaph Island], which was not above a musket-shot from our ships, and formed an establishment there for the time of our stay in port. We pitched tents for our sail-makers and smiths, and made a store for our water-casks, which we completely refitted. As all the Indian villages were on the main-land, we flattered ourselves, that we should be in security on the island, but we were soon convinced of our mistake. Experience had already taught us, that the Indians were great thieves; but we did not suspect them of sufficient activity and perseverance, to carry into execution difficult and tedious schemes. In a short time we learned to know them better. They spent the night in watching for favourable opportunities to rob us: but we kept a strict watch on board our vessels, and they were seldom able to get the better of our vigilance. I had established also the Spartan law: the person robbed was punished; and if the thief received no applause, at least we reclaimed nothing, to avoid all occasion of quarrel, which might have led to fatal consequences. That this extreme mildness rendered them insolent I will not disavow: but I endeavoured to convince them of the superiority of our arms; for which purpose I fired a cannon, to show them, that I could reach them at a distance, and pierced with a musket-ball, in presence of a great number of Indians, several doubles of a cuirass they had sold us, after they had informed us by signs that it was impenetrable to arrows or poignards.

We had already visited the head of the bay, which is perhaps the most extraordinary place in the world. To form an idea of it, it is necessary to conceive a basin of water, unfathomable in the middle, bordered by peaked mountains, of great height, covered with snow, and without one blade of grass to decorate this vast heap of rocks, condemned by nature to eternal sterility. I never beheld the surface of the water ruffled by a single breath of wind. Nothing disturbs it but the fall of enormous masses of ice, which frequently separate from five different glaciers, while the sound is re-echoed by the distant mountains. The air is so calm, and the silence so profound, that the single voice of a man may be heard half a league, as may the cries of a few sea-fowl, which deposit their eggs in the hollows of the rocks. It was at the head of this bay, that we hoped to find channels, by which we might penetrate into the interior of America. We conjectured it might lead to some large river, taking it's course between two of the mountains, and originating from one of the great lakes north of Canada. At length, after having rowed a league and half only, we found the channel terminated at two vast glaciers. We were obliged to push away the flakes of ice with which the sea was covered, to penetrate thus far; and the water was so deep, that I could find no bottom at half a cable's length from the shore with a line of a hundred and twenty fathoms. Messrs. de Langle, de Monti, and Dagelet, with several other officers, attempted to ascend the glacier. With unspeakable fatigue they advanced two leagues, being obliged at extreme risk to leap over clefts of great depth; but they could only perceive one continued mass of ice and snow, of which the summit of Mount Fairweather must have been the termination. While they were on this expedition, my boat remained on the shore. A fragment of ice, which fell into the water near half a mile off, occasioned such a swell along the shore, that my boat was upset, and thrown to some distance on the border of the glacier. This accident was soon repaired, and we returned on board, having finished our voyage into the interior of America in a few hours.

The day after this excursion, the chief came on board better attended, and more ornamented, than usual. After many songs and dances, he offered to sell me the island, on which our observatory was erected; tacitly reserving, no doubt, to himself and the other Indians, the right of robbing us upon it. It was more than questionable, whether this chief were proprietor of a single foot of land: the government of these people is of such a nature, that the country must belong to the whole society; yet, as many of the savages were witnesses to the bargain, I had a right to suppose that it was sanctioned by their assent; and accordingly I accepted the offer of the chief, sufficiently aware, however, that many tribunals would find a flaw in the contract, if ever the nation should think proper to litigate our title, for we could bring no proof, that the witnesses were it's representatives, or the chief the actual proprietor of the soil. Be this as it might, I gave him several yards of red cloth, hatchets, adzes, bar iron, and nails, and made presents to all his attendants. The bargain being thus concluded, and the purchase money paid, I sent to take possession of the island with the usual formalities, and buried at the foot of a rock several bronze medals, which had been struck before our departure from France, with a bottle containing an inscription recording our claim.

For a country so frightful, nature provides inhabitants differing as widely from civilized nations, as the land I have described from our cultivated plains. Rude and barbarous, as their soil is wild and rugged, they inhabit the country only to extirpate every thing that lives and moves upon it. At war with every animal, they despise the vegetables that spring up around them. I have seen women and children eat a few raspberries and strawberries: but these are no doubt insipid to the palates of men, who are precisely on the earth what the vulture is in the air, or the wolf and the tiger in the forest. Their arts are considerably advanced, and their civilisation in this respect has made great progress; but in every thing that polishes and softens the ferocity of manners, they are yet in their infancy. The manner in which they live, excluding every kind of subordination, renders them continually agitated by vengeance or fear. Choleric and prompt to take offence, I have seen them continually with the poignard unsheathed against each other. Exposed to perish with hunger in the winter, when the chace cannot be very productive, they live in the summer in the greatest abundance, as they can catch more fish in an hour than is sufficient for their family. The rest of the day they remain idle, spending it in gaming, of which they are as passionately fond as some of the inhabitants of our large cities. This is the grand source of their quarrels: and I do not hesitate to pronounce, that this tribe would be completely exterminated, if the use of any intoxicating liquor were added to these destructive vices. Philosophers may exclaim against this picture if they please. They may write books by their fire-sides, while I have been voyaging for thirty years. I have been witness to the knavery and injustice of these people, whom they depict as good, because they are so little removed from a state of nature; but this nature is sublime only in the great, in the minutiae of things it is negligent.

I have given the appellation of village to three or four sheds of wood, twenty-five feet long, by fifteen or twenty wide, and closed with planks or bark of trees only on the side exposed to the wind. In the middle was a fire, over which hung salmon and halibut drying in the smoke. Eighteen or twenty persons lodged under each of these sheds, the women and children on one side, and the men on the other. It appeared to me, that each hut contained a small tribe unconnected with it's neighbours; for each had it's canoe, and a sort of chief; each departed, left the bay, and took away it's fish and it's planks, without the rest of the village appearing to take the least concern in the business. I think I may venture to affirm, that this place is inhabited only in the summer, and that the Indians never pass the winter here. I did not see a single hut, that afforded shelter from the rain; and though there were never three hundred Indians collected in the bay at one time, we were visited by seven or eight hundred others. Every day we saw fresh canoes enter the bay; and every day whole villages departed, and gave place to others. These Indians seemed to have considerable dread of the passage, and never ventured to approach it, unless at the slack water of flood or ebb. By the help of our glasses we distinctly perceived, that, when they were between the two points, the chief, or at least the principal Indian, arose, stretched out his arms towards the sun, to which he appeared to address a prayer, while the rest paddled away with all their strength. In the course of our inquiries respecting this custom, we learned, that seven very large canoes had lately been lost in this passage, while an eighth escaped. This the Indians who were saved consecrated to their god, or to the memory of their comrades. We saw it by the side of a morai,[9] which no doubt contained the ashes of some who were shipwrecked.

The men of this country bore holes through the cartilages of the nose and ears, and append to them different little ornaments. They make scars on the arms and breast with a very keen iron instrument, which they sharpen by rubbing it on their teeth as on a whetstone. On occasions of high ceremony, they wear their hair long, braided, and powdered with the down of sea-fowl. A simple skin is thrown over their shoulders, and the rest of the body is left naked, except the head, which they commonly cover with a little straw hat, curiously woven; though sometimes they wear on their heads caps with two horns, eagle's feathers, and entire heads of bears fitted on a skullcap of wood. These kinds of headdresses are greatly diversified, but their principal object, like that of most of their customs, is to render them frightful, perhaps to awe their enemies. I saw no appearance of tatooing, except on the arms of some of the women. These, however, have a custom, which renders them hideous, and which I could hardly have believed, had I not seen it. All without exception have the lower lip slit close to the gum the whole width of the mouth, and wear in it a kind of wooden bowl without handles, which rests against the gum, and which the slit lip serves as a collar to confine, so that the lower part of the mouth projects two or three inches. The drawing made by Mr. Duche de Vancy, which is extremely accurate, will render more plain than any description this custom, the most disgusting perhaps that exists upon the face of the earth. These women, the most disgusting in the world, covered with stinking hides, often not even tanned, were still capable of exciting desire in the breasts of some persons, not of the most delicate taste. At first they raised difficulties, and declared, by signs, that they should hazard the loss of their lives: but when they were overcome by presents, they wished the sun to be witness of their actions, and refused to retire into the woods.

The grand work, however, for which we had put into port was accomplished. Our guns were mounted [for the Chinese seas], our hold was restowed, and we had taken on board as ample a stock of wood and water as at our departure from Chili. Not a port in the universe could afford more conveniences for accelerating a business often tedious in other countries. In short we considered ourselves as the most fortunate of navigators, in having arrived at such a distance from Europe without having had a single person sick, and without an individual of either crew being attacked with the scurvy. But here the greatest of misfortunes, and most impossible to be foreseen, awaited us. It is with the most pungent sorrow I proceed to give the history of a disaster a thousand times more cruel than disease, and all the other events incident to long voyages. Before our departure, we erected on the island in the middle of the bay, to which I gave the name of Isle du Cénotaphe, or Cenotaph Island, a monument to the memory of our unfortunate companions; and Mr. deLamanon wrote the following inscription and account, which he buried in a bottle at the foot of the monument:

> At the entrance of this harbour perished twenty-one brave seamen. Reader, whoever thou art, mingle thy tears with ours.
>
> On the 4th of July, 1786, the frigates la Boussole and l'Astrolabe, which sailed from Brest the 1st of August, 1785, arrived in this port. Owing to the care of Mr. de la Pérouse, commander in chief of the expedition; of the viscount de Langle, commander of the Astrolabe; of Messrs. de Clonard and de Monti, first lieutenants of the two ships; and of the other officers and the surgeons, the crew had experienced none of those diseases which usually

"Femme du Port des Francais," from drawing by *Duche de Vancy.* 1786. *Lapérouse portfolio, courtesy Bancroft Library.*

attend long voyages. Mr. de la Pérouse congratulated himself, as we all did, for having visited people reputed barbarians, without losing a single man, or spilling a drop of blood. On the 13th of July, three boats departed at five in the morning, to place the soundings on the plan that had been drawn of the bay. They were commanded by Mr. d'Escures, lieutenant of a man of war and knight of St. Lewis. Mr. de la Pérouse had given him written instructions, expressly prohibiting him from approaching the current; but at the moment when he thought himself at a distance from it, he was drawn into it. Messrs. de la Borde, two brothers, and Mr. de Flassan, who were in the boat of the second frigate, hesitated not to expose their own lives, to assist their comrades. But, alas! they only shared their fate. The third boat was under the command of Mr. Boutin, lieutenant of a man of war. This officer, bravely struggling against the breakers, made vain but useless attempts to assist his friends for some hours, and would have perished likewise, but for the superior construction of his boat, his enlightened prudence, that of Mr. Laprise Mouton, lieutenant of a frigate, his second, and the activity and prompt obedience of his crew, consisting of John Marie, cockswain, Lhostis, le Bas, Corentin Jers, and Monens, all four seamen. The Indians appeared to participate in our grief, which is extreme. Affected, but not discouraged, by our misfortune, we departed the 30th of July, to continue our voyage.[10]

Depicting the loss of Lapérouse's boats, Lituya Bay, 1786. Adapted from the original drawing by Duche de Vancy, Lapérouse portfolio. Engraving on copper, ca. 1790 (collection of the author).

Crepin pinxit

NAUFRAGE DE MM DE LABORDE SUR LES CANOTS DE LA
DÉDIÉ A MONSIEUR ALEXA

M.' de la Peyrouse avoit envoyé plusieurs chaloupes pour placer des sondes dans le port des français, dont il avoit fait lever le plan. M. de Lescure, qui commandoit cette pet. expédition, s'étant avancé trop loin fut entrainé par le courant et son canot brisé contre les rochers. M.M. de Laborde qui suivaient, se précipitèrent alors pour le sauver et eure. le même sort. M. de la Peyrouse, dans son rapport au Roi, rend ainsi compte de cet evenement. M.M. de Laborde étaient à un grand quart de lieue du danger, c'est-à-dir

Deposé à la Bibliothèque Impériale

...YROUSE AU PORT DES FRANÇOIS DANS LA CALIFORNIE.
...E DE LABORDE LEUR FRERE

Par son très humble Serviteur *Ostervald* l'ainé, Editeur et Proprietaire.

...s une mer aussi calme que celle du port le mieux fermé: Mais ces jeunes Officiers, poussés par une générosité sans doute imprudente puisque tous secours étaient impossibles dans cette circons-
...ce, ayant l'ame trop élevée, le courage trop grand pour faire cette réflexion, lorsque leurs amis étaient dans un si grand danger, volèrent à leur secours, se jetterent dans les mêmes
...sants et victimes de leur générosité et de leur desobéissance formelle à leur chef, périrent comme lui. *Voyage de la Peyrouse, Tome 2.*

A Paris chez Ostervald l'ainé Rue du petit Lion St Sulpice N.º 20.

Lapérouse disappeared beyond the horizon from which he had come. The journals were carried from Kamchatka overland across Russia by de Lesseps, in an epic journey, and delivered safely to Paris. But the *Boussole* and *Astrolabe* went down on the reefs of Vanikoro, with all hands either drowned or (probably) murdered, and France lost a remarkable sailor.

Lapérouse, although he may have doubted the validity of the bargain, at least purchased Cenotaph Island from the Indians, but the practice was rare among the powers of the day. Two years after Lapérouse, Russian sails appeared from the northwest. It was the galleon *Three Saints* under the Masters Gerassim Ismaïloff and Dmitri Bocharoff. They were under orders to cruise "in the sea near the shores of the main land of America, for the purpose of discovering new islands in the sea and bringing them under the rule of the Russian Empire, as well as to confirm the inhabitants of those places already discovered, in their allegiance to the Russian Government by communicating to them the satisfaction of Her Majesty."[11] They had on board a young Koloshi from the Yakutat Bay area, and he told them of the bay situated between high peaks, of the fish to be had there, of the big ship that had been there not long ago. At first the entrance could not be found, but on July 3rd, 1788, the *Three Saints* on the second try made it through the narrow opening and entered the bay their Koloshi guide called Ltua Gulf. They remained overnight just inside the entrance, but the flood tides made the position untenable, and the following day the ship was moved, apparently anchoring at Cenotaph Island:

> At first there were no inhabitants visible, but at one o'clock three bidars and some small canoes came in sight and paddled toward the ship, and when they approached the ship it was discovered that this bay was also inhabited by Koloshi. Among the savages in the bidar was a Chief by the name of Taik-nukh-Takhtu-yakh, who came on board with two old men. He was taken into the cabin and hospitably received and then a conversation was held through an interpreter. He was informed according to the instructions issued with regard to our course of action when meeting with native Chiefs, "that he saw before him people of the Russian Empire, and that as they were a numerous and very strong people, they had taken possession of all those regions in the name of Her Imperial Majesty the most gracious Empress." When this had been explained to him, he was allowed to look at the portraits of Her Imperial Majesty and Their Imperial Highnesses. Then he was told of the immense population, wealth and strength of the country and the almost limitless power of the ruler of all the Russias. This Chief appeared to be deeply impressed with the description of the power of our country and he was so anxious to be called a subject of the Empire and enjoy its protection that we showed him one of the beautiful Russian copper medals. His admiration of this was so great that it was concluded to bestow one of these medals upon him, as had been done with the first Koloshi Chief we had met, Il-Khak [Yakutat Bay, chief of all the Koloshi], and he received it with the same satisfaction and gratitude. As he desired to show his gratitude he went to his bidar and brought one fresh otter skin and six otter tails, which he tied together in a bundle on the ship and requested that they should be taken as a proof of his gratitude to the Court of Her Imperial Majesty and asked that the package might be sent there without fail. This otter-skin and tails were actually forwarded as requested.[12]

The Russians proceeded to trade with the natives, managed to do some fishing and raspberry-picking, and with the help of the Indians found and brought aboard a 780-pound anchor said to have belonged to the earlier ship. At least one copper plate was buried under a prominent rock, but no mention is made of the cenotaph of Lapérouse. If the Russians did find it, they very probably destroyed the evidence. On the 9th of July, Ismaïloff and Bocharoff weighed anchor and put to sea, leaving behind their new, but I suspect not overly-convinced, subjects.[13] And for more than three-quarters of a century after Ismaïloff, the history of the Bay is vague, unrecorded, shrouded in Tlingit legend, legend which speaks of monumental events in enormous country. Of course, there were additional visits by Russians under Baranof,[14] as the Bay was known for its sea otter population. But once that beautiful animal had been wiped out along the coast through the combined efforts of half a dozen nations, Lituya Bay ceased to be of interest except as a port in the emergency of a storm. Not until 1874 was history again accurately written.

In that year the Coast Survey schooner *Yukon*, with Mr. Marcus Baker aboard as astronomical observer and under the command of the surveyor-scientist William Healy Dall, anchored in Lituya Bay for four days. Dall, unlike many present-day scientists who would consider written discussion of scenery a breach of faith, later reported the expedition to his superior and, commenting on the region inland said, "The scenery is grand; the mountains, reaching 16,000 feet above the sea, are bedded in forest lowlands, and are scored by enormous glaciers."[15] And in his *Coast Pilot* of 1883, Dall compared the Bay to Yosemite Valley, a Yosemite which had retained its glaciers, however, and whose floor was submerged six hundred or eight hundred feet. The *Yukon* left the Bay on the morning of May 19, 1874, and sailed northwest up the coast to complete the voyage, during the course of which most of the Coast Survey names from Cape Spencer to Cape Fairweather were bestowed.

Then, historically at least, silence for another twenty years. But on August 17, 1896, the ugly fever of gold erupted at Rabbit Creek in the Yukon, and within five days Dawson City was born. Almost unbelievable scenes were subsequently acted out in Skagway, on the White Pass, on Lake Bennett, and in Dawson. No such activity took place on the Lituya Bay coast, but sporadic beach placer-mining occurred there during the 1890's, most of it not very profitable.[16] However, gold mining in any wilderness produces strange partnerships and often even stranger results. Lituya Bay, paradise though it may have been to Lapérouse when he first arrived, did not quite live up to his expectations.

And so to the Bay in summer 1898, in seventy-foot Siwash canoes, came Edith Whittlesey Nelson, born in rural England, and her husband Hans Nelson, an immigrant Swede. They had for partners three single men among whom was one Michael Dennin.[17] The group apparently set up camp on the present Portage Creek just west of the Bay, in a cabin built in the early 1890's. They prospected during the rest of the summer and on into the fall, producing about eight thousand dollars in gold dust, but waited too long in making a decision to leave and were trapped by snow and cold weather. Food was scarce and had to be rationed, and a certain amount of tension was unavoidable once mining activity had ceased. Then without warning, when the group still had four months of survival to live through, Michael Dennin shot and killed the two single men and was about to murder the Nelsons when they disarmed him. During the struggle, Dennin was knocked unconscious by Hans Nelson, who would have killed the murderer if his wife had not stopped him in his blind fury. Some minutes later Edith Nelson again stopped her husband from killing Dennin with the shotgun. Dennin was made a prisoner, two shallow graves were dug in the bitter December weather, and the Nelsons attempted to settle down to the endless task of guarding the man who would kill them if he broke loose. They tried to persuade Negook, head man of the very small Indian village nearby,[18] to take the prisoner down the coast in a canoe to a white settlement, but the Indian would have nothing to do with the affair. As the new year came in, the situation became intolerable and the Nelsons reached the soul-searching decision to hold a trial, with themselves as witnesses, prosecution, and jury, and in the event it was necessary, as executioners.

In a tiny cabin, in the silence of dead winter, the remarkable scene was then acted out. The evidence was presented, the jury deliberated, and as judge, Edith Nelson brought in the verdict. On the day preceding the scheduled execution, the Indians Negook and Hadikwan were brought to the scene to hear the confession, since Dennin had decided to talk. He said he had not been home to the old country for fifteen years, and wanted to return in style. He could not have accomplished that on his $1,600 share of the gold, so decided to take the entire $8,000 by murdering them all and reporting it as an Indian killing. Dennin signed the document Edith Nelson had written out as he spoke, and Negook and Hadikwan put crosses after their own names. The following January morning, at minus 25° Fahrenheit, Michael Dennin was hanged from a tree by Edith Nelson.[19]

The prospectors who ranged the coast near Lituya Bay, and there were not many, served as transition between the early history and the modern history of the Bay. They arrived as the age-old Indian hunting and fishing patterns were breaking down on contact with the white culture. The prospectors bridged a certain period between the old and the new, but they were part of neither. Some time during the year 1915 or the year 1917 a solitary man in a small boat landed on Cenotaph Island and proceeded to build a cabin. This man was to be the only white permanent resident in the history of the coast from Cape Spencer to Yakutat, a distance of one hundred fifty miles. For twenty-two years his home was Cenotaph Island in the middle of Lituya Bay, where he lived essentially alone, although he had a partner of sorts later on. The man was obviously a hermit in the extreme, but an extraordinary one, for all who met him were struck by his generosity and kindness. I would like to know why and how he chose Lapérouse's island for a home, but I do not have the answer. I only know he chose an indescribably beautiful place to live, and I know what the isolation must have been, especially in the winter. I never knew James Todd Huscroft of Lituya Bay, but in the early thirties during some of the first climbing expeditions to the area, Robert Bates and Bradford Washburn came to know him. So I wrote Washburn and asked him to reminisce on Huscroft. He wrote back and said he would be delighted, but that Bates should do it. I wrote Robert Bates and asked for his thoughts on Jim, and this is what he put down:

"Jim Huscroft was one of the kindest men I have ever known. When I first met him in 1932, he was living alone on Cenotaph Island in Lituya Bay, where he had lived for some seventeen years as a sort of modern hermit, going 'out' to Juneau once a year to buy supplies and to sell furs of the blue foxes that ran wild on the island. By 1932 the foxes had died from mange, however, and Jim had no visible source of income. A stocky, tremendously powerful man with a sad, kindly face, Jim had arms the size of a normal man's legs. The way he could saw up a whole pine tree into chunks to fit his stove was awe-inspiring. When a stranger arrived at Cenotaph Island, whether by boat or float plane, Jim was always there to greet him. His bald head gleaming dully, he would be waiting, watch in hand, with the words, 'I make it 11:20; what do you make it?' Watches compared and the hands adjusted, he would be likely to remark that his radio had not been working very well lately, which usually meant for the last seven or eight months. In June 1933, when we arrived at Cenotaph Island aboard the gas boat *Yakobi*, with Captain Tom Smith, Jim was there at his little dock, watch in hand, but this time the first thing he said was, 'Say it ain't so, Bob. Say it ain't so.' I said, 'What ain't so, Jim?,' and he replied, 'That the kids in New York City is eatin' out of garbage pails! I've been thinkin' about it all winter ... you know, my radio ain't been workin' so good lately. There's all those salmon in the Bay and goats in the hills, an' if I could just get some cans I could help some. Tain't right for kids to be eatin' that way, you know, an' I want to help 'em out. Been thinkin' about it all winter.'

"Jim would give away anything he had and was always thinking of other people's problems. He once told me he had been born in Steubenville, Ohio, had made three 'fortunes' and lost them all, and after the third—some kind of lumber business—had retired to Cenotaph Island where for seventeen years he had lived alone, except on occasions when Ernie Rognan, a Norwegian fisherman and owner of the *Ya Sure*, stayed with him. But nothing pleased him more than helping someone else. 'Take it,' he would say, lying gracefully, 'I got lots more.'

"Jim's needs were few, but the only time I ever saw him angry was a brief flare-up when someone threw out what looked like a pail of dirty water, which was in reality his 'potato water,' source of whatever rise there was in his sourdough. He grew lots of potatoes, ate salmon and goat, and every morning— three hundred sixty-five days a year—had the sourdough hot-cakes, heavy ones, the size of the fry pan. But he showed imagination in producing soups, one of his favorites a Norwegian milk soup with raisins. Near Jim's island, beds of delicious strawberries spread for miles along the coast at the mouth of Lituya Bay, and through his prospecting he had come to know the berries in other areas within thirty miles of the Bay. The beaches outside were known to other prospectors as well, so that each summer one or two would usually drop in to see Jim. On one occasion in 1933, we had just finished a salmon supper in Jim's cabin, and Bradford Washburn was proudly holding up a heavily iced cake we had baked in Jim's oven, when the door opened and in came six gaunt, bearded men. They were five Dutchmen and a Finn who had been prospecting and run low on food. When they saw the cake, our one cake of the whole summer, their eyes lit up. It turned out they had been living on bear meat for the past week and were sick and tired of it. We filled them up on salmon and beans before cutting the cake.

"When Jim took his small boat to Juneau on his annual trip to the outside, he always went first to a store where he could buy a tub of salt mackerel. He ate one or two on the spot and then put away the rest of the tub to take to the island. Next he would buy his most essential item, snuff, which he referred to as 'snuss,' in the Norwegian way. When he had a supply, Jim constantly kept a plug of it under his upper lip. One fall when he went to Juneau, he called at the post office to pick up his year's supply of mail, consisting usually of a bill or two and a small cheque. On this occasion, however, the man at the window said, 'Huscroft? Just a minute.' He raised the wicket and began pushing out stacks and stacks of letters to the thoroughly amazed hermit. Jim did not know that some months previously Bradford Washburn had written about him in the *National Geographic*. The result was a bushel basket of mail giving him recipes for salmonberry jam, asking philosophical questions about the advantages of life as a hermit, and even proposing marriage. The publicity and especially the seven marriage proposals startled Jim, and he scarcely took time to go to the Elks Club to get his year's supply of newspapers before starting back to the Bay. The papers were saved for him all through the year, and while he always read the very latest news when he made the annual voyage, he never cheated on returning to the island where, each morning over his enormous sourdough hotcakes and coffee he read the morning paper with news fresh to him and only one year old. He told me, 'It don't matter which year it is. The news is all the same anyway. Only if I peeked ahead, it'd take away the fun.'

"But the great climax of each year for Jim Huscroft was Christmas dinner. He planned the momentous affair months ahead, and always showed us strawberries and blueberries and salmonberries he had put up, to be used when the time came for Christmas baking. When the exciting occasion arrived Jim would sit down, entirely alone, to a roast goose dinner with a choice of fourteen different kinds of pie."[20]

In 1936 a great wave removed some of Jim's outbuildings, destroyed part of the vegetable garden, and partially inundated the floor of his cabin. He survived, and so did the boat, but on 23 March, 1939, Jim died, quite feeble toward the end,[21] the cabin in disrepair, the vegetable garden producing little because he could not give it enough attention. The following year Bradford Washburn had a plaque fixed to a huge rock on the northwest corner of the island:

"Near this spot Jim Huscroft, Alaskan, pioneer and frontiersman, made his home for twenty-two years. His kindness and generosity endeared him to all those whose work or travels brought them to this beautiful bay. This tablet is

Jim Huscroft, Cenotaph Island. 1933. Photograph by BRADFORD WASHBURN.

placed here in his memory by the members of the Harvard-Dartmouth Alaskan Expeditions of 1930, 1932, 1933, and 1934. 1940"

Forty years ago Allen Carpé, writing on the attempt on Mount Fairweather, referred to Jim Huscroft with this phrase: "According to a local man who has lived on Cenotaph Island for several years..."[22] In Webster's, the first definition of *local* is "relating to place." In that case, I guess Huscroft was as local as they come.

Lituya Bay, treacherous, wild, incomparable. The peaks of the range rise very nearly straight out of the waters and on a cold morning, after the north wind has cleared the fog and rain, there is often a small cloud plume from the high, brilliant summit of Mount Fairweather. With new snow on the trees to fifteen hundred feet, and Crillon surrounded by the luminosity of early light from the east, the scene becomes an eighteenth century engraving, delicate and vast, the water calm, occasional rumbles from the glaciers. At its best, Lituya Bay is certainly the paradise described by a number of observers, and from the air is an unbelievable gem. But at its worst, the Bay can be savage and utterly brutal, a paradise always poised just on the edge of violence, and when that violence comes it is overwhelming. The Tlingits knew, but it is one thing to read a legend and quite another to feel it. Camped alone high on the south shore in enormous wind and horizontal rain, I went back one hundred eighty years to Yeahlth, to a world-view encompassing Lituya Bay north to Icy Bay and south to Cross Sound. A world-view, however, that involved much thought about the nature of the land, dominated as it was by snow and ice. And if, as the Tlingits imagined, the glaciers were the children of the mountains, born in regions of eternal snow, if the sun as the arch-enemy looked down to destroy the glaciers, and the parents tore rocks from their sides and scattered them over the surface of the glaciers to protect their children, what of the legend of Kah Lituya,[23] the monster of the deep who dwelled in the ocean caverns near the entrance to the Bay?

Kah Lituya, it is said, resented any approach to his domain. He took as slaves those he destroyed. They became bears and from their watchtowers high in the Fairweather Range they warned of the approach of canoes, and with their master they grasped the surface of the water and shook it, causing tidal waves to rise and engulf the enemy. Perhaps only a reference to the dangers at the entrance, to the men lost in 1786, to the Tlingits who were no doubt lost in the same tide rips. But I think not. The legend hints at much greater events, for the rips, dangerous as they are, affect only a small area of water. If the entire surface of Lituya Bay is to be shaken as a sheet, a cataclysm is required, inestimable violence, chaos. And that chaos has come to the Bay three times at least, quite possibly four times since Lapérouse. The giant waves of Lituya Bay.

The Tlingits must have known, for in addition to the legend of Kah-Lituya, a somewhat vague story has come down[24] which tells of a village on the shores of the Bay, perhaps somewhere near Anchorage Cove. Most of the men of this village were hunting sea otter along the coast one day, and on returning to their homes found the village completely wiped out. The only survivor was a woman who had been gathering berries on a slope well above the site, and the catastrophe probably unfolded before her eyes. The great wave of 1853 may have been responsible for the lone survivor watching her people disappear beneath tons of water, although the vagueness of the legend probably indicates an earlier date.[25]

But the most recent was the worst, July 9, 1958. Weather clear, water calm. Eight Canadian climbers, just finished with the centennial climb of Mount Fairweather, were camped at Anchorage Cove off the north end of La Chaussee Spit. At about 9:00 P.M. this group was airlifted to Juneau, although they had originally planned to leave the following morning. An hour earlier the troller *Edrie* had entered the Bay and anchored off the south shore in a small cove east of The Paps. At 9:00 P.M. the troller *Badger* entered, went as far as Cenotaph Island, then returned to Anchorage Cove and dropped anchor near a third troller, the *Sunmore*. The sun was setting, the tide ebbing. The six people aboard (two on each boat) turned in for the night. At 10:16 the Fairweather fault, which runs directly through Gilbert and Crillon Inlets at the rear of the Bay, was wrenched in a violent earthquake. One minute later ninety million tons of rock with a displacement of forty million cubic yards plummeted from the northeast wall of Gilbert Inlet into the Bay.[26]

A colossal water surge climbed beyond 1700 feet on the steep spur southwest of Gilbert Inlet, stripping the headland to bedrock, and a giant wave front fifty to one hundred feet high raced from the rear of the Bay toward the ocean at an average speed of one hundred miles per hour. The *Sunmore* was swamped and went to the bottom, the *Edrie* with a snapped anchor chain rode out the giant and secondary waves, and the *Badger* was carried stern first over La Chaussee Spit eighty feet above the trees. The *Badger* foundered when the wave crest broke outside the spit, but the Swansons abandoned ship in a small skiff and were rescued at midnight. On the morning of 10 July, Don Miller, of the United States Geological Survey, and Ken Loken of Juneau flew over the Bay in a small plane. The scene was indeed chaos. The entire shoreline of Lituya was devastated and the vertical scar on the northeast wall of Gilbert Inlet reached to 3000 feet; thirteen hundred horizontal feet of ice was missing from the front of Lituya Glacier, and the delta at the terminus and underneath the slide area was completely gone. The upper two and a half miles of the Bay was solid with floating ice blocks, a stupendous raft of floating logs and other vegetation twelve hundred feet by three miles long hugged the outer north shore, and over the rest of the Bay and beyond to five miles at sea thousands of logs rode peacefully with the tides.[27] Six years later, Lituya Bay still bore the scars. The floating logs and the ice were gone, but the shorelines were naked. Great trees now bleached were lying in all directions, and here and there a solitary upright trunk, in place but broken off savagely head high. And in the middle of La Chaussee Spit, a lone tree, standing as a mast, a few branches at the top, the bark stripped clean.

Lituya Bay, wild and incomparable, the thread of violence. Tchirikov never saw it, Cook missed it, but by chance Lapérouse found it and left us a wealth of description. And Huscroft. What possessed him to select that spot? Did he merely need an island, any island, on which to farm foxes? Maybe and maybe not, but I think I can see him as he rowed over the first time back in 1917. It must have been a good day. It had to be a good day for I am sure he saw the peaks—all of them—and felt the immense space. The Isle du Cénotaphe became his that day. It still is, even though the great wave of 1958 removed the rest of the outbuildings, the cabin, and any trace of the vegetable garden.

NOTE: The Roman numeral within the parentheses refers to the major bibliographical section in which the citation may be found. As a rule, I have not used ellipses in the text.

[1] See place names for Lituya Bay.

[2] Golder (1922, IV) 1; 291.

[3] Ibid., 292-3.

[4] Ibid., 296-7.

[5] Ibid., 311—a long editor's note on the disappearance of Tchirikov's men, whose fate has never been determined.

[6] Cook (1784, IV) 2; 345-6.

[7] Yeahlth, the principal divinity of Tlingit mythology, symbolized by the Raven. After arranging the world, he was one day to reappear and reward those who followed his teachings, turn to stone those who disobeyed him.

[8] *Alaska Magazine* (1927, III) 1; 151-3, and Emmons (1911, III).

[9] Morai—Tlingit burial enclosure.

[10] Lapérouse (1799 London, IV) 1; Chapters VII, VIII, IX. I have retained Lapérouse's wording exact, but for the sake of continuity the paragraphs have been rearranged. I commend the reader to this fascinating account for further detail.

[11] Shelekhoff (1788, IV) 2; 76.

[12] Ibid., 108-109.

[13] Shelekhoff, according to the translation by Petroff, mentions a *permanent* Tlingit village only a short distance from the anchorage of the *Three Saints*. This is the only mention I have ever seen of Tlingit winter quarters in Lituya Bay, except for Jack London (1906, VI).

[14] From time to time large bidarka fleets under Baranof put into Lituya Bay (see Bancroft 1886, V), and Davidson (1867 pgs. 285-6 & 1869 pgs. 132, 134; IV) mentions Shiltz (Shields?) in Lituya Bay 1796, and Lipunski and Khromtchenko in Lituya Bay 1826, but I have been unable to verify these visits.

[15] Dall (1878, IV), quoted by Patterson, 64. There are a number of Alaskan placenames after W. H. Dall, as well as the Dall sheep.

[16] *Alaska Sportsman* (July 1936, VI) and Wright (1907, I).

[17] London (1906, VI). The story of the hanging incident was titled "The Unexpected" by Jack London. The details given here are taken from that account. In the copy of *McClure's Magazine* held by the State Museum and Library at Juneau, a handwritten note from Mrs. M. B. Keller, a personal friend of the Nelson's, has been inserted. The note attests to the authenticity of the story.

Williams (1952, VI) adds the fact that the Nelsons left Lituya Bay on board the steamer *Bertha* early the next summer.

[18] The mention of a winter village in Jack London's story raises some questions as to the exact location of the hanging incident. It is very doubtful the Tlingits ever had winter quarters in Lituya Bay.

[19] An unexpected sequel to this act of lonely courage occurred in 1962 when the Superintendent of Glacier Bay and Sitka National Monuments, L. J. Mitchell, submitted to the National Park Service Western Regional office a list of 18 proposed place names for Glacier Bay. Seventeen of those suggested were forwarded by Regional to the Board on Geographic Names. The 18th was held back. Mitchell wanted to name the fourth large creek northwest of Lituya Bay *Justice Creek*, in honor of the incident of 1899 which had occurred in that general area. In a magnificent example of bureaucratic timidity, Regional suggested he consider a more appropriate name for the creek, in the belief that it would be questionable for the Federal Government to officially recognize a name for a feature, based upon the consequences of the Government's inability to enforce law. Mitchell, in just as classic a rebuttal, wrote the following letter to Regional: "At about the time of this happening, Alaska had four main cities. They were Skagway with a population of 3,117, Juneau with 1,864, Sitka with 1,396, and Douglas with 825. The only other major city in the 1900 census was Nome where 'thousands' of stampeders were mining gold. Alaska then was a frontier territory of 586,400 square miles with about 34,000 miles of coast line; an area of about 1/5 the size of the 48 contiguous states, and a coast line of more than twice the length of that of all the other states. From 1867 to 1884 the only official representative of the United States government was a collector of customs at Sitka. Until 1884 it was not legally possible to make a will, punish crimes, own or transfer property, or even get married.

"In 1884 Congress created the District of Alaska, with an appointed governor and a district court system. In about 1900 Congress established a code of civil and criminal law for the territory but not until 1912 were there mechanics established for enforcing them. Around 1900 the notorious Soapy Smith gang held control of Alaska's largest city, Skagway. Soapy was finally killed and his gang driven from Skagway by a citizen's group known as 'the committee of 101.' This, then, was a frontier area where many stampeders were scattered about the land prospecting and mining gold. Certainly the government was not able to enforce law under these circumstances, and could not do so today if these conditions were to exist again. The overwhelming demands upon a law enforcement organization over such a great area, and with the lack of communications and transportation, certainly were conditions under which no government could afford to provide government services to the remotest gold sluice box. This is the background of the incident near Lituya Bay where citizens out of communication with the law constituted themselves a court and carried out the task for which there was no alternative.... The trial and execution was not the action of a mob, but a function of citizen government. Detailed records were kept of the trial, including a signed confession. This incident has become a bit of the history, and legend, of frontier Alaska. We do not see how the proposed naming of this feature would reflect discredit to our government." (L. J. Mitchell to Region Four, Feb. 1962, quoted by permission of L. J. Mitchell.)

[20] Personal communication from Robert Bates of the American Alpine Club. For further insight on the severity of the land Huscroft lived in, I call to the reader's attention the epic diary of V. Swanson quoted by Colby (1945) in *A Guide to Alaska*, Federal Writers' Project, The Macmillan Co., 218-20.

[21] USNPS correspondence, Regional Forester Heintzleman to Department of Interior, September 1939 re Huscroft's fur farm permit.

[22] Carpé (1926, VII); 444.

[23] Emmons (1911, III).

[24] Williams (1952, VI). Laguna (1964, III) further discusses Williams' account of Tlingit legend.

[25] Laguna (1964, III), Miller (1960, I).

[26] Miller (1960, I).

[27] Ibid.

II *Bay of Great Glaciers*

AT LATITUDE 58°13′, fifty miles south of Lituya Bay, the coastline turns east and becomes Cross Sound, a wide body of water open to the storms from the southwest, but at least almost entirely free of floating ice. It was not always thus. In July, 1794, H.M.S. *Discovery* anchored at Port Althorp, in the vicinity of which Captain George Vancouver was to carry out some of the last of his surveys and explorations. On July 10, under the command of Lt. Whidbey, the long boats pulled away into a world of ice and fog. Progress northwest across the Sound was immediately impeded by the floating ice, quantities of it, but Whidbey reached Cape Spencer and turned east to begin charting the continental shoreline.

> Having at length effected this object [Cape Spencer], the continental shore from the cape above-mentioned was found to take nearly a north direction for about 3 leagues to a low pebbly point; N.N.W. from which, five miles further, a small brook flowed into the sound, and on its northern side stood the ruins of a deserted Indian village. To reach this station, the party had advanced up an arm about 6 miles wide at its entrance, but which had decreased to about half that width, and their further progress was now stopped by an immense body of compact perpendicular ice, extending from shore to shore, and connected with a range of lofty mountains that formed the head of the arm, and as it were, gave support to this body of ice on each side. Their course was now directed across the arm, and on its eastern side, compelled by the inclemency of the weather, the party stopped until it should prove more favorable to their purpose. These shores are composed of a border of low land, which on high tides is overflown, and becomes broken into islands. Here were erected two pillars sixteen feet high, and four feet in circumference, painted white; on the top of each was placed a large square box; on examining one of them it was found to contain many ashes, and pieces of burnt bones, which were considered to be human; these relicts were carefully wrapped up in skins, and old mats, and at the base of the pillars was placed an old canoe in which were some paddles.[1]

The narration is by Captain Vancouver, and his lieutenant had discovered Taylor Bay. The immense body of compact perpendicular ice was the Brady Glacier. But the ruins of the deserted Indian village, even had they not rotted away, could not be seen today for the site lies under one thousand feet of ice, buried by the advancing glacier. Whidbey and his party, after spending a night of constant rain on the east side of the bay, pushed through the ice beyond Point Wimbledon and entered what is now Dundas Bay. Vancouver continues the narration:

> Up this opening the party advanced nearly in a north-west direction about 2 leagues, where their further progress was nearly stopped by shoals, rocky islets, and rocks, extending across the branch, which decreased to about a mile in width, and for the space of about two miles, was occupied by these islets and rocks; beyond them on the western shore was a small shallow opening, that appeared to communicate [in fact, it did not] with one of a similar description, and which had been noticed in the other arm a few miles below the icy barrier, but was too shallow to be approached by the boats. About 4 miles from hence in a northerly direction this branch finally closed, being in most places greatly encumbered with ice. On the return of the boats, they were much incommoded by the shoals that extend from the north-east side of the arm, to within half a mile of its south-west side. About its entrance the soundings were regular, of a moderate depth, and afforded good and secure anchorage; but at this season, vessels would be much inconvenienced by the immense quantities of floating ice; this impediment, in addition to the weather being again very foggy, stopped the progress of their researches early in the afternoon, and obliged them to retire about a league within the entrance on the eastern shore. About ten of the natives in two canoes had been met with, who had conducted themselves in a very civil and friendly manner...
>
> The morning of the 12th, though unpleasant, was rather more favorable to their pursuit, which was still greatly impeded by the ice. From the east point of this branch, which I have called Point Dundas, situated in latitude 58°21′, longi-

Tarr Inlet from the north. 1940. Russell Island top left, thirteen miles distant. Grand Pacific Glacier foreground, Margerie Glacier right. Photograph by BRADFORD WASHBURN.

tude 224°1', the coast takes an irregular E.N.E. direction about seven miles to a point [Point Carolus], from whence this branch of the sound appeared to be very extensive in an E.S.E. point of view, and was upwards of 3 leagues across. The party proceeded from Point Dundas to this station, through a channel from 2 to 3 miles in width, between the continental shore, and an island [Lemesurier Island] about seven miles long and three miles broad, lying in a N.E. and S.W. direction. This spacious inlet presented to our party an arduous task, as the space between the shores on the northern and southern sides, seemed to be intirely occupied by one compact sheet of ice as far as the eye could distinguish. Whilst the boats remained at this point they were visited by the natives in several canoes, that had come from out a small shallow brook a little to the westward of the point. Excepting a few indifferent sea otter skins, these people brought with them no articles for traffic. To the north and east of this point, the shores of the continent form two large open bays, which were terminated by compact solid mountains of ice, rising perpendicularly from the water's edge, and bounded to the north by a continuation of the united lofty frozen mountains that extend eastward from Mount Fairweather. In these bays also were great quantities of broken ice, which having been put in motion by the springing up of a northerly wind, was drifted to the southward, and forcing the boats from the northern shore, obliged them to take shelter round the north-east point of the above island.[2]

Whidbey and Le Mesurier continued east on their explorations, turning Point Couverdeen and thence up the Lynn Canal, but there is no need to follow them further, for the last two sentences of the narration just quoted contain the recorded discovery of Glacier Bay, and discovered as it should have been: under conditions of rain and occasional fog and beset by extreme quantities of floating ice, a brooding wall of solid ice looming close by, Indian visitation, a north wind clearing. But where *exactly* was Whidbey when he saw his compact solid mountains of ice on July 12, 1794, and how far away were they? The assumption is that the Lieutenant and his party were ashore at Point Carolus, and that the glacier front was six miles north of them, or approximately on a line with Rush Point.[3] Whidbey's remarks were casual but his charts were far from that, and the conclusion is staggering even if obvious. From Point Carolus today one moves sixty-five miles north in Glacier Bay to the terminus of the Grand Pacific Glacier, or the entire length of the Glacier Bay National Monument. In other words, there really was not much Glacier Bay for Whidbey and Le Mesurier to discover. Just a rather small indentation of ten miles or so, and a glacier destined to calve uncounted billions of cubic yards of ice in the following one hundred and seventy years.

And prior to Captain George Vancouver of H.M.S. *Dis-*

Section from Captain Vancouver's map portfolio. 1794. Large indentation east of Pt. Dundas was the Glacier Bay of 1794. Courtesy Bancroft Library.

"A Sea Otter." 1778. Captain Cook portfolio, courtesy Bancroft Library.

covery? Mostly legend, Indian legend which mentions harsh events in harsh country. Handed down from Tlingit mother to daughter, chanted by rote, the story of Glacier Bay relates events which almost certainly happened although some observers, notably G. F. Wright, suggested the Indian traditions should be ignored. The Reverend Wright was apparently not very pleased with folklore[4] even though that folklore adhered with remarkable accuracy to his own geology, to say nothing of the glacial geology of today. Of course no exact dates can be realized from the Indian traditions, but a long-lived Tlingit patriarch could have witnessed the entire drama, living as he did so near the great glacier, listening as he surely did to one of his wives handing down the tale, perhaps within hearing distance of the thundering ice wall.[5]

It is very hard to describe our history and our Father's origin. Our Father's Father lived with his people in Glacier Bay when it was a great valley with a single river running through it. It was our country, the Tcukanadi, and we called it Sitt-eeta-ghaee, bay from where the ice receded. Our people lived at Klemshawshiki, or city on the sand at the base of the mountains [Beardslee Islands], and there were many fish in the river. But our people were always worried about the great Glacier because they could see it and knew it might come down. They always talked to it saying "My son's daughter, be very careful. You might come down on me." Only those of our people who hunted seal and goat went very near the Glacier. It was long, long ago, but one time a young girl known as Kahsteen was kept in seclusion while in puberty. She was very lonely and it was unbearable for her. She decided to call the Glacier down for spite. She got fish bones filled with the charm of supernatural power and whistled through them, calling the ice down. When the ice started to move, the people asked why. So then it was known. It came down in a day and would not go away in ten years, and a great wave rushed in from the ocean and swept away most of the village and knocked down the forest with icebergs. And there were no more fish in the river. Our people counseled among themselves and decided to move away. But they knew the Glacier would follow them until it found the one who called it. So someone must stay. It was to be Kahsteen. But an old lady named Shaw-whad-seet stopped them and said, "She is young and can have many children yet. I am old and have little usefulness. Let me stay in her place." It was agreed.

Our Father's Father picked a protected place and our people called the town Hoonah, meaning in the lee of the north wind. And then all the people moved there and Shaw-whad-seet waited alone in her house for the Glacier to pass over her. Then after that she lived under the ice with the ice people and gave birth to their children. And when the great sheets of ice fall away from the glaciers and crash into the Bay, you can sometimes see bright things in the water. They are Shaw-whad-seet's ice-children, playing.[6]

The terminus Whidbey and Le Mesurier saw in 1794 had already started the great recession, and as the mammoth ice front retreated, it left behind a chaotic landscape, a landscape of austere beauty to some, to others a worthless sea of boulders on top of rocks on top of dying ice. No trees, no bushes, nothing green, nothing living. Or so it seems. The facts are otherwise. There are many living things, some of them only a few feet from the ice, already taking possession of the land just released by the glacier. But for almost a century after Vancouver the record is written only in tree rings and carbon-dating. There is not even Indian tradition, although the Tlingits took possession of their old land again and established temporary summer camps for sealing and fishing, and since the best sealing was near the ice front, those temporary villages moved a little farther north each year. Of course the willow and the alder were moving north too, if more slowly, and so were birds and small ground animals, and more occasionally Alaskan brown bear, the mammoth, unpredictable carnivore, supreme in a landscape as wild as himself, new-born nameless landscape with the ice front always close at hand, thundering across the decades, receding at an incredible pace, the rain, fog, screeching birds, seals calling, the Hoonah kwan people huddled in their smoky bark huts chanting legend, hunting, fighting, moving in canoes across frigid waters, through masses of floating ice and enormous tides.

* * *

It is not possible to say for certain when a white man first heard of Glacier Bay. There are rather vague references[7] to Russian pilots having been in the area, and it is very probable Russian ships did get into the Bay before Alaska was purchased by the United States. But two years after the Russian flag was lowered at Sitka, definite word was passed about the ice country. In that year, 1869, Professor George Davidson of the U. S. Coast and Geodetic Survey visited the eminent Indian chief Klohkutz at Chilkat.[8] Klohkutz drew a map covering many hundreds of square miles, not quite including the country as far southwest of Chilkat as Glacier Bay. But the chief told Davidson about the bay of great glaciers, a thirty mile journey on snowshoes.[9] Had George Davidson made that trip with Klohkutz, it would have been well recorded, for Davidson was a prolific writer. But there was not time, and the first exploration of the Bay was to be written elsewhere.

When Russell Island, some fifty miles up Glacier Bay from Point Carolus, was not yet an island, its southern end just protruding from the ice front, a white man came to the still nameless bay to visit the Indians and see the country. Lieutenant Charles Erskine Scott Wood[10] had initially set out from Portland, Oregon in early April 1877, with C. H. Taylor of Chicago, on an expedition to climb Mount St. Elias. The two gentlemen arrived at Sitka aboard the steamer *California* and, failing to engage a trading schooner for the trip to Yakutat, immediately set about negotiating with the natives for a canoe and guides. After the usual prolonged bargaining, the explorers succeeded in contracting for a vessel which would hold four tons of goods, and passengers. Some days after mid-April they left Sitka and paddled north, the canoe jammed with supplies, four natives, a prospector, and Taylor and Wood. On April 27 they turned west from Chatham Strait and, fighting headwinds all the way, moved through Icy Strait into Cross Sound and reached Cape Spencer. Near the Cape they made camp on a small island occupied by a summer encampment of three Hoonah families. They were now within five days of Yakutat but at this point the expedition collapsed. The natives refused to go farther and with devastating logic (apparently pointing at Mount Fairweather) said, "One mountain is as good as another. There is a very big one. Go climb that if you want to."[11] The expedition turned back to Cross Sound, briefly explored the unnamed Taylor Bay, where they found a summer camp of Hoonah seal hunters,[12] then paddled south to Sitka. Taylor decided to return to Chicago, but Wood was not satisfied. He re-engaged his native interpreter, Sam, and Myers the prospector, and with a new crew once again set off for the north, to explore a bay which he estimated lay twenty miles southeast of Mount Fairweather. Thus, some time around the middle of May 1877, C. E. S. Wood arrived in the glacier country.

My purpose was to explore the bay, cross the coast range, and strike the upper waters of Chilkáht. On the shores of the bay we found hospitality with a band of Hoonáhs. Leaving the crew with our large canoe under the charge of Myers at this place, I took a smaller one and went with Cocheen, the chief of the band, northwesterly up the bay. After about forty miles' travel, we came to a small village of Asónques [Hugh Miller Inlet?]. They received us with great hospitality, and as our canoe had been too small to carry any shelter, the head man gave me a bed in his own cabin. He had a great many wives, who busied themselves making me comfortable. The buckskin reinforcement of my riding trowsers excited childish wonder. I drew pictures of horses and men separate, and then of men mounted on horses. Their astonishment over the wonderful animal was greater than their delight at comprehending the utility of the trowsers.

From this Asónque village I went, with a party of mountain goat-hunters, up into the Mount St. Elias alps back of Mount Fairweather—that is, to the north-east of that mountain. For this trip our party made elaborate preparations. We donned belted shirts made of squirrel skins, fur head-dresses (generally conical), seal-skin bootees fitting very closely, and laced half-way to the knee. We carried spears for alpenstocks, bows and arrows, rawhide ropes, and one or two old Hudson Bay rifles. The climbing was very laborious work. The mountains, where not covered with ice or snow, were either of a crumbling schistose character or ice-worn limestone, and sometimes granite. The sides were terribly rugged; some of the face walls were about eight hundred feet sheer, with a foot slope of shellrock or debris of two hundred or three hundred feet more. Ptarmigan were seen on the lower levels where the ground was bare, but I saw nothing on which they could feed. The goats kept well up toward the summit, amid the snowfields, and fed on the grass which sprouted along the edges of melting drifts. They were the wariest, keenest animals I ever hunted. After crossing this coast range the country seemed much the same—rugged, bleak, and impassable. The Indians with me, so far as I could understand them, said it was an exceedingly rough country all the way over, and that the Chilkáht River had its rise among just such alps as those around us, only it was warmer in the Chilkáht mountains, and there was more grass and plenty of wild goats, sheep, and bears. We found a bear that, so far as I know, is peculiar to this country. It is a beautiful bluish under color, with the tips of the long hairs silvery white. The traders call it "St. Elias's silver bear."[13] The skins are not common. Being unable to go further overland I returned to the Asónque camp. There we fitted ice-guards to a small canoe, and with ice-hooks pulled our way through, and carried our canoe over the floes and among the icebergs, to the extreme limit of so-called open water in that direction. The ice-guards were merely wooden false sides hung to a false prow. From this point, also, I found the interior impenetrable, and went to a temporary camp of seal and goat hunters, who were camped on a ledge[14] of rocks above the crunching and grinding icebergs. The head man of this camp was a young fellow of about thirty, who was both Shamán and hereditary chief. He was the most thoughtful and entertaining Thlinkit I had met. He told me that within his own lifetime this place where we now were had been solid ice. He would listen with breathless attention whenever I spoke, and then reply in low, musical intonations, almost like chanting. His narration of the traditions of his people was pathetic in its solemn earnestness.

He said: "You are the only white man that has ever been here, but I have heard of your people. Before I was born—a

long time ago—a ship came to the mouth of this bay, and gave the Thlinkits iron to make knives like this one [Russian traders?]. Before that they had made knives from copper or from stone, like this. Then the Thlinkits had many furs,—foxes, and bear, and sable,—all the people were warm, all were happy, and lived as Yéhl had set them to live. There was plenty to eat, and plenty to wear. Now, sometimes we are hungry and wear ragged robes." Here he paused again, picked up the corner of his squirrel robe and raised it with a sweeping forward gesture, which he maintained till his words had produced their full effect, when the sing-song intonation would begin again.[15]

Leaving Coon-nah-nah-thklé's camp of seal and goat hunters, Wood briefly visited Cocheen's village again, picked up the large canoe, and headed south for Sitka. In Chatham Strait he ministered to the sick boy of an old Hoonah head chief, though with hesitation because of the Tlingit custom of killing the doctor if the patient died. After building a fairly extensive medical practice at the village, Wood prepared to leave, but not without a proper send-off from the chief:

> In the gray dawn, as we were about to push from shore, the old chief came to us accompanied by two of his wives. My blanket was wrapped round him. He said I had a good heart. I was a young chief now, but some day I would be a great one. Among the Thlinkits, he said, when a friend was leaving on a long journey, they watched him out of sight, for he might never return. I was his friend. I was going away to my own land. He would never see me again. Therefore he had come to watch me out of sight. He then motioned to his elder wife, who handed me a beautiful sable skin, and he continued: "Wherever you go among Thlinkits, show them this and tell them I gave it to you." The breeze was freshening. I wrapped my capote about me and stepped aboard. We paddled rapidly out to sea, and it was not long before the three figures were lost to view.[16]

Lieutenant Wood did not receive credit for the discovery of Glacier Bay because he failed to make his explorations known to the public until 1882, when he wrote the article for *Century Magazine*. It made no difference to Wood, however, and in later correspondence he disclaimed any desire to be known as the discoverer.[17] Wood was much more interested in the Indians than the glaciers and did not pay much attention to topography. As a result, he left us no observations on where the glaciers stood as of 1877, and his travels must be followed vaguely. By contrast, the next visitor to the bay of glaciers not only observed the ice fronts, he loved them with a passion. And he told the world about what he had found.

* * *

Two years passed after Wood's visit, and then on October 14, 1879, a canoe left Fort Wrangell, about two hundred fifty miles by water south of Glacier Bay. There were four natives and two white men aboard. The party paddled west from Wrangell through Sumner Strait, north between Kupreanof and Kuiu Islands, northwest across Frederick Sound, and north up Chatham Strait. The plan had been to continue to the Chilkat country, at the north end of the Lynn Canal, but rumors of fighting among the Chilkats reached the group on October 21 when they were just opposite Icy Strait. The decision was to turn west and search for the ice mountains. It was indeed late in the season to look for glaciers in an unknown and, in fact, only rumored country. The thirty-five-foot canoe had already encountered severe winds, and winter was almost upon the North.

Nevertheless, the party headed into Icy Strait and late in the day reached Hoonah, the main village of the Hoonah kwan, where they were met at the water's edge by Kashoto the chief, as he stood robed, dignified, serene, and barefoot. The expedition was entertained hospitably, staying three nights, during the course of which a good deal of discussion occurred about the country the party proposed to visit. The existence of a bay of glaciers was confirmed at this point, but the Hoonahs did not add to the peace of mind of the four natives in the canoe. The Hoonahs said the bay was full of vast masses of floating ice, with a constant noise of thunder in the air. There were said to be deadly bays and passages full of evil spirits, making navigation very perilous. In fact, a giant devil-fish with arms as long as a tree, another creature with an arm with a thousand suckers, a rapacious killer whale in a stretch of swift water and, most dangerous of all, Kooshta-kah the land otter man, the mischievous Puck of Indian lore—all these and more were waiting in Glacier Bay for unwary canoes.[18] But the oratory of the whites prevailed and the expedition pushed off for the glaciers on October 24. They reached Pleasant Island about noon, made some coffee, and took aboard a supply of wood, for one of the guides in the crew had warned there would be no more fuel. Since none of the other natives in the party had ever seen a woodless country, the supposed fact was found hard to believe, and lent an additional sense of mystery and foreboding to the undertaking. The weather worsened as the canoe left Pleasant Island, with rain and then sleet. Darkness came but the explorers continued on their northwesterly course for several hours, finally landing on a desolate, snow-covered beach at a small inlet on the west mainland of Glacier Bay. The leader of this so-far intrepid party of six was, in spite of the wet and the cold, extremely excited at the prospect of discovering some glaciers, and if his four Indians were not entirely dauntless about the dangers lurking beyond, he was. The camp made that night, October 24, 1879, was at Berg Bay, and John Muir had at last reached the rumored bay of great glaciers.[19]

That the party had made it this far so late in the season was due in no small part to the selection of the personnel. Both Muir and S. Hall Young, the Presbyterian missionary, were skilled in the type of oratory which had already and would again carry the day. Toyatte, a Stickeen nobleman to whom the canoe belonged, was captain of the crew, an imposing figure and a great seaman. Kadichan, the son of a Chilkat chief, was chosen specifically for that kinship, for his knowledge of Indian lore, for his powers of oratory, and for his expertise in Tlingit etiquette.[20] In other words, Kadichan was chief of protocol for the party. Sitka Charley, who as a boy had hunted seal in the bay of ice, was a general utility man, as was Stickeen John, who also acted as interpreter. Especially in view of the fact a Tlingit contract for work could be broken at any time by returning the goods paid, no such undertaking was ever assured success, natural obstacles aside. If, in addition, weather turned for the worse,

Kooshta-kah the land otter man, Tlingit gravestone. 1966

and evil spirits began to close in on the Indians—a state of affairs made likely when one is extremely wet and extremely cold—they would more than probably turn around and go home. But the Tlingits along the way were fascinated with both Hall Young and John Muir, although of the two, Muir made much the stronger impression on the native mind. In the canoe the four Indians were strongly under the influence of the two white men, indeed, had to be, for what fools would dash around looking at ice mountains with winter coming on?

On the morning of October 25, Muir peered expectantly through the icy rain and gloom hoping to see a glacier, but saw only storm clouds hanging far down the mountains. The group shoved off, theoretically guided by Charley, who was now lost. Noting smoke across the inlet, they steered in that direction and were shortly greeted by a shot fired over their heads. After Stickeen John had established who they were and Kadichan had sufficiently rebuked the Hoonah for meeting a missionary with a loaded gun, friendlier relations prevailed and the visitors were invited into the bark hut. And here, in a circle of nineteen natives peering at him through a pall of oily smoke, John Muir learned a little bit about the country. The Hoonahs told him they called the bay Sit-a-da-kay or Ice Bay, that there were indeed many ice mountains but no gold mines, that the greatest ice mountain, the one they knew best, was at the head of the bay where large numbers of seal were to be found. Muir wanted to leave immediately, but Charley was now quite uncertain of his supposed knowledge of the area because it had changed so drastically since his boyhood. It was agreed they should take one of the seal hunters as a guide, but this required prolonged consultation, further stretching Muir's patience. At last they got away, and about noon discovered the first ice front, afterward named by Muir the Geikie Glacier. Muir was now in his element, excited beyond measure. He wanted to push on until dark, but the guide said no, and they camped in a small indentation on a low shoreline, probably about three miles north of Geikie Inlet. The following day, Hall Young refused to leave camp because it was Sunday, and the natives did not care for the weather, so Muir, not yet having really seen the country because of the low clouds and mist, climbed alone up the ridge just east of what is now Charpentier Inlet:

Pushing on through rain and mud and sludgy snow, crossing many brown, boulder-choked torrents, wading, jumping, and wallowing in snow up to my shoulders was mountaineering of the most trying kind. After crouching cramped and benumbed in the canoe, poulticed in wet or damp clothing night and day, my limbs had been asleep. This day they were awakened and in the hour of trial proved that they had not lost the cunning learned on many a mountain peak of the High Sierra. I reached a height of fifteen hundred feet, on the ridge that bounds the second of the great glaciers. All the landscape was smothered in clouds and I began to fear that as far as wide views were concerned I had climbed in vain. But at length the clouds lifted a little, and beneath their gray fringes I saw the berg-filled expanse of the bay, and the feet of the mountains that stand about it, and the imposing fronts of five huge glaciers,[21] the nearest being immediately beneath me. This was my first general view of Glacier Bay, a solitude of ice and snow and newborn rocks, dim, dreary, mysterious. I held the ground I had so dearly won for an hour or two, sheltering myself from the blast as best I could, while with benumbed fingers I sketched what I could see of the landscape, and wrote a few lines in my notebook. Then, breasting the snow again, crossing the shifting avalanche slopes and torrents, I reached camp about dark, wet and weary and glad.[22]

That evening, as the expedition crouched around a very small fire of fossil wood[23] in the snow and the rain, the crew became fearful of continuing. Toyatte said his heart was not strong and the Hoonah guide refused to go any closer to the head of the bay because of the danger of icebergs rising from the bottom. But Muir made a speech, Toyatte's heart grew strong again, and the next morning they shoved off into the sleet, a south wind behind them. They reached the Hugh Miller Glacier, paddled up its fjord and examined the terminus, then moved on toward the head of the bay. Off the north end of Gilbert Island they set sail and raced toward the greatest of the ice mountains, the Grand Pacific Glacier. From camp on the west side of the terminus, Muir climbed again and was rewarded with a magnificent view of the storm-ridden Fairweather Range. Returning at dusk he found the crew in high spirits because the weather was clearing and they had reached the far point of the journey. At daybreak they crossed to the rock that was then dividing the front of the ice wall, and Muir climbed once more, this time to glacier level by cutting steps where ice and rock met.[24] The next day they pushed around the headland between the Grand Pacific and the Rendu, Muir sketching from the canoe because masses of floating ice prevented a close approach to the glacier. Off Rendu Inlet the explorers were reminded again of the lateness of the season. It was now October 29 and the water areas between the bergs in that inlet were covered with a film of new ice, the beginning of the pan ice of winter. They paddled slowly past Queen Inlet, while Muir sketched the features of the Carroll Glacier, then moved on down the eastern shore and camped between the two glaciers of Tidal Inlet. The irrepressible Muir, in constant exultation over the wild, inhospitable country he was discovering, stole from his sleeping bag late that night and climbed the 3500-foot peak directly above camp. By the light of stars with luminous glaciers lying below him, Muir saw all the western arm of Glacier Bay, then descended for an early breakfast.

Crossing to the west mainland, the group headed south, and as they moved across the front of the Geikie Glacier saw, thirteen miles distant, the last of the ice mountains, the one which would soon bear Muir's name and attract visitors from all over the world, the Muir Glacier. Stopping long enough at Berg Bay to return the seal-hunter safely to his wife, John Muir, Hall Young, and their native companions left the still nameless Glacier Bay country on October 30 and headed for Chilkat and Fort Wrangell.

* * *

On August 8 of the following year, Hall Young was standing on the dock at Fort Wrangell watching the steamer *California* unload passengers and goods, when down the gangway bounded John Muir, back to find the glaciers he had failed to see the

"The Pacific Glacier." 1879. Russell Island and the Fairweather Range, drawn by J. A. Fraser from a sketch by John Muir, Century Magazine, June 1895.

previous season. Muir wanted to leave almost instantly, insisting that Young accompany him, but an entirely new crew had to be recruited, for the sad news was that Toyatte, the noble Stickeen to whom both Muir and Young had become greatly attached, had been shot and killed early in January during an Indian quarrel in which he played no part. On 16 August they left Wrangell in a twenty-five-foot canoe belonging to their captain, Tyeen, with his son-in-law Hunter Joe, an interpreter Billy Dickinson, and Hall Young's dog, whom Muir named Stickeen. After visiting Sum Dum (now Holkham) Bay and Taku Inlet, the expedition paddled and sailed north and then west around Admiralty Island and through Icy Strait, reaching Taylor Bay in mid-afternoon of 29 August. While their camp was made near the east side of the terminus (now the Brady Glacier), Muir and Young went off together toward the sloping ice wall, a grounded ice front no longer calving bergs and with a push moraine across the front of it. Nevertheless, the glacier was advancing and had been for some time, although Muir was apparently not aware of the fact that Vancouver's deserted Indian village site of 1794 was now buried deep under the west side of the glacier. Early the next morning, Muir set off into a wild rainstorm, unable to wait for coffee but at least eating the usual piece of bread. Even for this truly incredible man of the mountains it must have been quite a storm: "Instead of falling, the rain, mixed with misty shreds of clouds, was flying in level sheets, and the wind was roaring as I had never heard wind roar before. Over the icy levels and over the woods, on the mountains, over the jagged rocks and spires and chasms of the glacier it boomed and moaned and roared, filling the fjord in even, gray, structureless gloom, inspiring and awful."[25] As he left sea level at the east end of the ice wall, Muir was face to face with forest that was even then being carried away by the ice, and out on the flats he saw dead stumps in place, where a hundred years before there had been forest also.

Unable to persuade the dog Stickeen to return to camp, Muir and his small companion now moved alongside the glacier for about three miles, then struck west across the ice into the mist, the mountains of the other side not visible. They reached the west shore in three hours, explored north to an ice-dammed lake, and at 5:00 P.M. started back, now tracing a line across the glacier somewhat farther north than their previous tracks. In two hours, probably about mid-glacier, Muir reached crevasses of great depth and width, and with early darkness coming on found himself in a very unhealthy situation. Soaked to the skin and with no food, he was well aware of the distinct possibility of a night out on the ice in the wind and rain. And it was starting to snow. But Muir worked out of the situation, making a good many frightful leaps over crevasses, crossing others by ice bridges which he carefully flattened on top so Stickeen could follow. Reaching what appeared to be the final crevasse, with smooth ice beyond, Muir hesitated to jump, because the side he was on seemed to be about one foot higher than the other. And if there happened to be an impassable opening beyond, he was afraid he would not be able to retrieve the leap. He jumped anyway, the dog followed suit, and two hundred yards farther on they came to the impassable crevasse, which connected both north and south into the one they had just leaped. With two choices open, to retrace his steps or cross an ice bridge which he no doubt aptly called a "sliver bridge," Muir chose the knife-edge, weathered sliver. After first solving the problem of getting down to the level of the bridge—a feat in itself—Muir crossed à cheval, carefully ignoring the dark space on either side of him while cutting a four-inch wide surface along the top for Stickeen. Safely on the other side, he spent some minutes persuading the dog to follow, which Stickeen finally did, moving slowly and with utmost concentration, at the far end springing past Muir in a paroxysm of joy that the ordeal was over. They reached the moraine at dark, and in three hours stumbled into camp to supper and a roaring fire. Seventeen years later John Muir published the story of the Brady Glacier episode, although the two who shared that long evening on the ice never saw each other after the expedition of 1880 ended, for Stickeen was stolen by a tourist at Fort Wrangell in the summer of 1883 and taken away on a steamer.[26]

While Muir was out in the storm observing the evidence of the Brady Glacier advance, Hall Young was hearing the human side of the story. Camped near the terminus of the glacier was an old Hoonah subchief, surrounded by abandoned summer houses, a quantity of salmon weirs, and his wives. But the old gentleman was not happy about the salmon stream close by, for the ice had encroached upon it and even then the fish could move only a short distance upstream before returning bewildered to the salt water. Unable to let a major opportunity slip by, the chief finally decided to ask Young for a conference. The answer was yes, whereupon considerable preparations were undertaken. With ceremony, presents of a suitable nature were exchanged, and when all the preliminaries were out of the way, both groups sat down in the chief's hut. The initial oratory was lengthy, for the chief took pains to compare the missionary with the great things of the universe; Young thus was not only a father to all the Hoonahs, he was as the sun, the stars, the moon—and on and on. Not wishing to sit into the night, Young at last broke in upon the old man's eulogy and asked him what he wanted. "I wish to pray to your God," he replied. "For what do you wish me to pray?" asked Young.

The old man raised his blanketed form to its full height and waved his hand with a magnificent gesture towards the glacier. "Do you see that great ice mountain? Once I had the finest salmon stream upon the coast." Pointing to a cliff of rock five or six miles beyond the mouth of the glacier, he said: "Once the salmon stream extended far beyond that rock. There was a great fall there and a deep pool below it, and here for years great schools of king salmon came crowding up to the foot of that fall. To spear them or net them was very easy; they were the fattest and best salmon among all these islands. My household had abundance of meat for the winter's need. But the cruel spirit of that glacier grew angry with me, I know not why, and drove the ice mountain down towards the sea and spoiled my salmon stream. A year or two more and it will be blotted out entirely. I have done my best. I have prayed to my gods. Last spring I sacrificed two of my slaves—members of my household, my best slaves, a strong man and his wife—to the spirit of that glacier to make the ice mountain stop; but it comes on; and now I want you to pray to your God, the God of the white man, to see if he will make the glacier stop."[27]

The missionary was somewhat less than pleased at news of the sacrifice, and so informed the chief, but nevertheless went ahead and petitioned as requested. Eight years later, while still at Wrangell, Hall Young was visited by the old Hoonah of Taylor Bay and informed the glacier was retreating and the salmon were beginning to return to the stream.[28]

On the morning of 31 August, the little group beat around Point Wimbledon, still fighting high winds and excruciatingly cold rain, and camped with another Hoonah subchief and his family in Dundas Bay. Muir made a brief exploration of the upper part of Dundas, and on the following day the canoe pushed on through Icy Strait and all the way to the terminus of the Muir Glacier. Camped alone on the east shore, because the Indians refused to stay so close to the ice wall, Muir spent a few days along the east margin of the glacier, making several small ascents of peaks along the way, writing ecstatically from their summits of views of the enormous, prairie-like glacier and of the Fairweather Range to the west.[29]

But it was not easy country to write about. It was almost too vast and too wild to be comprehended, as later attempts at description would clearly show. And while it had been only eighty-five years since Vancouver, the changes in the landscape were already monumental. The Gustavus foreland in 1794 was flat and bare, and Bartlett Cove was only just emerging from the ice. Twenty years later at Bartlett Cove the first spruce seed blew in on the wind and took root, and in 1817 was a tree four inches high. For a good many years that pioneer spruce struggled in rather hostile soil conditions, remaining a sickly yellow-green, starved for nitrogen. But the alder was fixing the nitrogen necessary to support the spruce forest, and by 1835 Bartlett Cove was nearly choked with an almost-continuous sea of the impenetrable bush with more than occasional spruce in evidence. In that year, the glacier was just north of Beartrack Cove and the massive, thundering front was eight miles across and two hundred and fifty feet high. An impressive height indeed for an ice cliff, but small compared with what the thickness of the ice had been in 1794 at the same place. A thousand feet above Beartrack Cove rested the evidence of that earlier depth, for there was the ancient spruce forest, intact, healthy, extending north along the east shore of Glacier Bay in a gradually rising line until the elevation of timberline was intersected. By 1855 the glacier had retreated to Sandy Cove, and at this point the terminus was a magnificent fifteen miles across, the entire width of Glacier Bay from east shore to west shore. I would not be foolish enough to try to reduce the scene of 1855 to written description, for any such attempt becomes absurdity. The reader can easily enough visualize something fifteen miles long and about two hundred fifty feet high, but that is about as far as the visualization will go, for a calving terminus has to be heard before it can be even dimly related to experience, an experience thousands of years behind most of us. The Hoonahs were much closer to the kind of existence I am talking about, and they were so exactly right when they called the country a bay filled with vast masses of floating ice with the constant noise of thunder in the air. But the quality of the sound of that thunder is what is important here. It is a primeval sound and has in it all of infinity. It is a sound absolutely associated with the concept of space in the same way silence is associated with space, and both sounds, silence and thunder, are awesome.

Some time after 1855 the west side of the enormous trunk glacier began to retreat faster than the east side, but the fifteen mile front probably remained intact until shortly after 1860 when the headland at Tlingit Point split the terminus, the major width of the glacier (the Grand Pacific) retreating northwest in Glacier Bay proper, the eastern arm (Muir Glacier) retreating due north into Muir Inlet. The speed of recession of the Grand Pacific in the twenty years following 1860 was phenomenal. If the northwest point of the entrance to Geikie Inlet is assumed as the western edge of the glacier in 1860, with a concave terminus to Tlingit Point, the Grand Pacific retreated about twenty miles in those years, exposing about one mile of the southern end of Russell Island by the time John Muir arrived in 1879. Muir Glacier, on the contrary, after separating at Tlingit Point was receding toward one of the narrowest points in Muir Inlet, and as the terminus width continued to decrease, recession slowed almost to a standstill, the Muir retreating about four miles in the same years the Grand Pacific retreated twenty, and only about two miles from 1880 to 1892. On the east shore of Glacier Bay and on into Muir Inlet, colonizing vegetation kept pace a normal distance from the ice front, usually about six miles for the first alder thickets, but on the west shore and northwest in Glacier Bay the speed of recession of the Grand Pacific was so great that colonizing vegetation was left far behind, catching up somewhat while the glacier spent another twenty years bringing forth Russell Island, but to this day well behind the advance of vegetation in Muir Inlet.

One can perhaps better understand Muir's excitement, then, as the canoe pushed through the ice during those two expeditions. He was seeing the evolution of landscape and that evolution was proceeding with remarkable speed. In 1880 the young spruce forest at Bartlett Cove was more than half a century old and the alder was starting to die out. At Beartrack Cove alder was dominant but a host of ten-year old spruce trees was established and competing. At Sandy Cove there were small alder thickets, an occasional tiny spruce, and round patches of dryas mat—the mat-forming ground cover—on the gravel. North into Muir Inlet the green disappeared entirely, except for an occasional bit of moss or a minute perennial herb, the landscape now a mass of boulders and mud, high gravel banks just back from the shoreline, then at last the glacier, two and one half miles across and still thundering, but destined to slow down for a few years at least. Muir wasted no time gaining a summit, as already indicated, for the evolution he was witnessing by no means ended at the ice front; far back from the terminus and beyond to the horizon were the glaciers and the nunataks, country exactly as Glacier Bay had been before the ice retreated, except that the fjords did not extend indefinitely under the glaciers. The endless back country of ice and rock, far from the water and the trees and the birds where everything slows down and, except when the wind is blowing—which is often enough—the silence is immense. There are occasional flashes of action when an avalanche streaks down a mountain face, but then the silence again. During clear summer days on the glaciers when there is no wind, the silence is blistering, and exactly as the sun goes over the peaks, the silence becomes cold, sometimes breathlessly cold. The finest description I know of such country was actually written about land one hundred miles northwest of the Glacier Bay of 1880, but it could just as well have been written from one of John Muir's summits. The description is from Israel C. Russell of the United States Geological Survey, on his second attempt to climb Mount Saint Elias in 1891. He was about to reach the divide (now Russell Col) between Mount Newton and Saint Elias, he was alone, and he expected something very different from the scene which unfolded before him as he looked into the Yukon:

> I was now so near the crest of the divide that only a few yards remained before I should be able to see the country to the north, a vast region which no one had yet beheld. As I pressed on, I pictured in fancy its character. Having crossed this same system of mountains at the head of the Lynn Canal, and traversed the country north of it, I imagined I should behold a similar region north of Mount Saint Elias. I expected to see a comparatively low, forested country, stretching away to the north, with lakes and rivers and perhaps some signs of human habitation, but I was entirely mistaken. What met my astonished gaze was a vast snow-covered region, limitless in expanse, through which hundreds and perhaps thousands of barren, angular mountain peaks projected. There was not a stream, not a lake, and not a vestige of vegetation of any kind in sight. A more desolate or more utterly lifeless land one never beheld. Vast, smooth, snow surfaces, without crevasses stretched away to limitless distances, broken only by jagged and angular mountain peaks.[30]

But it was time for the expedition of 1880 to end. John Muir came down from his glacier, packed away the notebooks, and the party headed south. There was a brief stop at Hoonah, then a fast voyage to Sitka where Muir caught the steamer for Portland and home. He was to return to Glacier Bay ten years later, but would not find quite the solitude he had found there in 1879 and 1880, for by then there would be tourists coming to the Muir terminus and poking around the tents at Camp Muir.

* * *

On August 19, 1880, when John Muir was still in Sum Dum Bay, a small ship left Willoughby Cove on Lemesurier Island headed for the bay of ice mountains. It was the Northwest Trading Company steamer *Favorite*, and aboard were Commander Lester Anthony Beardslee and Dick Willoughby. The Commander wanted to interview Hoonahs at their summer

Alder leaves, Stump Cove. 1966

camp (Berg Bay) on the west shore and make a running survey for a chart. The ship did not reach the Hoonahs, and went only as far as Willoughby Island when the fog shut down,[31] but Beardslee came away with a chart incorporating his own observations, those of Willoughby, Hoonahs at Willoughby Cove, and a member of the *Favorite's* crew, an old Russian who told Beardslee he had been up the Bay in command of a schooner. It is tantalizing to know Beardslee had taken Dick Willoughby along because of the prospector's previous explorations of the Bay, but the naval officer made no comment on the extent of those explorations nor did he suggest when they first occurred.[32] Nevertheless, the Commander wrote the report of the *Favorite's* voyage on September 1 aboard his ship, the U.S.S. *Jamestown*, in Sitka harbor, posting the dispatch on the same steamer John Muir took to Portland. And in Beardslee's handwriting at lower left on Hydrographic Office chart 225 appeared this short legend: "Chart 225 Important changes by Jamestown indicated in red ink."[33] When submitted, the most important addition on that map was the name Glacier Bay, a confirmation of the old Indian name Sitadakay.

One writer[34] later commented that Beardslee had the new name accepted by the Coast Survey only as the result of persistent argument, Glacier Bay winning out over an obscure statesman, but again the Commander had no comment on the details. He simply said, "A deep bay, named by me 'Glacier Bay,' which is not on the chart, penetrates the northern coast of Cross Sound, between longitude 135°38' west, and 135°56' west. This bay is 35 miles deep, and at its head are five immense glaciers [this according to Dick Willoughby], from which the icebergs we have encountered are derived."[35] After the *Favorite* returned to Sitka, naval officers aboard the *Jamestown* apparently bestowed two more names in the bay, Willoughby Island and the Beardslee Islands, for both these names appear on the chart.

At least as far as the white man was concerned, then, the bay of glaciers was no longer nameless. Of course, it never *had* been nameless for the Hoonah, but as is usually the case white men found it difficult to explore new country and bother about native names. And while Glacier Bay National Monument has probably fared better in place names than other areas, it seems very unfortunate a good many native words are not today on the maps. Among over two hundred place names covering a land and water area of 4400 square miles, there is exactly *one* Indian name surviving, and that is Lituya Bay. Other Indian names have been added, about seven of them, one of which—Sitakaday Narrows—is misspelled from John Muir's original rendition of Sitadakay. What happened to the Hoonah names for Taylor and Dundas Bay and the Grand Pacific Glacier, for example, all three of which were intimately known to these people? As far as I know, they are lost as are the native words for all the other inlets and glaciers in Glacier Bay. For perhaps five hundred to a thousand years of Indian history to be represented by seven place names in two hundred, speaks rather poorly for the white man, but that is certainly nothing new.

In a very real sense it was the end of an era when John Muir paddled away from Glacier Bay in early September 1880. The Hoonahs were about to fade from the scene as a vital part of the history of the Bay and the coastal region north to Lituya Bay. It was not a sudden disappearance, for there were Hoonahs fishing and sealing in Glacier Bay well past the turn of the century. The end of the era was subtler than that, but it was quite final. Glacier Bay belonged to the Hoonahs until August 19, 1880 when the *Favorite* moved north past Point Carolus. Steam power had been substituted for the cedar canoe and as a result the Bay ceased to be Indian country at that moment in time. Those who understand wilderness know of the transition, which is irreversible. Most future visitors to the bay of ice mountains would come by steamer, some of them hardy enough to scramble a few feet over the moraine, touch the edge of the glacier and hurry back to the ship for sumptuous dining. A far cry from that night in 1879 when Muir, returning from his first view of the Glacier Bay solitude, crouched at the tiny fire with the natives and Hall Young; the natives fearful of continuing the journey, talking in "tones that accorded well with the wind and waters and growling torrents about us, telling sad old stories of crushed canoes, drowned Indians, and hunters frozen in snowstorms."[36] A lament at the passing of that scene, for the seven men around the small fire three miles north of Geikie Inlet were part of the wind and the growling torrents. But in the next eighty years, although Glacier Bay would be seen by more and more people, the observers—with notable exceptions—would know less and less about the land and the silence.

[1] Vancouver (1799, IV) 3; 242.

[2] Ibid., 243-5.

[3] Klotz (1899, I); 528, suggests that Pt. Carolus either emerged or moved east after Vancouver's visit. This is not necessary because Pt. Dundas is just seven miles from Pt. Carolus. As for the glacier terminus, Tebenkov's chart (1852), as taken from Vancouver, shows the ice at 58°28′ latitude, which is the present-day Rush Pt.

It has been suggested Whidbey mistook floating ice for a terminus. This cannot be the case since Whidbey clearly mentions *both* floating ice and solid mountains of ice.

[4] Wright (1887, I) not only ignored Tlingit tradition but doubted Whidbey had seen the ice terminus. But Wright three years later (1890, I) had decided that Whidbey's reference to the ice terminus was "irresistible inference" that the ice had extended that far.

[5] The legend is written here as a Tlingit might have repeated it, as taken from notes provided by Hall (1960, III), Scidmore (1899, VI), Laguna (1960, III), Swanton (1909, III), Lawrence (1958, II).

[6] Lawrence (1958, II) mentions a button blanket of recent origin which commemorates the Tlingit legend of Glacier Bay. I located and photographed this felt blanket in 1966. It is still owned by Helen Clements of Elfin Cove, and was made ca. 1944. Unlike pre-contact Tlingit art, the decoration includes an actual likeness of a human face, supposedly the old woman who was overwhelmed by the glacier.

[7] Beardslee (1882, IV), Scidmore (1899, VI).

[8] Davidson (1901, IV).

[9] Scidmore (1899, VI), but I find no mention of this conversation in any of Davidson's writings.

[10] Aide-de-camp to General Howard in the Nez Perce campaign, author of *Heavenly Discourse*, poet, lawyer, painter.

[11] Wood (1882, III); 332.

[12] Ibid. Wood comments on the size of the glacier (Brady Glacier) and the amount of floating ice.

[13] Now the 'Glacier Bear.'

[14] Since in 1877 the Muir Glacier was somewhat north of Tlingit Point and the Grand Pacific Glacier at Russell Island, I suspect Coonnah-nah-thklé's camp was perched on a ledge just at the mouth of Queen Inlet. There are more rock ledges in that area by far than in Muir Inlet, and the Grand Pacific Glacier was probably much more active in those days than the Muir Glacier.

[15] Wood (1882, III); 333-35.

[16] Ibid., 339.

[17] Scidmore (1896, VI).

[18] Young (1915, VI); June 23. Kooshta-kah in particular is very much a part of Tlingit stories of today, and is by far the most interesting character. In September 1966, I spent considerable time with Mrs. George Dalton at Hoonah, listening to her fascinating and intense stories of the land otter man, who steals people both dead and alive. Once a person is stolen alive by Kooshta-kah, he will remain alive—with the land otters—but may never return to his own people. The land otter men are especially dangerous because they can look just like people, and are constantly seen (though not recognized) in that guise.

[19] Muir (1915, VI).

[20] Young (1915, VI); June 23.

[21] John Muir saw the Geikie, Hugh Miller, Grand Pacific, Rendu, and Carroll Glaciers. He did not see the Muir Glacier until later in the trip.

[22] Muir (1915, VI); 144-5.

[23] Wood from the ancient interstadial stumps.

[24] Muir was cutting steps alongside Russell Island which was in 1879 emerging from the ice (see Muir's drawing, pg. 48). The 'Hoona Glacier' mentioned by Muir in *Travels in Alaska* is the Reid Glacier of today.

[25] Muir (1915, VI); 246-7.

[26] Muir (1897 & 1909, VI).

[27] Young (1915, VI); July 28.

[28] Ibid.

[29] Muir climbed Tree Mountain and up the northwest shoulder of Mt. Case.

[30] USGS 13th Annl. Rept. 1891-92; 47.

[31] Scidmore (1899, VI).

[32] The old Russian was Cozian. Scidmore (1899, VI) says Cozian had never heard of Glacier Bay. But since he had worked for the Russian-American Co. prior to 1867, and as a commercial-government pilot after that date, Cozian may well have been in Glacier Bay long before C. E. S. Wood got there.

Dick Willoughby was one of Alaska's noted pioneers. He apparently took up residence at Willoughby Cove on Lemesurier Island in the summer of 1879. According to Bruce (1899, VI), who spent six weeks with him in Glacier Bay in 1889, Willoughby was in the vanguard of the California forty-niners as a boy (at Sutter's Mill), moved north into Fraser River, Cassiar and Cariboo mining camps, and was among the early placer miners in the gold camps of southeastern Alaska. Scidmore (1885, VI) has Willoughby arriving on the northwest coast scene in 1858, and places him as far north as Bering Strait, with mines and possessions scattered all along the Alaskan coast.

Willoughby was instrumental in organizing the second mining district in Alaska. On August 20, 1880, a group of miners met on Willoughby Island in Glacier Bay. The Berry Mining District was created with Dick Willoughby as recorder. L. A. Beardslee was also present. The minutes for this meeting appear in the *Alaska Mining Record*, Juneau, March 4, 1895.

Relative to credit for the discovery of Glacier Bay, in the C. L. Andrews collection at the Sheldon Jackson Junior College Library in Sitka, there are two letters from former Alaskan governor John G. Brady to C. L. Andrews, July 17, 1914 and Nov. 9, 1915. In these letters, Brady claims he discovered Glacier Bay prior to Muir's arrival, aboard the steamer *Rose* in 1878, including a stop in Taylor Bay. I am not able to verify Brady's claim, but based on the letter of 17 July—which is certainly rather vague—I believe Brady did precede John Muir in Glacier Bay. The discovery—or first exploration—of Glacier Bay by a white man of course still remains with C. E. S. Wood, who preceded Brady by one year.

[33] Beardslee (1882, IV); 100.

[34] Scidmore (1896 & 1899, VI).

[35] Beardslee (1882, IV); 71.

[36] Muir (1915, VI); 146.

White marble and algae, Glacier Bay. 1964

"Glacier Bay, Alaska," ca. 1885. Oil on canvas by A. Langsford, courtesy Glenn Daugherty.

III *The Wondrous Scene*

PERHAPS ONE of the notable exceptions was Captain James Carroll, who first saw Glacier Bay not from the deck of a steamer, but from the bridge. It was July 1883, and Captain Carroll had with him a tracing of Beardslee's chart.[1] The ship was the sidewheeler *Idaho*[2] and was the first tourist steamer to enter Glacier Bay. Navigation was more than dangerous because the chart was extremely vague, but Carroll wanted to find a new trading post said to be in a cove in the southern part of the bay, and he wanted to see the great glacier Muir had talked about after the expedition of 1880. On the bridge with the Captain was Elizah Ruhamah Scidmore[3] who, although she was not inclined to see the glaciers from a canoe, nevertheless understood the Indians and the country she later wrote about, particularly Glacier Bay. The *Idaho* found the cove on the southeast shore, and the pilot, Captain W. E. George, named it Bartlett Bay in honor of the owner of the small fishery that was still under construction there.[4] As the ship moved slowly toward the tiny settlement, a canoe paddled from shore and, as Miss Scidmore saw it, "a wild figure rose in the stern and shouted to the captain to 'go close up to the new house and anchor in thirteen fathoms of water.' "[5] The wild figure was Dick Willoughby, now running the trading post at the cove and ready to assist the Captains Carroll and George in locating John Muir's ice mountain. The rest of the day the *Idaho* unloaded supplies for the fishery and trading post while the passengers examined the Indian camp close by Willoughby's log house. And the fact that those passengers were the first tourists in Glacier Bay is forever verified by these words from Elizah Scidmore: "A small iceberg, drifted near shore, was the point of attack for the amateur photographers, and the Indian children marvelled with open eyes at the 'long-legged gun' that was pointed at the young men, who posed on the perilous and picturesque points of the berg."[6] It was only 1883 but the photographers were hard at it.

The following morning the *Idaho* sailed out of Bartlett Bay and headed north with Scidmore and Willoughby on the bridge alongside pilot George and Captain Carroll. As they passed the first island, the captain and the pilot named it for Scidmore in the ship's log,[7] although the name unfortunately did not survive, that domain now known as Strawberry Island. When the *Idaho* rounded Willoughby Island the group on the bridge saw the full front of the huge glacier, and Carroll took the ship to within an eighth of a mile of the terminus, casting anchor in eighty-four fathoms at low tide. Into the log went Muir Inlet and Muir Glacier as named by the Captain, and Scidmore wrote her impressions of the scene as she saw it from the ship, and a little while later as one of the first party landed at the Muir Glacier:

Words and dry figures can give one little idea of the grandeur of this glacial torrent flowing steadily and solidly into the sea, and the beauty of the fantastic ice front, shimmering with all the prismatic hues, is beyond imagery or description. The vast, desolate stretch of gray ice visible across the top of the serrated wall of ice that faced us had a strange fascination, and the crack of the rending ice, the crash of the falling fragments, and a steady undertone like the boom of the great Yosemite Fall, added to the inspiration and excitement. There was something, too, in the consciousness that so few had ever gazed upon the scene before us, and there were neither guides nor guide books to tell us which way to go, and what emotions to feel.[8] We left the stewards cutting ice from the grounded bergs near the ship, and, putting off in the lifeboats, landed in the ravine on the north [west] side of the glacier. We scrambled over two miles of sand and boulders, along the steep, crumbling banks of a roaring river, until we reached the arch under the side of the glacier from which the muddy torrent poured. Near that point, on the loose moraine at the side, there was the remnant of a buried forest, with the stumps of old cedar-trees standing upright in groups. They were stripped of their bark, and cut off six and ten feet

above the surface, and pieces of wood were scattered all through the debris of this moraine.

Reaching the sloping side of the ice-field, we mounted, and went down a mile over the seamed and ragged surface towards the broken ice of the water front. The ice was a dirty gray underfoot, but it crackled with a pleasant mid-winter sound, and the wind blew keen and sharp from over the untrodden miles of the glacier field. The gurgle and hollow roar of the subterranean waters came from deep rifts in the broken surface, and in the centre and towards the front of the glacier, the ice was tossed and broken like the waves of an angry sea. The amateur photographers turned their cameras to right and left, risked their necks in the deep ravines and hollows in the ice, and climbed the surrounding points to get satisfactory views. Every one gathered a pocketful of rounded rocks and pebbles, and shreds of ancient cedar trees carried down by the ice flood, and then, having worn rubber shoes and boots to tatters on the sharp ice, and sunk many times in the treacherous glacier mud, we reluctantly obeyed the steamer's whistle and cannon-shot, and started back to the boats.[9]

Miss Scidmore was back in Glacier Bay a year later, this time aboard the side-wheeler *Ancon*, anchored near the east shore. A small party was landed, climbing over the moraine to glacier level, then descending to the beach where they walked up practically under the sheer ice cliff. She wrote: "From this south-side [east] landing we easily approached the base of the ice cliffs by following up the beach to the ravine that cut into the ice at the edge of the moraine. We got a far better idea of the height and solidity of the walls by standing like pigmies in the shadow of the lofty front, and looking up to the grottoes and clefts in the cobalt and indigo cliff. It was dry and firm on the beach, and the golden sand was strewn with dripping bergs of sapphire and aquamarine that had been swept ashore by the spreading waves. These huge blocks of ice on the beach, that had looked like dice from the ship, were found to be thirty and forty feet long and twenty feet high.

"The nearer one approached, the higher the ice walls seemed, and all along the front there were pinnacles and spires weighing several tons, that seemed on the point of toppling every moment. The great buttresses of ice that rose first from the water and touched the moraine were as solidly white as marble, veined and streaked with rocks and mud, but further on, as the pressure was greater, the color slowly deepened to turquoise and sapphire blues. The crashes of falling ice were magnificent at that point, and in the face of a keen wind that blew over the icefield we sat on the rocks and watched the wondrous scene. The gloomy sky seemed to heighten the grandeur, and the billows of gray mist, pouring over the mountains on either side, intensified the sense of awe and mystery. The tide was running out all of the afternoon hours that we spent there, and the avalanches of ice were larger and more frequent all of the time. When the anchor was lifted, the ship took a great sweep up nearer to the glacier's front, and as we steamed away there were two grand crashes, and great sections of the front fell off with deafening roars into the water."[10]

When Captain Carroll anchored the *Idaho* in front of the just-named Muir Glacier in 1883, he began a series of visits to that ice stream which would span more than twenty years, the years during which the steamers were carrying hundreds of passengers into Glacier Bay every summer. More so than any other steamship captain, James Carroll's name became practically synonymous with a sightseeing trip to the famous Muir Glacier, especially aboard the magnificent 330-foot steamer *Queen*, owned by the Pacific Coast Steamship Company. Carroll was noted as the genial host,[11] constantly regaled his passengers with stories of the bay and his narrow escapes from collisions with icebergs, and even constructed a boardwalk over the moraine, from the beach on the east side of Muir Glacier, so that passengers could easily reach glacier level. As for the *Queen*, she was one of the great ships of the day and from 1890 on, because of her speed, made more trips into Glacier Bay than the other steamers on the Alaska route.[12] Tourists for the north country boarded at Seattle, Tacoma, Port Townsend, and Victoria, those boarding at San Francisco and Portland often changing at the former ports if they were continuing on to Alaska. The trip was an unforgettable one for most who took it, and if they managed to find space aboard some of the larger ships, passengers were fortunate enough to see the terminus of the Muir. Competition among reputable steamship companies was aggressive and when fly-by-nights cut a slice from the pie, occasionally became a bit vitriolic. A fine example of this occurred in 1897 when the Pacific Coast Steamship Company, in answer to a telegram which had appeared in the *San Francisco Bulletin* announcing the sailing for the Klondike of the ancient side-wheeler *Eliza Anderson*, had the following printed for the edification of potential passengers:

QUEER OLD CRAFTS FOR THE KLONDIKE. The Eliza Anderson is a sample of the kind of crafts running to Alaska, which passengers are asked to risk their lives on. The Pacific Coast Steamship Co. has been running steamers to S. E. Alaska for over 20 years, Summer and Winter. It was the only company running there before the Klondike excitement. Since that date all kinds of inexperienced parties with all kinds of old coffins and with all kinds of swindling schemes have been trying to induce people to patronize them. Look out for them. Remember, the Pacific Coast Steamship Co. owns the only vessels built especially for the Alaska trade, and also has the experienced officers and pilots. The following vessels are being operated on the Alaska route by this Co. viz: City of Topeka, Corona, Willamette, Queen, Al-ki and Geo. W. Elder.[13]

Most of those ships, plus the *Idaho, Ancon, Olympian,* and *Spokane,* are to be seen in many of the old photographs and drawings of the terminus of the Muir, with the *Queen* and *City of Topeka* at the top of the list.

After the season of 1884, the Muir Glacier was established as a wonder of the world, and descriptions of it became more and more complicated and ponderous. In other words, Scidmore's evaluations had been mild and straightforward compared to what followed. In 1884 or 1885, probably from the steamer *Idaho*, Charles Hallock took notes on his impressions of icebergs, Glacier Bay, and the Muir Glacier, and shortly thereafter published this contribution:

The chunks cut off [from an iceberg, for the ship's ice chest]

Riggs Glacier. 1966

seem colorless, but the central core of the berg itself glows like a great blue eye, sentient and expressive, with that sort of poetical light termed *"spirituelle."* You never tire of gazing into the translucent depths of the glacier ice, whose radiance emulates the blue and green of beryl, turquoise, chrysoprase and emerald. You gaze into them as into the arcana of the empyrean, with some vague awe of their mysterious source, and the intangible causes which gave them birth. And the grand icebergs!—so cold, yet so majestic; so solid, yet so unsubstantial; so massive, yet so ethereal!—whose bastions are mighty enough to shiver an onset, and yet so volatile that the warmth of wooing spring will dissipate them into vapor. Children of the Arctic frost, conceived in the upper air, inspired by the effulgent sun, and molded in the bowels of intensest congelation: the human mind can not contemplate them without a sympathetic inspiration, for their duplex entity is so like our combination of soul and body!

With the ice chest filled, the ship moved north past the Beardslee Islands and Hallock proceeded to describe Glacier Bay itself:

> It is twelve miles from the entrance to the head of the bay, and over the entire landscape nature seemed dead. Not a living thing appeared—not a gull on the wing, nor a seal in the gloomy fiords. Desolation reigned throughout, for there was nothing to sustain life. The creation was all new, and the glacier was still at work gradually preparing it for the abode of organic life. Darkness only was needed to relegate us to the primordium of chaos.

Finally, Hallock describes the Muir Glacier from a pinnacle overlooking the icefield:

> Looking afar off into the blank perspective the icy re-enforcements which pour out of the mountain fastnesses like gathering clans seem compacted into indefinable fleecy masses, while in the immediate van they pass in review in serried phalanxes of cowled and hooded monks twenty feet tall, wrapped in dirty toques and capuchins, snow powdered, and bedraggled, and pressing forward with never-ceasing march, as if all the life-long denizens of the Gothard and St. Bernard had set out at once to temper their frigid tongues in the tepid waters which are warmed by the Kuro-Siwo. In other places, where the mer-de-glace is level like a plain, its surface is seamed with deep crevasses and slashed with rifts and chasms whose sides and walls deep down for sixty feet are dazzling blue. Thus the incipient bergs are split and carved and chiseled and prepared for their final segregation, so that they will break off easily when they reach the front.[14]

Any further attempts at description of Glacier Bay and the Muir Glacier should have ceased after Hallock's appeared, but the stampede was on, to see the great glacier and write about it, or else from the more commercial point of view, to make the best of the Muir while it lasted. The Pacific Coast Steamship Co. had a monopoly on excursions into Glacier Bay, but nevertheless produced some prose of their own to entice passengers. In a travel folder for the steamship *Spokane*, they had this to say about the glacier:

> Witness its vastness! Let eyes and senses feel the terrible suggestion of this powerfully silent sea of resistless ice. It is the culmination of all seen before or that may be seen again. Rivers may be bridged, valleys may be filled and mountains may be razed to the ground, but MUIR GLACIER, slow-moving monument of time, may only be measured by man as an unconquerable evidence of eternity itself.[15]

As a result of John Muir's various lectures on the Fairweather glaciers and the written publicity Glacier Bay received after the expedition of 1880, science was attracted to the study of the country, especially the remarkable glacier. In 1884, the English geologist G. W. Lamplugh visited the Bay for one day and made some observations at the terminus of the Muir. He published two reports of his findings, in the second of which he took exception to the inevitable exaggerations found in newspaper accounts. "In a recent number of *Nature* an abstract is made of a San Francisco newspaper account of the 'Great Glacier' of Alaska. This account is not very accurate, and as I spent a few hours on this glacier during a flying visit to Alaska in the summer of 1884, I think my observations may be worth recording. I have heard that some descriptions by American observers have already been published, but have not been able to procure them. However, as there are one or two features to which it may be useful to draw the attention of future explorers in this region, I will give my observations just as I made them, and apologise beforehand if they should be found to overlap those of others. On August 1, 1884, I took passage from Victoria, Vancouver Island, on the steamer—on this occasion the *Ancon*—which carries the monthly mail from ports on Puget Sound to Sitka, Alaska, and eight days later we steamed up the long fiord known as 'Glacier Bay.' All around us the waters of the bay were strewn with masses of floating ice of beautiful colour and fantastic outline, but none were large. Right ahead, a gleaming wall of ice rose up out of the water and completely blocked the fiord, extending with a slight outward bulge from shore to shore. This was the 'Great Glacier,' or the 'Muir Glacier,' of Alaska."[16] Lamplugh need not have apologized, for there was really nothing to overlap. But his objections to the newspaper article were justified, for the *San Francisco Courier* had reported the height of the terminus at five hundred feet and the length of the glacier at one hundred fifty miles. The former figure was only double what it should have been, but the latter was nearly four times over-estimated. Lamplugh spent the day climbing on the east moraine, ascending to glacier level and making sketches of gravel sections, and estimated the terminus at 350 feet in the center at most, 240 feet high at the sides, three miles in breadth. The estimates were quite accurate, and in closing his article, Lamplugh requested the following from geologists to come: "This whole region forms a magnificent field for the study of glacial phenomena, and to any geologist who may follow I would especially say—examine the hollow between the ice and the mountains; go to the foot of the ice-cliff at low water; and, wherever there is stained ice on the top of the glacier, trace out the source of the discolourations."[17] That final suggestion was made because Lamplugh thought he had found evidence of a decomposed meteorite on the top of the glacier.

The next scientist on the scene was Rev. George Frederick Wright who spent a month at the Muir in 1886 attempting to measure the rate of flow. His subsequent book, and particularly the chapter on Muir Glacier, was received without pleasure by a

Plateau Glacier. 1965

Muir Glacier 1893, from 1800 feet on the shoulder of Mt. Wright. Frank LaRoche standing, T. J. Richardson seated. John Muir's cabin (not visible), near shore, right of stream outlet between two groups of grounded bergs. Photograph by LaRoche, courtesy American Geographical Society, New York.

number of reviewers,[18] notably McGee, an anthropologist, who tore it to shreds with a vehemence unusual even for scientists. Wright and his companions, Rev. J. L. Patton and Prentiss Baldwin, attempted to set out stakes in the ice and, failing in this, triangulated on eight pinnacles on top of the glacier and the front point of the terminus. Wright concluded that seventy feet of ice a day moved past a given point in the center of the glacier, ten feet a day at the sides, and the front point of the terminus was stationary. Combined with his estimate of a 5,000-foot breadth (in 1886 the Muir terminus was actually about two miles across) and a 1,000-foot height, which of course included the ice underwater, Wright's average rate of motion of forty feet a day required 200,000,000 cubic feet of ice a day breaking away from a stationary terminus.

And then on June 14, 1890, John Muir sailed from San Francisco on the steamer *City of Pueblo*, destination Glacier Bay. Muir was suffering from a recurring bronchial cough and nervous indigestion, and against the advice of his physician decided the best cure was a sled trip on the Muir Glacier.[19] At Port Townsend Muir met Henry Loomis, who had climbed Mount Rainier with him in 1888, and the two boarded the steamer *Queen*, Captain Carroll commanding. Also aboard for Alaska was Israel C. Russell of the U. S. Geological Survey, headed for his first attempt to climb Mount St. Elias. Nine days later the *Queen* arrived in the bay and Muir and Loomis went ashore on the east side about a mile from the terminus. They built a tent platform with lumber brought by the ship, and in the next few days set stakes on the glacier to measure the motion. It rained almost constantly, but as usual Muir was all over the hills and the edge of the glacier examining the geology.

Early in the morning of July 1, the two were awakened by the shrill whistle of the steamer *George W. Elder,* and the ship disembarked a party of five, led by Professor Harry Fielding Reid of the Case School of Applied Sciences in Cleveland. Reid knew nothing about Glacier Bay and the Muir Glacier except what he had read in G. F. Wright's book, but he was intrigued by the reports of remarkable ice motion on the Muir, and decided to see for himself:

A desire to see the Alaskan coast more thoroughly than is possible to ordinary tourists led to the formation of a party to spend the summer of 1890 encamped there. The description of Muir glacier by Professor Wright turned our attention to that point. Its accessibility and the interest awakened by its reported motion of 70 feet a day decided us to camp at its mouth and study the glacier and its neighborhood as thoroughly as time would permit. The first requisite was a reliable map of the region. None such existed, and we determined to devote much time to a survey and to make a map which would show with some accuracy the extent and form of the glacier and the positions of the mountains which surmount it, and also serve to determine what changes may take place in the future. We also planned a careful measure of the motion of the ice, a determination of the magnetic elements, a regular meteorologic record, a study of the geology of the region, a collection of plants, and observations of all indications of change in the extent of the glacier, the amount of glacial erosion, etc. The party consisted of Mr. H. P. Cushing, who took charge of the meteorologic records, the geologic observations, and the collection of plants; Messrs. H. McBride, R. L. Casement,[20] J. F. Morse, C. A. Adams, and the writer.

On July 1st the *George W. Elder* cast anchor in Muir Inlet, not far from the glacier, and landed our instruments, tents, personal baggage, and provisions on the eastern shore. We found Professor Muir and Mr. Loomis encamped there. They had come also to study the glacier, and added much to the pleasure of our stay. We immediately set to work to put up our tents, and before evening everything was in good shape. We brought boards from Juneau for flooring, tables, etc., which added materially to our comfort and convenience. A book-shelf held our small library of works on glaciers, logarithmetic tables, etc. A gasoline stove enabled us to cook our meals with ease, and campstools permitted us to eat them in comfort. This was to be our base-camp, and, in honor of Professor Muir, we named it *camp Muir*.[21]

In the weeks that followed, Reid accomplished the first accurate measurements of the rate of motion of the glacier, and surveyed Muir Inlet and the areas immediately adjacent. The map subsequently published,[22] then, is the first real map of any part of Glacier Bay, the previous charts inaccurate and essentially sketches. It carries Reid's own place names of 1890, plus those of Commander Beardslee, Captains Carroll and George, and John Muir.

On July 7 the steamer *Queen* returned and in brilliant weather dumped ashore a good many of the two hundred thirty tourists on board. John Muir wrote lightly of the mob, although I suspect he was not at the time overjoyed at the commotion. "What a show they made with their ribbons and kodaks! All seemed happy and enthusiastic, though it was curious to see how promptly all of them ceased gazing when the dinner-bell rang, and how many turned from the great thundering crystal world of ice to look curiously at the Indians that came alongside to sell trinkets, and how our little camp and kitchen arrangements excited so many to loiter and waste their precious time prying into our poor hut."[23] Earlier that morning Muir sat in front of the tent (the hut was actually built a month later) and completed a letter to his wife which he posted on the *Queen* when she left late in the day:

To Mrs. Muir. Glacier Bay. Camp near eastern end of ice wall. Dear Louie: The Steamer Queen is in sight pushing up Muir Inlet through a grand crowd of bergs on which a clear sun is shining. I hope to get a letter from you to hear how you and the little ones and older ones are. I have had a good instructive and exciting time since last I wrote you by the Elder a week ago. The weather has been fine and I have climbed two mountains that gave grand general views of the immense mountain fountains of the glacier and also of the noble St. Elias Range along the coast mountains, La Pérouse, Crillon, Lituya, and Fairweather. Have got some telling facts on the forest question that has so puzzled me these many years, etc., etc. Have also been making preliminary observations on the motion of the glacier. Loomis and I get on well, and the Reid and Cushing party camped beside us are fine company and energetic workers. They are making a map of

the Muir Glacier and Inlet, and intend to make careful and elaborate measurements of its rate of motion, size, etc. They are well supplied and will no doubt do good work. I have yet to make a trip round Glacier Bay, to the edge of the forest and over the glacier as far as I can. Probably Reid and Cushing and their companions will go with me. If this weather holds, I shall not encounter serious trouble. Anyhow, I shall do the best I can. I mean to sew the bear skin into a bag, also a blanket and a canvas sheet for the outside. Then, like one of Wanda's caterpillars, I can lie warm on the ice when night overtakes me, or storms rather, for here there is now no night. My cough has gone and my appetite has come, and I feel much better than when I left home. Love to each and all. Ever thine. J.M.[24]

Four days later Muir started off on the long-awaited trek across the glacier, hauling a three-foot wooden sled on which was lashed a sack of hardtack, a bit of tea and sugar, and a sleeping bag. He was assisted the first day by two Indians and Loomis, but was alone the rest of the way. As mentioned earlier, this was the cure he had prescribed to rid himself of a severe bronchial cough which had troubled him for three months. He skirted the southern edge of the Muir Glacier inland, then crossed north to Snow Dome which he climbed. From the summit near sunset he planned his route west across the icefield and wrote of the scene before him, then descended. Glissading a ravine on the way down, Muir hit an ice patch and burst out of control into the talus at the bottom, but was not injured. The following day he started for the west shore, and camped the evening of July 16 about eight miles out from Snow Dome, after getting over a good many dangerous crevasses. Writing in his diary that night, Muir reveled in solitude: "I am cozy and comfortable here resting in the midst of glorious icy scenery, though very tired. I made out to get a cup of tea by means of a few shavings and splinters whittled from the bottom board of my sled, and made a fire in a little can, a small campfire, the smallest I ever made or saw, yet it answered well enough as far as tea was concerned. I crept into my sack before eight o'clock as the wind was cold and my feet wet."[25] When he awakened the next morning after a night of cold glacier winds, Muir's cough was gone according to prescription, and he continued across the mass of crevasses, hummocks, and glacier streams, reaching the west shore at evening.

By afternoon of the next day he began to suffer from the glare of the snow, and on July 19 was forced to stay at the sled until late afternoon, a snow poultice bound across his eyes. That evening he camped with the main tents in sight across the inlet and the following morning, with his eyes in better condition but still seeing double summits on all the peaks, he continued on toward the terminus. When only about two miles from the moraine, Muir suddenly plunged into a concealed, water-filled crevasse, going down over his head. He spent the night shivering in his sleeping bag, and the next day wrote into his diary the final events of his trip, having traversed some forty miles of the Muir Glacier:

July 21. Dressing this rainy morning was a miserable job, but might have been worse. After wringing my sloppy underclothing, getting it on was far from pleasant. My eyes are better and I feel no bad effect from my icy bath. The last trace of my three months' cough is gone. No lowland grippe microbe could survive such experiences. I have had a fine telling day examining the ruins of the old forest of Sitka spruce that no great time ago grew in a shallow mud-filled basin near the southwest corner of the glacier. The trees were protected by a spur of the mountain that puts out here [Morse Creek area], and when the glacier advanced they were simply flooded with fine sand and overborne. Stumps by the hundreds, three to fifteen feet high, rooted in a stream of fine blue mud on cobbles, still have their bark on. A stratum of decomposed bark, leaves, cones, and old trunks is still in place. Some of the stumps are on rocky ridges of gravelly soil about one hundred and twenty-five feet above the sea. The valley has been washed out by the stream now occupying it, one of the glacier's draining streams a mile long or more and an eighth of a mile wide. I got supper early and was just going to bed, when I was startled by seeing a man coming across the moraine, Professor Reid, who had seen me from the main camp and who came with Mr. Loomis and the cook in their boat to ferry me over. I had a good rest and sleep and leisure to find out how rich I was in new facts and pictures and how tired and hungry I was.[26]

Near the end of July Captain Carroll brought in on the *Queen* the lumber for Muir's cabin, ready cut and designed for a structure with two windows and a door. During a rainy period when both parties remained in camp, the cabin was erected, and a few days later Reid commented in his diary on the use of the new hut: "Prof. Muir takes his meals with us and we use his house to sit in. The fire-place is progressing; in the meanwhile, we have built a fire on some sand in the middle of the floor, which warms the house but causes a good deal of smoke. Morse developed some of my photographs today; they seem pretty good. Under Professor Muir's directions I worked on my sketches and improved their appearance and effect."[27] When the building was essentially finished, Morse took the memorable glass negative which shows Muir on the left, Reid on the right, Cushing, Adams and McBride in the middle, and Casement at the top of the chimney. Including the photographer, every man in the photograph has a glacier in the bay named for him, five of the names occurring during the expedition of 1890.

The seventh man who was with the Reid party that year was one William York, hired as a camp-helper when the *Elder* was at anchor in Pyramid Harbor, Lynn Canal. He worked as agreed until the 1st of August, then went over to John Muir's employ. In the narrative of the 1890 expedition[28] Reid mentions York briefly, saying only that he found the work at Camp Muir too confining, and with the consent of the group left overland via Main Valley (now Endicott Valley) for Pyramid Harbor. However, Reid's notebook indicates there may have been more serious problems, for apparently trouble developed between Muir and York a few days after York switched employers. On August 9 Reid had this to say in the diary: "Prof. Muir had a rough experience with York. York followed him apparently with the intention of shooting him, but the Professor kept out of his way, and came back some fifteen hours ahead of him. York left yesterday for Chilcat via the glacier."[29] William York went his

John Muir's cabin, Camp Muir, Muir Inlet. 1890. Left to right John Muir, H. P. Cushing, C. A. Adams, H. McBride, H. F. Reid, and top of chimney R. L. Casement. Photograph by J. F. Morse, courtesy American Geographical Society, New York.

Captain James Carroll, ca. 1890, from Lewis and Dryden Marine History of the Pacific Northwest.

2 P.M., and had some lunch and pushed on to the summit, some two hundred feet higher. I made one or two sketches of the beautiful view and tried to get some angles on the peaks, but the lower circle of the transit could not be kept stationary and the angles were worthless. We descended the grassy southern slope, starting at 5:25, worked on to the glacier, walked its full length, and reached the large floodplains of its discharging stream. We walked over this when it was quite dark and after wandering about for some time, found our boat at 10:15 P.M. We soon rowed across the inlet, luckily finding but little ice in the water, and reached camp, a very tired out party. This is the first peak up which I have ever led a party. It is about seven miles from camp, about 4000 ft. high, and required some care in the couloir. We were out from camp 18 hours.[30]

A small climb, yes, and not very important. But it was the first roped ascent in that country. There would not be another one for forty-one years.

On August 22 the *Queen* returned with more tourists and more lumber for the hut, and late that day John Muir boarded

solitary way, then, skirting the southern edge of the Muir Glacier east, southeast through Endicott Valley and down the Endicott River to the Lynn Canal. The details of that journey are lost, as far as I know, as are the reasons for the trouble at Camp Muir.

On the same day York disappeared to the east, Cushing, McBride, and Reid rose at 3:30 A.M., breakfasted, and pushed through the ice across Muir Inlet for an attempted climb of Pyramid Peak. From Reid's diary, here is the terse account of that small climb:

On landing we crossed the moraine, and struck up the valley of the Dying Glacier; we reached Glacier front at 7:20 and took breakfast. We then ascended the glacier to the divide. Pyramid Peak rises in a steep uniform grass slope from the water to its summit, 4000 ft. The height of the divide was 860 ft. by barometer. We descended some 200 ft. and had some more breakfast at a stream which poured under the glacier from the right. We then skirted a ridge between us and Pyramid Peak and entered a second valley. We wound up the left side of the valley, over a small part of the glacier and then struck a snow couloir which led straight up the N. face. This couloir became steeper and steeper; at first one kick was sufficient to make a step, then two were necessary, and finally the slope was so steep that four or five kicks were needed to make a sure step. We of course were roped on this slope. In the steepest places the slope was certainly 50°. This couloir was about 1200 ft. high. We reached its top about

"Crevasse in Muir Glacier," from painting by C. Dahlgren.
Californian Illustrated Magazine, May 1892.

"Steamer Queen at Muir Glacier," ca. 1890. Photograph by LaRoche (collection of the author).

for the journey south. The Reid party continued their studies, moving by water in a sixteen-foot rowboat with sail, plus a three-man dugout canoe purchased from the Hoonahs, and trudging the eastern part of the Muir in a five-day excursion of mapping and exploration, the sleds—constructed from Muir's recommendations—piled high with all their instruments, food, and blankets. They had the most difficulty with measurement of the glacier's motion, for the area close to the terminus was badly crevassed, and they never quite succeeded in setting stakes all the way across the glacier. Reid commented in the narrative on such problems, although to anyone who has traveled a glacier near its front, he obviously understated the case: "Shorter excursions were made on all clear days to points more easily accessible. Among these the most interesting were connected with the measure of the motion of the ice. To plant our flags where we wanted them required us to make a way among the crevasses, which offered great difficulties. Some experience in the Alps had taught me what means were necessary for progress in such places and what precautions should be taken to avoid accidents. We were always roped together, and were provided with ice-axes which served to cut steps in places where we could not otherwise stand. Balancing on narrow ridges, creeping along steep walls, or crossing crevasses on pieces of ice that had fallen in and bridged them over, were the usual methods of progress. Our precautions, however, rendered accident impossible."[31] By mid-September they were finished and followed John Muir south. The cabin they left behind stood a lonely sentinel on the moraine for many years, then about 1920 began to disappear in the advancing vegetation. Today there is nothing left but the pile of chimney stones overgrown with moss, surrounded by dense alder fifteen feet high.

The next year a luxuriously equipped camping party occupied the cabin at Camp Muir. Miss Scidmore was back for her fifth and final visit and brought with her the artist[32] T. J. Richardson, a female companion, the sportsman C. S. Johnson, a small boy with his dog, a Russian hunter, and a maid. The cabin was jarred constantly by the icefalls, awakening the party frequently during the night, especially the dog. Scidmore does not say how the maid fared in the midst of the thundering wilderness, but Richardson worked sixteen hours a day most

of the time, as Scidmore put it, "trying to record a fraction of his impressions of sea and sky, mountains and snow-peaks, and of the changefull, glistening ice wall."[33] She was right. It is not possible to record for others all the impressions from such country. A suggestion of insight here and there, perhaps, but the rest has to be filled in by the viewer or the reader.

Harry Fielding Reid returned in 1892 to continue mapping Glacier Bay, occupying the hut for two months and making several trips away from Camp Muir to survey the west side of the bay and to recheck the ice shrinkage on the eastern portion of the Muir Glacier. The small party—two hired hands and Reid—lost their boat three times when it floated away on the twenty-foot tides, but after the third brutally cold (38°) bath, they learned to carry the boat far enough up on shore. At the end of the 1890 season Reid had concluded from his measurements that the Muir moved at the rate of ten feet a day at the center and about six or seven at the sides, and of course there was some controversy over the figures and those of 1886 by G. F. Wright. In the report of 1896 Reid finally sought to answer the discrepancy:

> The very different rates obtained by Professor Wright in 1886 and by me in 1890 for the velocity of flow of Muir Glacier have been discussed by Professor Wright, Professor Cushing, and Mr. Baldwin.[34] The two latter, one of whom was with me and the other with Professor Wright, have both concluded that the observations are irreconcilable, and either that one set was in error or that there was a remarkable change in the motion of the glacier between our visits. If such a change had taken place the quantity of ice breaking off from the glacier in 1886 and 1890, respectively, must have been quite different. Allowing for a large temporary retreat of the glacier's end during the summer of 1890 [about five hundred yards in the center], I find that the amount of ice breaking off would correspond to a maximum velocity of about 27 feet a day if the position of the ice front had remained unchanged. Professor Wright tells us that this was the case during his visit. According to his measurements, therefore, there must have been more than twice as much ice discharged in 1886 as in 1890. This could not have escaped the notice of officers commanding the steamers which enter Glacier Bay. I wrote to Captain Carroll of the steamship Queen, who makes several visits annually to this region, and questioned him on this point. He answered: "For the years 1890, 1891, and 1892 there was more ice coming from Muir Glacier than there was in any of the seven years previous to 1890. I never saw so much ice coming from the glacier, before or since, as there was in that year (1890)." Again, if an increase of 1,000 yards in length corresponds to a tenfold increase in velocity, it is evident—though the problem can not be solved as a simple proportion—that when the glacier was several miles longer than at present its velocity must have been far greater than we can possibly admit. These considerations, I think, make it probable that some undiscovered source of error has crept into Professor Wright's observations.[35]

At the end of August 1892 the *Queen* made her last trip to the Bay for that year. Captain Carroll boarded Reid's party and took the ship up Glacier Bay, the first vessel north of Tlingit Point in that fjord. The route of the ship can be traced by the soundings on the map of 1892 as Carroll stayed close to the east shore, swung north of Composite Island, and took the steamer to the end of Rendu and Queen inlets. The names Carroll Glacier and Queen Inlet commemorate that voyage. Reid stayed in the Rendu Inlet vicinity for three days surveying and photographing, then returned to Camp Muir on the night of September 1, a brilliant aurora overhead. Reid's report, issued four years later as "Glacier Bay and Its Glaciers," is a beautiful publication. The map includes the results of the surveys of 1890 and 1892, and is the first complete chart of Glacier Bay. A few of the photographs are superb, especially the plate of Rendu Glacier, which is one of the finest of the old photographs of the Bay.

In the second week of June 1899, perhaps the most remarkable scientific, artistic, and literary expedition of all time entered Glacier Bay for five days aboard the steamer *George W. Elder*. This was the Harriman Alaska Expedition, and the roster included an amazing spectrum of experience and knowledge. In late 1898, Edward H. Harriman, the railroad magnate, had suffered a nervous breakdown, and his doctors ordered a vacation at sea. Harriman asked if he could have some friends along, and the answer was yes, provided none of those friends were railroad men.[36] Harriman proceeded to put together an enormous party, which included among others eight members of the Harriman family; John Muir and John Burroughs, the naturalists; the scientists William Healy Dall, Grove Karl Gilberg, Henry Gannett, C. Hart Merriam, and Charles Keeler; the artists R. Swain Gifford, Fred S. Dellenbaugh, and Louis Agassiz Fuertes; and the great Indian photographer, Edward S. Curtis. A large library was carried aboard to keep everyone happy, and twelve committees were formed to function in planning the expedition's activities. Fourteen volumes of material resulted from the studies, plus a magnificent souvenir album of photographs by G. K. Gilbert and Edward Curtis,[37] later presented to each member of the party. As might have been expected, there were some loud disagreements among the scientists during the voyage, most of the sparks probably provided by Muir and Burroughs, two adamant personalities who did not always see eye to eye. In the narrative of the expedition, Burroughs later could not resist needling the Scotsman about his Howling Valley of 1890:

> We lingered by the Muir and in adjacent waters five or six days, sending out botanical, zoological, and glacial expeditions in various directions; yes, and one hunting party to stir up the bears in Howling Valley. Howling Valley, so named by Muir, is a sort of coat tail pocket of the great glacier. It lies twenty or more miles from the front, behind the mountains. The hunters started off eagerly on the first afternoon of our arrival, with packers and glistening Winchesters and boxes of ammunition, and we had little doubt that the *genius loci* of Howling Valley would soon change its tune. Some of us the next afternoon were exploring the eastern half of the glacier, which is a vast prairie-like plain of ice, when we saw far off across the dim surface to the north two black specks, then two other black specks, and in due time still other black specks, and the conjecture passed that the hunters

Interstadial stump. 1965

were returning, and that the heart of the mystery of Howling Valley had not been plucked out. Our reluctant conjectures proved too true. Just at nightfall the hunters came straggling in, footsore and weary and innocent of blood—soberer if not sadder, hardier if not wiser men. The undertaking involved more than they had bargained for. Their outward course that afternoon lay for a dozen miles or more across the glacier. They had traveled till near midnight and then rested a few hours in their sleeping bags upon the ice. One may sleep upon the snow in a sleeping bag, but ice soon makes itself felt in more ways than one. When the cold began to strike up through, the party resumed its march. Very soon they got into snow which became deeper and deeper as they proceeded. Hidden crevasses made it necessary to rope themselves together, the new hunting shoes pinched and rubbed, the packs grew heavy, the snow grew deeper, the miles grew longer, and there might not be any bears in Howling Valley after all—Muir's imagination may have done all the howling—so, after due deliberation by all hands, it was voted to turn back.[38]

While the glacier-study parties—usually Burroughs, Muir, Gilbert, and Palache—were visiting the Muir, Reid, Hugh Miller and other glacier fronts, the botanists and ornithologists were encamped on the Gustavus foreland where they observed and collected over forty species of birds, studied the plants and the first generation trees, and climbed on the low peaks bordering the foreland to the east, observing first hand the line of the ancient forest. In the meantime, Gannett mapped the glacier fronts, Curtis photographed with the view camera, and John Burroughs wrote:

> We were in the midst of strange scenes, hard to render in words, the miles upon miles of moraines upon either hand, gray, loosely piled, scooped, plowed, channeled, sifted; the towering masses of almost naked rock, smoothed, carved, granite-ribbed, that looked down upon us from both sides of the inlet, and the toppling, staggering front of the great glacier in its terrible labor throes stretching before us from shore to shore. We saw the world-shaping forces at work; we scrambled over plains they had built but yesterday. We saw them transport enormous rocks, and tons on tons of soil and debris from the distant mountains; we saw the remains of extensive forests they had engulfed probably within the century, and were now uncovering again; we saw their turbid rushing streams loaded with newly ground rocks and soil-making material; we saw the beginnings of vegetation in the tracks of the retreating glacier; our dredgers brought up the first forms of sea life along the shore; we witnessed the formation of the low mounds and ridges and bowl-shaped depressions that so often diversify our landscapes—all the while with the muffled thunder of the falling bergs in our ears. We were really in one of the workshops and laboratories of the elder gods, but only in the glacier's front was there present evidence that they were still at work. I wanted to see them opening crevasses in the ice, dropping the soil and rocks they had transported, polishing the mountains, or blocking the streams, but I could not. They seemed to knock off work when we were watching them. One day I climbed up to the shoulder of a huge granite ridge on the west, against which the glacier pressed and over which it broke. Huge masses of ice had recently toppled over, a great fragment of rock hung on the very edge, ready to be deposited upon the ridge, windrows of soil and gravel and boulders were clinging to the margin of the ice, but while I stayed not a pebble moved, all was silence and inertia.[39]

On the 11th of June, Burroughs and a companion climbed the shoulder of Mount Wright to an elevation of 3,000 feet, and under a hot summer sun looked out over the miles of snow and ice and nunataks. They spent most of the day up there, and the silent immensity did not escape Burroughs' pen: "But the largeness of the view, the elemental ruggedness, and the solitude as of interstellar space were perhaps what took the deepest hold. It seemed as if the old glacier had been there but yesterday. Granite boulders round and smooth like enormous eggs, sat poised on the rocks or lay scattered about. A child's hand could have started some of them thundering down the awful precipices. When the Muir Glacier rose to that height, which of course it did in no very remote past, what an engine for carving and polishing the mountains it must have been."[40]

As it turned out, the minimum observations the Harriman Expedition made at the termini of the various glaciers were very important, for in the early fall of 1899 another era of Glacier Bay's history ended abruptly. It had been the era of first explorations, of initial measurements at the terminus of the Muir, of the first accurate maps of the Bay and its glaciers, of the first photographs and paintings of that wild country. But in historical perspective, I think it was above all the era of the steamer moving slowly to the front of the Great Glacier and disgorging scores of passengers, who wanted to reach glacier level and have a group photograph taken on top of the ice; of Captain Carroll and his boardwalk across the moraine, of Captain Carroll unloading John Muir's cabin, Captain Carroll of the *Idaho* and the *Ancon* and the steamer *Queen*, on the bridge pushing his ships through the ice up Muir Inlet and casting anchor under the remarkable ice cliff.

At 12:20 P.M. on September 10, 1899, the coast of Alaska and adjacent areas were jarred by a violent earth tremor, the severest of all the shocks felt during the preceding week and earlier that day. At the epicenter in Disenchantment Bay, one hundred fifty miles northwest of Glacier Bay, eight prospectors in two camps survived nearby shoreline uplifts of as much as forty-seven feet, and managed to stay alive amidst swaying and cracking earth, avalanche and flood from above, and tidal waves from the sea.[41] The Muir Glacier was apparently shattered beyond recognition, but there were no eyewitnesses to the devastation of the ice front. In Bartlett Cove, August Buschmann was waiting for lunch at the red salmon saltery when the quake hit. His trunk came sliding across the room at him, and in a moment or two the cook's helper—a boy of twelve—ran into the cabin in great alarm. He had been up the hill at the Hoonah cemetery and thought the Indians were coming to life as the ground heaved. No one at Bartlett Cove was injured, but shortly after the great tremor Glacier Bay became almost a solid mass of floating ice. The saltery at the cove could not be reached by a ship for two weeks, and the cannery boats operating out of the Dundas Bay cannery were unable to make their regular

Interstadial stump. 1965

trips into the station.[42]

In view of the accounts of the amount of ice in the Bay immediately following the earthquake of the 10th, combined with what observers later saw in Muir Inlet, it seems that the terminus of the Muir Glacier may simply have collapsed, calving unbelievable quantities of ice as it retreated past Adams Inlet in the few years following. The first ship to get close to the glacier arrived late in July the following summer. It was the steamer *Queen*, of course, and presumably Captain Carroll was on the bridge. The *Queen* moved west of Willoughby Island because the main channel was jammed with ice, and pushed opposite the mouth of Muir Inlet, at which point the captain gave up. Aboard was O. H. Tittman, commissioner for the United States on the International Boundary, and as he looked ahead the ten miles to the front of the Muir, he saw a floating ice pack from shore to shore.[43] There was no possibility of reaching the glacier that summer, nor the next summer, when the steamers were stopped a minimum of five miles away. In December 1901, the *City of Topeka* reached within a mile, but the following summer the steamers once again could get no closer than five miles. Those aboard the *Topeka* in late 1901, then, were the first really to see what had happened to the world-famous ice front, and although accounts vary, the descriptions from the *Topeka*[44] essentially agree with what Fremont Morse wrote five years later:

> Formerly the Muir presented a perpendicular front at least 200 feet in height, from which huge bergs were detached at frequent intervals. The sight and sound of one of these vast masses falling from the cliff, or suddenly appearing from the submarine ice-foot, was something which once witnessed was not to be forgotten. It was grand and impressive beyond description. Unfortunately the recent changes in the Muir have not increased its impressiveness from a scenic standpoint. Instead of the imposing cliff of ice, the front is sloping, and seems to be far less active than formerly. The eastern arm discharges but little, and appears to be nearly dead. The front of the western arm is in [the] shape of an elongated basin, and, as above stated, slopes gently.[45]

In 1907, Captain Carroll put the steamer *Spokane* to within a mile of the sloping terminus, but the quantity of floating ice in the years to follow was so great that excursions to Glacier Bay were finally eliminated from the schedules. The Muir Glacier terminus, once it was slightly north of Adams Inlet, retreated with considerable speed, probably as a result of the combined factors of the earthquake as a triggering device and the broader and deeper waters of the inlet acting on the ice front. In 1931 C. W. Wright predicted the glacier would ground itself shortly[46] but the Muir continued to remain a tidewater glacier as it drew back further and further to the north. In 1934 it was clear of Nunatak Cove, in 1941 it was even with McBride Glacier coming in from the east, and in 1961 it turned the corner at Riggs Glacier and disappeared to the west. Today it is five miles from Riggs, still retreating and still calving into the sea, the front twenty-five miles from where it was when John Muir first saw it at a distance in 1879.

As far as the tourists were concerned, Miss Scidmore's "wondrous scene" of 1884 no longer existed. Unknown to the world in 1879, Muir Glacier became prominent by 1884, reached world fame by 1886, was unattainable behind the masses of floating ice after 1899. But if the tourists disappeared with the glacier, the scientists did not. Lamplugh in 1884 was only a beginning. The descriptions which had poured forth for twenty years were finished. Now came the explanations, and they have not yet stopped coming.

Alder with colonizing spruce, Beardslee Islands. 1966

Interstadial forest, Forest Creek. 1965

[1] Scidmore (1899, VI).

[2] See Lewis & Dryden (1895, V); 372, *Idaho* history, pg. 93 picture.

[3] E. R. Scidmore traveled widely and wrote extensively about her experiences. In 1892 she joined the staff of the *National Geographic*, and in 1898 became an associate editor for the magazine.

[4] Scidmore (1885, VI). The place name is now Bartlett Cove.

[5] Scidmore (1885, VI); 124.

[6] Ibid., 125.

[7] Ibid., 131.

[8] Scidmore wrote *Appleton's Guide Book to Alaska and the Northwest Coast* in 1899.

[9] Scidmore (1885, VI); 135, 139-40.

[10] Ibid., 145-6.

[11] The following, quoted in part, appears in footnote 27, Lewis & Dryden (1895, V); 150, on Captain James Carroll: "In the fall of 1870 he received his first command, the steamship *Montana*, . . . From that time he remained continuously in charge of the Holladay steamships and those of its successor . . . until 1878, when he took command of the big sidewheeler *Great Republic*, running to Portland as an opposition steamer. After her wreck . . . Capt. Carroll went to the *Idaho, Eureka* . . . and various other steamships on the Alaska route in the course of the past ten years, among them the finest which have plied to the land of the midnight sun, and during that time has entertained thousands of tourists from all parts of the world. He is regarded as the prince of good fellows by all who travel with him, but never allows his gallantry and hospitality to interfere with his duty aboard ship. A story indicative of this characteristic is told by a passenger who made the Alaska trip with him, in the summer of 1894, on the steamship *Queen*. A large party of tourists were aboard, and they were very anxious to visit an Indian village near a point which the steamer was to reach in the night. The passengers knew that they were scheduled for a brief stop only, but they concluded to attempt to accomplish their purpose by persuading the Captain to remain there until the next day. A petition was accordingly drawn up and signed by nearly every one on board, and the duty of presenting it to the genial skipper was assigned to a charming lady who at meal time occupied the seat of honor next to the Captain. She approached the Captain with a most engaging smile and handed him the document. He read it carefully, and, returning it to her, said: 'My dear madam, I regret very much to disappoint you and your friends, but this steamship is not run by petitions. We will sail on schedule time.'"

[12] *Pacific Coast Steamship Company's Alaska Route*; Goodall, Perkins and Co., notes on Chilcoot and White Passes folder 1897-98, under *Sailings*: "Note: During the summer months the Steamer *Queen* is the regular Alaska Excursion Steamer, and on account of her high speed, etc., is expected to call at more points of interest to the tourist than the other steamers. The other steamers attend more especially to the local traffic. The Al-Ki does not ordinarily extend her run beyond Juneau, and does not call at either Sitka or Glacier Bay." (Bancroft Library)

[13] Ibid., 1.

[14] Hallock (1908 and 1886, VI). In the latter 171-72, 174-5.

[15] World Data Center A: Glaciology. At the Am. Geog. Soc., N. Y.

[16] Lamplugh (1886, I); 299. Note also Lamplugh (1885, I). The exaggerated description is in *Nature* 32, June 18, 1885; 162.

[17] Lamplugh (1886, I); 301.

[18] Wright (1890, I). McGee's review of Wright's book may be found in *The American Anthropologist* 6, Jan. 1893; 85-95. Prior to that, McGee quartered Wright in *Science*, December 2, 1892; 317.

[19] Linnie Marsh Wolfe, *Son of the Wilderness*—The Life of John Muir.

[20] McBride and Casement arrived aboard the *Queen* on 7 July.

[21] Reid (March 1892, I); 21-2.

[22] Reid (March 1892, I).

[23] Muir (1915, VI); 293.

[24] In W. F. Badè, *The Life and Letters of John Muir*, 2; 246-8.

[25] Muir (1915, VI); 302.

[26] Ibid., 310-11.

[27] Reid (1890, IV); Aug. 9.

[28] Reid (March 1892, I).

[29] Reid (1890, IV); Aug. 9.

[30] Ibid., Aug. 8.

[31] Reid (March 1892, I); 22-3.

[32] The account is in Scidmore (1892, VI). In addition to T. J. Richardson, at least the following artists visited Glacier Bay: Thomas Hill (1887), William Keith (1886), J. E. Stuart (1898), F. S. Dellenbaugh, R. S. Gifford, L. A. Fuertes, and E. S. Curtis (the great Indian photographer), the last four all with the Harriman Expedition of 1899.

[33] Scidmore (1892, VI); 711.

[34] Referring to Wright (1890, I), Cushing (1891, I), Baldwin (1893, I).

[35] Reid (1896, I); 445.

[36] *SCB*, December 1965, interview with William Colby.

[37] Both volumes at the University of Washington Library, Seattle.

[38] Burroughs (1901, VI); 38-40.

[39] Ibid., 42-3.

[40] Ibid., 46-7.

[41] Tarr and Martin (1912, I).

[42] Ibid.; also Buschmann (undated ms. with USNPS, Bartlett Cove), who was managing the saltery for his Father. Since Dundas Bay will not appear again in the narrative, but actually has quite a history of its own, I will give a brief resume here. The Dundas Bay cannery site, on the west shore, was erected in 1898 by James Baron of Hunter Bay, and was briefly known as The Tlingit Packing Co. Baron sold to Pacific Navigation and Trading Co., who sold to Northwestern (or Western) Fisheries in 1900. Even by 1900, the community was large, for in that year the cannery employed sixty-one hands, thirty of them Chinese, and thirty-five fishermen. A fine early photograph (by Dodge 1912, courtesy Frank Shotter of Hoonah) shows the cluster of about forty houses ranged along the shore north of the cannery, although today there is no trace of these homes, and the cannery site is in ruins.

In 1928, prospector William Horsman (Doc Silvers) and his wife arrived in Dundas Bay, and during the next eleven years built three homes in the area. Three years later Stanley 'Buck' Harbeson arrived to work on Horsman's claims, subsequently building his own trap line and two homes. About 1935, the Horace Ibachs settled in Dundas Bay at the abandoned cannery site, by then owned by Pacific American Fisheries. Finally, Nina and Jimmy White became the last Tlingits to live in Dundas. Of the above, only Buck Harbeson stayed beyond the 1940's, essentially alone in his cabin on the east shore, except for his pet dogs and a black bear who often called at the back door for handouts. Occasionally, Harbeson would row to Elfin Cove (about twenty miles) for supplies, and even to Juneau, an eighty-mile pull on the oars. On or about 6 May, 1964, Buck died alone in his immaculate cabin after thirty-three years in Dundas Bay. (For information on Dundas Bay, I am indebted to Frank Shotter of Hoonah, and Mrs. F. M. Smith—Buck Harbeson's sister. Brief mention of Dundas Bay appears in *The Salmon and Salmon Fisheries of Alaska*, Moser, Govt. Prtg. Off., Washington, D.C., 1902).

[43] Gilbert (1904, I).

[44] Davidson (1904, IV).

[45] Morse (1908, VI); 78. Additional accounts of the Muir Glacier following the earthquake of 1899 may be found in Reid (1895-1916, I), Andrews (1903, VI), *Alaska-Yukon Magazine* (1908, VI).

[46] Wright and Wright (unpublished ms., I).

IV *A Lone Prospector*

THE FIRST attempt to present a comprehensive picture of all that had happened and was happening was made in 1906 when the brothers Fred E. and Charles W. Wright spent one month total in Lituya Bay and Glacier Bay. A good many photographs and a long manuscript devoted to glaciology and geology resulted, but the photographs were misplaced when the USGS moved its headquarters and were not found until 1930.[1] The following year Charles Will Wright revisited the country with Harry Fielding Reid and made additional observations, incorporating them in a partly revised manuscript which, however, was never published by the USGS because a good deal of the Wright brothers' work had by then been superseded. But in 1906 the Wright brothers, in a few words, outlined the events that probably occurred over centuries: "The valley glaciers began to push forward and finally to coalesce into piedmont glaciers at the mountain bases. The piedmont glaciers increased in size and importance until they rose above perpetual snow limit and overshadowed the valley glaciers to which they owed their existence. As they grew they filled all depressions in the region and, like the continental glaciers of Greenland today, passed from the piedmont type, fed by tributary valley glaciers, to the continental or glacial-cap type whose surface is in large measure above the limit of perpetual snow and is in turn drained by glacier offshoots overflowing from its margins down tributary valleys."[2] It was at this time that Lieutenant Whidbey, of H.M.S. *Discovery*, arrived off Point Carolus. The ice at the narrows in Muir Inlet was then probably 2500 feet thick, and almost 4000 feet thick farther north. As the glaciers receded, a feature emerged that was commented on in all the early studies, namely the remarkable gravel deposits; some were at elevations exceeding 1,000 feet and others, especially in Muir Inlet, were high gravel banks near the shore. In 1896 H. F. Reid explained another part of the story which spanned centuries:

The gravels accumulated in large quantities higher up the valley during the long period when the glaciers of this region were smaller than at present. When Muir Glacier began to advance, its center must have pressed out beyond the sides, and it may thus have caused the drainage streams on each side to flow between it and the mountains and deposit their material along the sides of the valley only, where the floor was about at the level of the present surface of the inlet. As this projecting tongue became thicker and thicker it would gradually spread over the gravels deposited on its sides, forcing the streams closer to the mountains, near which the deposits would thus reach a higher level. The sides of the glacier would also advance, stopping deposition under themselves, but allowing the accumulations to increase in front. This would continue until the spreading of the projecting center and the advancing sides covered the deposits. All the low-level gravels were probably deposited about the same time, just before or during the last great advance of the ice, for we find the glaciers in all the inlets overriding them, and they themselves cover old forests in many places. The high level deposits occur in greatest development in Geikie and the three upper inlets of the bay. I did not see any indication of them in or south of Muir Inlet. They form a more or less thick lining, resting against the mountain slopes at all altitudes up to 1,000 or 1,500 feet. They seem to have been deposited by streams flowing along the sides of the glaciers when the latter were much thicker than at present. Since the glaciers have become smaller, streams formed by rain and melting snow have cut numerous gullies in these deposits, causing a vertical, streaky appearance.[3]

Reid saw no gravels in Muir Inlet, but they were there. By 1923 the southeast corner of the old Cushing Plateau, now the southeast corner of Wachusett Inlet, was starting to emerge from the ice, gravel-laden. At that time Wachusett Inlet was only a

mile long, and it was predicted that the lowlands under the ice to the northwest would also be mantled with gravel deposits. The inlet—Wachusett Inlet—now runs for ten miles and the low country uncovered by the recession of the Burroughs and Plateau glaciers is strewn with hundreds of acres of gravel, providing for the strangest and most austere setting in all the inlets of Glacier Bay.

A few days before his sled trip on the glacier in 1890, John Muir had written: "On my way back to camp I discovered a group of monumental stumps in a washed-out valley of the moraine and went ashore to observe them. The largest is about three feet in diameter and probably three hundred years old. They are Sitka spruces and the wood is mostly in a good state of preservation. How these trees were broken off without being uprooted is dark to me at present. Perhaps most of their companions were uprooted and carried away."[4] Muir mentioned such trees constantly in his narrative of the 1890 expedition, and had used the "fossil wood" for fuel in 1879 and 1880. He was probably very close in his estimation of the three-hundred year-old stump, and no doubt correctly identified it as Sitka spruce. All the early observers who spent any appreciable time in Muir Inlet mentioned the old trees, and well they might have, for those stumps told the story of an ancient forest which covered much of Glacier Bay. The first observers were essentially geologists, however, and it remained for the ecologist, working with additional knowledge and better tools to treat the broken but, in some cases, extraordinarily beautiful old remnants.

William Skinner Cooper of the University of Minnesota first entered Glacier Bay in the summer of 1916. Cooper, an ecologist, wanted to conduct a series of studies in an area where the major parts of a developmental cycle could be observed during the span of a single lifetime. Lawrence Martin, geologist and foremost authority on the great earthquakes of 1899, suggested to Cooper that Glacier Bay would be unique for the ecologist's purpose, and four expeditions to that country resulted, during which Cooper conducted classic studies of plant succession.[5] Paradoxically, Cooper became acquainted that first year with Captain Tom Smith who owned and piloted the *Lue* and provided the transportation for the party. In later years, as will be seen, Smith and Cooper held fundamentally opposing views on the use of an area such as Glacier Bay, but they have retained the friendship to this day. The 1916 expedition was the first time either of the men had been in the Bay, but in ten days they visited all the inlets and ice fronts except the Johns Hopkins, and Cooper established nine permanent quadrats in localities where the dates of ice recession were accurately known. It was during this trip that Tom Smith had his first brush with a glacier. Smith took the *Lue* up close to the front of the Rendu Glacier, put Cooper and Hubbard ashore, and anchored farther back from the terminus. A huge part of the front of the glacier then calved, tossing the boat rather violently, and according to Cooper,[6] they could never get Tom close to a glacier again.

In 1921 Cooper returned to Glacier Bay, re-charted the quadrats, which he located by a complicated system of compass bearings, cairns, pacings, and white crosses on rocks, but devoted most of his fifteen days there to a study of the vegetation in Muir Inlet and the remains of the interstadial forests, the old stumps referred to by so many of the early observers, *in situ* and still being uncovered as the ice retreated and the gravels eroded away. Cooper returned again in 1929, with Tom Smith and the *Yakobi*, made an extensive collection of flora, studied recently exposed remains of the interstadial forests, and re-charted the quadrats. For the first time Johns Hopkins Inlet was entered, and the party reached to within four miles of the terminus of the glacier before they were stopped by the pack of floating ice. The fourth expedition occurred in 1935, once more with Tom Smith and the *Yakobi*, during which Cooper continued the quadrat and interstadial forest studies, and spent three days on the Gustavus foreland observing the glaciological and botanical aspects. The terminus of the Johns Hopkins Glacier was finally reached, even though Tom Smith had earlier sworn never to get near a glacier again. Out of these four expeditions came nine[7] publications on Glacier Bay, mainly on its ecology, ecology that had to include the glacial history of the area as well as all the earlier observations. In other words, it remained for Cooper to pull together the works of Muir, Wright, Reid, Gilbert, Tarr and Martin, and the Wright brothers (and others), combine them with his own detailed and precise studies, and produce a major contribution to the story of a magnificent piece of land.

In 1916, but for the most part in 1921, Cooper visited the nine new localities of the ancient forest and also covered all the sites mentioned by his predecessors. Eighteen pages of conclusions were presented in 1923[8] as he sketched the probable history of the trees at each of the recent locations. At the beginning of the studies, Cooper assumed that the forest stage would become less mature farther north, giving way from a hemlock-spruce climax stage to pure spruce stands to willow-alder thicket as the sources of the glaciers at minimum ice extension were approached. To follow Cooper north, then, as he examined the succession of ancient times in Glacier Bay:

(*1921, Beartrack Cove*) At the head of Bear Track Cove there is a stretch of salt marsh, under water at high tide, in the middle of which stands a single large stump. At first this seemed of no significance, but when microscopic examination showed it to be a hemlock, it immediately assumed large importance. Other stumps, mostly overturned, were seen scattered over the flat, but these might possibly have been carried down by flood waters. It is hard to conceive, however, of this particular stump having been carefully deposited right side up, with no signs of abrasion visible upon it. We are fully justified in assuming it to be a remnant of the ancient forest. During the interglacial period the mountain slopes to the north were forested to timberline, which may well have been higher than now. This forest still remains above the upper limit of the ice at its recent maximum (less than 1,000 feet in this locality), and the line separating the old forest from the new growth below is vividly distinct. The stump, now below high tide level, agrees with those of station 38 [west shore] in indicating a recent subsidence of at least twenty feet. It seems, then, that the forest cover of the mountains stretched out over the lowland to the south, which was at least twenty feet higher than now. It was probably dense and in climax state, since the hemlock is the last tree to appear in the course of the succession. In its advance down the bay the ice, upon

Spruce and hemlock, Bartlett Cove. 1966

reaching the corner of the mountains at Bear Track Cove, being relieved of its confining walls, spread out in a piedmont bulb, its margin, following the mountain slope, making an abrupt turn to the eastward. Ahead of it poured glacial streams loaded with gravels, destroying the life of the lowland forest and burying its remnants. The overriding ice swept on to its maximum a few miles farther and then melted back. It is very possible that beneath the uneroded lowlands to the south many more remnants still lie buried, but on account of the dense covering of young forest these must remain concealed for an indefinite period.[9]

(*1921, north side of Adams Inlet at Muir Inlet, twenty miles north of Beartrack Cove. Here Cooper found the oldest tree sampled in Muir Inlet, 383 years*) If the former stations represent the climax, the condition here—a somewhat equal mixture of spruce and hemlock—subclimax, since the spruce normally precedes the hemlock in the succession. We will find this state general in the Muir Inlet region, and it is to be expected, since we are here from twenty to twenty-five miles nearer to the sources of the glaciers of that time. The period during which forest development was possible was shorter here at both ends, for in the previous retreat the ground was laid bare at a later date, and it was sooner covered up in the advance which closed the interglacial period. Number 3 in the list of trees furnishes a minimum for the length of the ice-free interval at this point —383 years. The narrowness of the first 60 rings in all probability indicates suppression beneath an earlier generation of trees, and therefore a much longer period.[10]

(*1921, southeast corner of Wachusett Inlet, one and one-half miles from the Muir terminus*) Four stumps were found in place; two were spruce, two hemlock. The presence of the hemlock showing a rather advanced stage of successional development, would seem to indicate a probable further extension of the forest northward beneath the Muir Glacier.[11]

In 1935, Cooper studied three groups of remnants at Goose Cove and Nunatak Cove, on land that had been under the ice in 1929. In one of those groups, out of twenty-two stumps, six-

Captain Tom Smith, Hotel Juneau. 1965

William S. Cooper, Blue Mouse Cove. 1966

teen were hemlock. In other words, he had overturned the assumption of 1921, for at Goose Cove in 1935, thirty miles north of Beartrack Cove, there was no indication of a near approach to the end of the forest; the group of hemlocks there were as mature as any in the lower part of the inlet. Twenty years later, in 1955, the old remnants contributed further to the history of the Bay. Samples for radiocarbon dating were taken from a good many of the localities, and near the upper end of Muir Inlet the most ancient stump in the Bay was found. It was Sitka spruce, four hundred years old when overwhelmed by gravel—and it was seven thousand years ago that it was alive on the same spot. The other dates represented were from 4000 years on down to the modern remnants of less than three hundred years, and while the picture is far from complete and there are conflicts in present-day theories, it appears that Wisconsin or Late Wisconsin ice in Muir Inlet retreated to positions even farther back than currently, after which followed some five thousand years of relative warmth. This geologically short interval, called the Hypsithermal, was a period during which the forest reestablished itself at least over all the Muir Inlet area, and tremendous quantities of outwash poured forth. To the west in Glacier Bay, the retreat of the ice was probably far less extensive because the glaciers there are fed by high accumulation areas near the great peaks of the Fairweather Range.

Then three thousand years ago, or perhaps somewhat earlier, the ice in Muir Inlet advanced, destroying certain parts of the forest. It is not known how far this ice moved nor when it stopped, except that the advance which started three thousand years ago *may* have culminated in Whidbey's compact solid mountains of ice at Bartlett Cove, or there may have been oscillations in between. What *is* known is the fact that the great glacier built a sizable terminal moraine sometime between 1650 and 1750, and over this hill of boulders and rocks stands today the silent hemlock-spruce-moss forest of Bartlett Cove. The so-called modern group of trees, then, were those destroyed at the end of the last great advance, and they stood at Bartlett Cove. Cooper had predicted this in 1921 and verified it himself in 1935. Donald B. Lawrence in 1958 wrote of that forest, buried not long before Vancouver laid down the shoreline of his map:

> On the shores of Bartlett Cove near the mouth of the Bay stand the youngest fossil groves of all, the wood well preserved even with bark still in place below the surface of the beach from which the stumps protrude. But they stand at a level where trees could not possibly grow now. Some are indeed rooted among seaweeds between the tides at levels at least 20 feet below the most venturesome young spruces living along the adjacent shore today. Less than 300 years ago when the fossil stumps were living trees the ice advanced from some unknown line of retreat to the mouth of the Bay, overwhelming the forests as it moved ahead and depressing the land as the load of ice increased where none had been immediately before. Though the ice has been gone now from the mouth of the Bay for about two centuries, the land surface had not yet rebounded to the level at which it stood in relation to sea surface before the ice advanced. But the land is rising rapidly,[12] from one half to one inch per year in this general vicinity, for the forest of young spruces is migrating out on strands which a few years ago were covered only with salt-tolerant shore plants. It may take another 250 years before the land can rebound from the depression produced by the load of the latest glacier extension. And even then rebound may not be complete because previously unconsolidated strata have very likely been permanently compressed and because of the heavy mineral deposits left by the ice, and meanwhile the sea level is rising because of the world-wide trend of glacier melting."[13]

Succession involves many events preceding the forest stage as the land is literally prepared for the hemlocks, and Cooper's quadrats helped him establish the appearance of the different communities after recession. He spent a large percentage of his time during those four expeditions down on his knees looking for new arrivals, and subsequently grouped the vegetation into three units; the pioneer community, the willow-alder thicket, and the forest. The earliest arrivals are the mosses, then variegated horsetail and dryas mat, and later on prostrate willows. The willow-alder stage begins with the shrubby willows, which start prostrate but later stand erect, completing the transition from pioneer to thicket stage. Alder gradually becomes dominant in the thickets and plays the vital part in preparing the soil for the forest stage, fixing the nitrogen necessary to support spruce, the earliest of which usually arrive much too soon and are severely stunted, not only from lack of nitrogen but from suppression under later arrivals. Finally the hemlocks, which are shade-tolerant, establish themselves, compete with the spruce, and eventually dominate.

As for the modern era of studies in Glacier Bay, an entire volume—and a detailed one—could be written. Ecological observations were continued, following Cooper, by Donald B. Lawrence of the University of Minnesota, including his major contribution on the importance of the nitrogen-fixing properties of alder. Most recently, a comprehensive program—including glaciological, geological, and ecological studies—has been developed by Richard P. Goldthwait of Ohio State University, under the auspices of the Institute of Polar Studies, Columbus, Ohio. Using tools not available to Reid and Cooper, especially radiocarbon dating, Goldthwait, Haselton, Taylor, and others

The Yakobi at Reid Inlet. 1940. Photograph by BRADFORD WASHBURN.

have reached a better understanding of the geological and glaciological history of the Bay, particularly Muir Inlet. They have shown, for example, that the gravels predicted by H. F. Reid were predicted for the wrong reason, were not in fact laid down just ahead of the advancing glaciers, but accumulated over the land when the glaciers were back in their mountain valleys, during which time—perhaps for five thousand years—enormous quantities of those gravels were covering most of the Muir Inlet area. Additional adjustments in theory have been made, and will continue to be made as a result of Goldthwait's program—a program which increases in complexity and importance with each passing year.[14]

Fifty years ago, then, Lawrence Martin was certainly right when he told Cooper Glacier Bay was the unique ecological setting. Cooper achieved the classic successional studies, and was at the same time instrumental in the establishment of Glacier Bay National Monument. But over the years he could never convince his long-time friend that a Monument, or in fact any kind of a reservation, was the proper way to deal with land. Tom Smith never stopped arguing with Cooper against the concept of a Monument, and to this day is convinced a mistake was made when the lands were withdrawn. Some months before Cooper started north in summer 1956 for another look at the country, he received from Tom a letter which rather clearly enunciated the positions of the two men:

Dear Bill: Pleased to hear from you. I think you better be prepared for the worst when you start for Alaska again. You may not be pleased with the going ons in Glacier Bay. If the mineing company finds a large body of nickel ore there, there will be a long, dirty greasey stinking cabel running from the Bradey Glacier right into the head of the Bay—and could be several thousand dirty mineres working there—and freighters hundreds of feet in length with dirty black smoke roeling out of the funnells—turning that beautifull blue ice to an awful color. Then next would be a smelter and from past sad experience we know what happened at Treadwell Mine on Douglass Island just killed all that fine young groth of timber. The worst is yet to come. The Canadians may open a port in the head of the Bay—and they would have dozens of steamers plowing through the Bay—and hundreds of deck hands, longshoremen, greace pots etc. It is really too awful to contemplate. I almost forgot the hundreds of outboard motors. The Coast Guard would be first to build a dock and station in the entrance to the Bay. Hope you will excuse my punctuation, as I do not have the book larnin that you have. Best regards to you and Mrs. Cooper. Tom Smith.[15]

The argument between Cooper and Smith is of course one that occurs on a large scale whenever there is a suggested withdrawal or reclassification of land. Relative to Glacier Bay, the argument occurred in the early 1920's, as will be seen, and it will almost certainly occur again in the near future, as will also be seen. And over and above the argument, the recurring paradox; namely, that those who move away from the crowded centers of population—for many reasons but always at least to find more space for themselves, proceed not only to ruin the land for any who would follow, but also proceed to do their utmost to bring as many as possible to crowd the very space they sought. In the history of this country, the multitude almost without exception *has* followed. And almost without exception the land has been ruined. But not always.

In the early summer of 1924, while the fight for the establishment of Glacier Bay National Monument was going on in Washington, a lone prospector landed at Ptarmigan Creek, three miles to the northwest of Reid Glacier, and moved southeastward up the stream and over the hill toward the ice, which in that year was almost at the mouth of what is now Reid Inlet, the sandspit on the west just emerging from under the glacier. A short distance below the two-thousand-foot level on the hillside facing Reid Glacier, the prospector hit two gold-bearing veins in a granodiorite fracture, and at the one-thousand-foot level and farther south hit another vein in the same fracture zone. The discoveries were staked and registered later in the summer as the *Monarch 1* and *Monarch 2*, and the *Incas*.[16] The prospector was Joe Ibach, beginning a thirty-two year association with the Reid Inlet area, during which time he and his wife, Muz, would become almost legendary figures in the Monument. And the Ibach home at Willoughby Cove on Lemesurier Island became, over those same years, an important part in the lives of many visitors. But I think it was farther north, in the Glacier Bay country, that Joe was in his element— austere, wild land, the freedom of immense space, and rarely a visitor.

Writing in 1940 about a hunting trip taken with Joe thirty-five years earlier, author Rex Beach describes the fierce independence that stayed with Ibach all his life: "Joe was not a guide when we first met him—there were none in that part of the country— he was a prospector, miner, trapper, and when we undertook to pay him for his services he at first declined to accept anything, asserting that he was having as much fun as we were. What's more, the idea of working for anybody kind of made him sore, because he was his own man and he didn't like to take orders. He was indeed the nearest to a free soul of anybody I ever knew and anything less than complete independence irked him like a shirt of nettles. Venturesome, self-reliant, restless and as solitary in his habits as a rogue elephant he had covered that part of Alaska like the dew."[17]

In the summer of 1935, Beach finally renewed the old friendship and visited the Ibachs at Willoughby Cove, where Joe told the novelist of his troubles following the discovery of the Monarch and Incas veins. The Monument had been created the very next winter, thus closing the lands to mining activity, but under the provisions of the act, Ibach should have been able to work his claims, which were prior and almost certainly valid. According to Beach, Joe related the mixup as follows: "My claims were recorded and under the terms of the proclamation they were legal, nevertheless the land office warned me against working them. If I moved a stone or stuck a pick in the ground, they said I'd be defacing the park and it would constitute a trespass. On the other hand, I had to do a hundred dollars' assessment work every year to hold my property and it had to be sworn to. Well, if I did that I'd swear myself into jail. I've been ten years trying to clear those titles and I haven't succeeded yet. It was President Coolidge who issued the proclamation. I've written to the Department of the Interior and pulled every wire

Forest floor, Bartlett Cove. 1966

I can reach: Tony Dimond, our Delegate to Congress, has tried time and again to straighten out those titles but the best he can get is the promise of a field examination. The examiner never comes. Well, I finally got fed up so I bought this little rig. Muz and I steal off up there when we can and bootleg the ore out, like a couple of burglars. Our own ore! Imagine it! We don't dare tell anybody what we're doing so I dig the stuff and sort it, she drags it down to the boat, a sack at a time, on a barrel-stave go-devil. Its an outrage!"[18]

It is quite possible a local land office did in fact give Ibach incorrect information on working his claims, but in view of what happened later, it seems unlikely that Delegate Dimond was unable to straighten out the affair. Ibach was either a victim of bureaucratic indifference, or else Beach had been less than accurate in reporting Ibach's story. Whichever the case, Ibach persuaded Rex Beach to go to Washington in an attempt to have the Monument opened to mining, which Beach succeeded in doing by the following summer. Joe, after receiving discreetly worded telegrams from Beach informing him of the new law, proceeded immediately to Reid Inlet, where he discovered and staked the Rainbow and Sentinel veins and, joined later in the year by Beach, the Highland Chief veins, almost three thousand feet above Reid Glacier. The rush of prospectors to Glacier Bay never quite materialized, however, and Beach realized nothing from the joint claims in Reid Inlet.[19]

But for Joe, always over the next slight rise was the possibility of a fabulously rich strike, for like all prospectors, Ibach was a dreamer. Reminiscing at age eighty-eight two summers ago, Captain Tom Smith related to me his two years of partnership with Ibach at Reid Inlet. There was no elaboration but great affection as Smith described how he first built a blacksmith shop in that summer of 1938, but as soon as the building was finished, Joe and Muz moved in. As Tom said, "That finished the blacksmith shop. They wanted to live *alone*, not on the boat." Tom went on to relate how Joe would hold the hand rock drill while Tom would swing the sledge, and pretty soon the drill would begin to wave in the breeze as Joe's gaze wandered up and over the hillsides, searching for a promising fracture. Failing in that combination, they would switch positions so Tom could hold the drill steady, but Joe's mind still wandered to the next possible discovery, and he would smash Tom's hands. Failing in that combination also, Tom would call for Muz who would take over the sledge and swing a true stroke. In other words, mining was too confining for Ibach. He was a prospector, first and last, and as Tom Smith said with a far-away glint in his eyes, "Joe ran all over the hills, constantly bringing in a new rock."[20]

Some time during that first summer with Joe, Tom took a load of ore on the *Yakobi* to Juneau, and from there it was shipped to a smelter in Tacoma. The smelter reported the amount of gold recovery was just sufficient to pay for the smelting costs, and then billed Joe for the freight.[21] Tom stuck with the mining through the second summer, but then decided he wanted to go back in the charter boat business. So Joe and Muz and Tom, as the three partners, sat down in the Ibach house at Lemesurier Island to split the profits. They came out with thirteen dollars apiece for the two years, which Tom thought was not so bad considering they had paid for all their supplies. Tom went back to his boats, but Joe and Muz stayed on the job summers at Reid Inlet, and took the ore to Lemesurier Island to process in the Gibson Mill during the winter.

The cabin at the entrance to the inlet was built about 1940, and Muz landscaped the ground immediately surrounding it, filling in the terraces with dirt carried from Lemesurier Island in the bags used to drag ore from the mines. A vegetable garden was planted, including strawberries and flowers, and it prospered even though the terminus of Reid Glacier was only three miles distant.[22] Three spruce trees were planted on one of the terraces, within a few feet of the cabin, and those trees today are fifteen feet high and doing well as a completely isolated colony of imported pioneers. For another sixteen years Joe and Muz went north from the island each summer to the cabin at Reid Inlet, and the site today speaks of the unique relationship that produced the cabin and the landscaping and the vegetable gardens, with Reid Glacier and all the space a man could want.

Make no mistake about it, an enormous amount of personality was invested in that tiny plot of land in the wilderness, which is another way of talking about the investment the Ibach's had in each other. Tom Smith knew, and he understood. In 1964 he said: "Joe told me he and Muz had agreed that if one of them died when they were out in the wilds together, the other would die right away. I can understand that kind of an arrangement. After all, they had lived in the wilds together for over forty years, and I think I would feel the same way if I had lived out there all that time with a wife."[23] The last year at Reid Inlet for Joe and Muz was 1956. They were getting on, and the work at the mines could no longer be handled. In May 1959, Muz became ill and was taken to St. Ann's Hospital in Juneau, where she died. According to Tom, Joe was not able to convince himself she was gone, for Muz should have died in the wilderness, not in a noisy, dirty city. Joe returned to Lemesurier Island, where Muz was buried, and lived in the small cabin near the big house. He was lonely, of course, lonely beyond measure, but still doing pretty well. By spring of 1960, however, he was drinking too much and eating less and less. Nevertheless, Joe still talked a great deal about Reid Inlet, and in June made plans with Don Gallagher, of the mail boat *Forester*, to visit the cabins. And then the morning after those plans were made, Joe shot himself. He left a will on brown wrapping paper, at the bottom of which he said, "There's a time to live and a time to die. This is the time."[24]

It is a certainty Joe Ibach was against establishment of a Monument, and I am just as certain he would have been against scores of men crawling all over the Reid Inlet area dragging ore out of the ground, although I question whether he would ever have admitted such heresy. But had the rush occurred, as Rex Beach so wrongly predicted, Ibach would not have stayed at Reid Inlet. He needed space, which fortunately is still there along with the wilderness cabin and the three ecologically premature spruce.

Reid Inlet. 1964. Ibach cabin right.

Salmon trap cabin, Reid Inlet. 1965
Horsetail, Johnson Cove. 1966

[1] Wright and Wright (unpublished ms., I).

[2] Ibid.

[3] Reid (1896, I); 435-8.

[4] Muir (1915, VI); 292.

[5] These expeditions occurred in 1916, 1921, 1929, and 1935.

[6] Personal conversations with W. S. Cooper, Boulder, Colorado, December 1964.

[7] See Cooper under Bibliography I and II.

[8] Cooper (1923, II).

[9] Ibid., 108-10.

[10] Ibid., 110.

[11] Ibid., 122.

[12] Twenhofel (1952, I), Hicks and Shofnos (1965, I).

[13] Lawrence (1958, II); 101-2.

[14] The reader who wishes to pursue in detail the glacial geology of Glacier Bay and Muir Inlet should see in particular: Field (1947, I), Goldthwait (1960, I & 1966, II), Haselton (1965, I), Lawrence (1958, II), Cooper (1937, I), Mercer (1961, I).

[15] Smith to Cooper, correspondence 1956. The "Canadian Port" Tom Smith refers to in this letter caused considerable excitement in the fall of 1964. At that time a Canadian lumberman and roadbuilder, Leo Proctor, suddenly discovered the Grand Pacific Glacier had retreated behind the border, giving Canada a deep-water port. Various press releases were made and Canadian and American newspapers carried the great story. The story, including the optimistic plan for a road down the east side of the Melbern and Grand Pacific glaciers, may be found in part in the *Whitehorse Yukon Star,* October 5 and 8; *The Ottawa Citizen,* October 14; *Juneau Empire,* October 6; *New York Times,* November 5, all of these 1964. There was one minor difficulty which collapsed all the excitement, however. In the fall of 1964 the terminus of the Grand Pacific Glacier was approximately 850 meters into Alaska on its east side, and 1150 meters on the west side, and had not in fact been behind the international boundary since 1947.

[16] Rossman (1959, I).

[17] Beach (1940, VI); 228-9.

[18] Ibid., 241.

[19] Rossman (1959, I) and Beach (1940, VI). Additional notes on mining in the Reid Inlet area may be found in Black (unpublished ms., V), and in Trager, *Glacier Bay Expedition of 1939,* USNPS files, Juneau.

Rossman (above) treats in some detail the Le Roy mines owned by A. L. and L. F. Parker. The story of the finding of the Le Roy vein is fascinating, if short, and I quote in full from Rossman, pg. 38: "The LeRoy veins, now owned by the Mount Parker Mining Co., were found in 1938 by Mr. Abraham Lincoln Parker and his son, Mr. Leslie F. Parker. The father was a resident and a founder of Gustavus. In his old age, when he had become almost too incapacitated to work, he decided that he wanted to own and operate a gold mine. For several seasons he worked on designing and building a small two-stamp mill at his home at Gustavus. Upon completion, the mill was dismantled, and he and his son towed it by raft to the upper part of Glacier Bay. They anchored in the small indentation in the shoreline opposite Ptarmigan Creek and decided to start prospecting from this location. Within a few hours, they had discovered the LeRoy vein and had ascertained that it contained a considerable amount of gold. Within a few days they had moved the mill up Ptarmigan Creek to a position below the vein. An aerial tram was built, and mining was started. This is the only instance known to the author in which the mill was actually built before the prospect was discovered."

[20] Personal conversations with Tom Smith, Hotel Juneau, July 1964.

[21] Trager, op. cit.

[22] F. T. Been, inspection trip of August 1942, USNPS files, Juneau.

[23] Tom Smith, op. cit.

[24] Personal conversations with Don Gallagher, aboard the *Forester,* September 1966.

Reid Inlet. 1965. Cabin group (one inch from bottom) right center.
Photograph by CHARLES V. JANDA.

V *Democracy at Work*

WHILE COOPER was still working on the manuscripts of the 1916 and 1921 expeditions, he attended the annual meeting of the Ecological Society of America in Boston in late 1922. Barrington Moore, former president of the Society, was impressed by the uniqueness of the area Cooper reported on, and suggested the Society initiate studies to determine the advisability of establishment of a national park or a national monument.[1] Although Cooper was chairman of the committee subsequently appointed, and would carry much of the load in the next two years, it was thus Barrington Moore who made the initial suggestion for the project. Shortly thereafter Cooper communicated with the three other members of the committee[2] and asked for opinions on what recommendation the committee should return to the Society. From the alternatives presented by Cooper, the committee unanimously voted for the fourth, namely that immediate action should be taken looking toward the establishment of a national monument for, as Robert F. Griggs pointed out to the other members of the committee, "A national monument is created by presidential proclamation, whereas a national park is made by act of Congress. In the first case it is necessary only to convince one man of the advisability of the action, while in the second, six hundred, more or less, must be converted to the idea."[3] The establishment of a national monument is still difficult, because persuading the President is the final step in a long chain of persuasions. For Glacier Bay, there were a good many organizations and individuals involved in that chain, but when the Monument was thrown open to mining ten years later, only a handful of people sat in on the decision.

In recommending that the area be set aside, the committee gave five pertinent reasons: the tidewater glaciers, no example of which was included in other protected areas; the large stand of coastal forest in natural condition (plus the forests to come); certain scientific features which included the ancient forest remnants and the opportunity to study the developmental cycle; the historical associations beginning with Vancouver's visit to the area; the area was deemed more accessible to ordinary travel than the other similar (i.e., tidewater glacial) regions of Alaska. Of the five, the last would seem to have been peripheral, but was included for obvious reasons. In the final proclamation, the last reason given was left out entirely; the other four were quoted almost verbatim from the committee's original recommendations to the Society. At the annual meeting in December 1923, the Society adopted the recommendations of the committee and passed a resolution urging withdrawal of the region, with copies to the proper officials and the President. The usual campaign followed and in April 1924 President Coolidge ordered temporary withdrawal of 2,560,000 acres (about 4,000 square miles). The withdrawal included essentially what is now Glacier Bay National Monument, except that the eastern boundary extended to Lynn Canal. The reaction was predictable and swift, especially on the part of local newspapers and chambers of commerce, the latter watchdogs, then as now, of the provincial economic scene. The not-unfamiliar charges were leveled at the bug hunters and the conservation faddists, and in late April the *Juneau Daily Empire* fired a classic editorial:

A MONSTROUS PROPOSITION: The proposal to establish a National Monument of all that territory between Lynn Canal and the Chilkat River and the Pacific Ocean and between Mount Fairweather on the north and Icy Strait on the south is a monstrous proposition. Within this area there are more than 30,000 acres of surveyed agricultural lands and three or four times more than that which are capable of agricultural development. There are canneries, operating mines, patented mineral claims and a number of settlers on homesteads within the area, and vast opportunities for min-

Dory, Beardslee Islands. 1966

eral prospectors, water power development, lumbering and other industries. The Strawberry Point region, said to contain the largest and best tract of agricultural lands in Southeastern Alaska, containing approximately 90,000 acres suitable for farming and grazing, is in this proposed National Monument, which contains in all something like 2,500,000 acres.

It is said the proposed National Monument is intended to protect Muir Glacier and to permit of the study of plant and insect life in its neighborhood.

It tempts patience to try to discuss such nonsensical performances. The suggestion that a reserve be established to protect a glacier that none could disturb if he wanted and none would want to disturb if he could or to permit the study of plant and insect life is the quintessence of silliness. And then when it is proposed to put millions of acres, taking in established industries and agricultural lands and potential resources that are capable of supporting people and adding to the population of Alaska, it becomes a monstrous crime against development and advancement. It leads one to wonder if Washington has gone crazy through catering to conservation faddists![4]

Cooper defended the concepts of the proposed monument in the same newspaper on July 11, 1924, also pointing out all the things the newspaper had not bothered to ask him about, and elsewhere the argument continued for the rest of the year. Early in 1925 a compromise was reached, reducing the proposed boundary to include somewhat less than half of the temporary withdrawal, and on February 26, 1925, President Coolidge signed the proclamation establishing the Glacier Bay National Monument, an area of 1820 square miles.

* * *

In the January 1936 issue of Hearst's *International-Cosmopolitan*, Rex Beach, who had visited Joe Ibach the previous summer, opened a two-fold campaign which included the aerial mapping of Alaska to encourage prospecting, and the opening of the Monument to mining. He sent a copy of the article with a covering letter to Franklin D. Roosevelt, and at about the same time[5] wrote the Director of the National Park Service, Arno B. Cammerer. Referring to the Monument, Beach said in part: "The greater portion of it is absolutely barren and the only timber, such as there is, lies along the southern edge. It is not a good game refuge, nor are there any fishing streams or lakes in which salmon spawn. Presumably there are some sheep and goats in the St. Elias Range but it is the last place anybody would go for bear, moose or caribou. In fact the whole area is like a haunted house and I doubt if ten white men have visited it in the last ten years aside possibly from some surveying parties."[6] On all counts, except for the mention of moose and caribou, Beach was utterly wrong. On January 9 President Roosevelt answered Beach, noting that Delegate Dimond had already introduced a bill into the House of Representatives to permit mining in Glacier Bay.[7] Roosevelt was entirely noncommittal on the Glacier Bay proposal in his letter to Beach, but in a memorandum to Secretary of the Interior Harold Ickes a week later, he was favorable:

> January 15, 1936—Memorandum for the Secretary of the Interior: Rex Beach says that if we open the Glacier Bay National Monument in Alaska for prospectors for gold and silver, thousands of unemployed will immediately go there on grub stakes, and that it is generally agreed that the area is highly mineralized. As I understand it this monument is wholly unfit for human habitation and I do not see why mineral development could seriously affect its scenic beauty. In regard to wild life, if the monument here was opened to mineral exploration, why not adopt the Canadian system of allowing no firearms to be carried by prospectors. This has worked in Canada and the wild life has remained. Will you let me have a report on this. F.D.R.[8]

In the meantime Beach had proceeded to Washington and was making the rounds of all the Government agencies that would have any interest in either of his plans. He encountered opposition to the Glacier Bay proposal from the National Park

Joe and Muz Ibach, Lemesurier Island. 1954. Photograph by BRUCE BLACK.

Reid Glacier. 1929. Cabin group spit is still under ice. Photograph by USN, courtesy USGS, Menlo Park.

Service, but discounted the reasons—which in part had to do with wildlife—as more or less absurd. A few weeks later he saw Roosevelt who, according to Beach, "could see no good reason for keeping the Glacier Bay area posted against trespassers."[9] On February 21, Delegate Dimond sent a letter to Roosevelt, the closing paragraph of which said: "This is written to call your attention to the subject again since it is of considerable importance to the people of Alaska, and to request that you amend the Proclamation creating the Glacier Bay National Monument so as to permit mineral development therein. No injury can be done to anyone or anything by such an amendment and it will probably result in definite benefit to quite a number of individuals who will engage in mining on the mineral grounds of that region."[10]

After introduction, the House bill had been referred to the Committee on Public Lands, which in turn referred it to Interior for a report.[11] And Cammerer, after receiving Beach's second letter, wrote W. S. Cooper informing him of the situation and asking for an appraisal of the effect of prospecting and mining upon the wildlife of the area and upon the ecological relationships the Monument was especially designed to protect. Cooper answered, outlining the probable damage, and made an important point for the future:

> It is evident, too, that the problem presents implications affecting the fundamental policy of the Park Service with regard to the National Monuments. If Congress passes the proposed bill, a precedent will be established which may lead to future attempts to invade other reservations. I cannot imagine a precedent more dangerous to each and every reservation under control of the Park Service—the assumption by Congress of authority to override the settled policy of the Service in special instances, under pressure of local interests. A firm stand in this case may prevent endless future difficulties.[12]

The Ecological Society then reactivated the original committee, except for Barrington Moore, and Cooper flew to Washington to confer with National Park Service officials and other interested parties. The Park Service was adamant against the bill, but felt a vigorous effort had to be made if it were to be defeated. As a result of that conference, the Ecological Society asked for help from several hundred organizations, more than one hundred fifty of which protested to the Committee of Public Lands of both House and Senate. And on March 18, Roosevelt answered Dimond with a letter drafted by Interior:

> Washington, March 18, 1936—My Dear Mr. Dimond: I have given considerable thought to your letter of February 21, concerning the Glacier Bay National Monument. The Act of June 8, 1906, under which the Monument was established, apparently contemplates that such reservations shall be free of the acquisition of claims or their disposition under the public land laws, except bona fide claims initiated prior to the establishment of the reservation. It also appears that Con-

[97

gress has excluded the national parks and monuments from the operation of the Mineral Leasing Act. Therefore, in order that mining claims may be located within this reservation, it would appear to be necessary to have Congressional legislation. The action which you propose would have far-reaching implications with respect to the integrity of our National Park System and should, therefore, be fully justified by unquestionable evidence. The area was open to prospecting until 1925 without valuable minerals being found in sufficient quantities and under conditions economically justifying important mining developments. In the absence of more specific information as to the potential mineral resources of the area, it would appear inadvisable to take any action that might adversely affect the major object and best utilization of this area for the purposes for which it was set aside as a national monument. Therefore, until an investigation of the presence, distribution, and extent of possible mineral areas in the Monument has been made by the Geological Survey, and the results made available for study in relation to the other factors involved, I should hesitate to consider favorably the bill you have introduced into Congress to permit unrestricted prospecting in Glacier Bay National Monument. Very sincerely yours, (F.D.R.)[13]

The bill was not acted upon, and Cooper and the Ecological Society apparently felt the matter was closed. But the matter was not closed, and in late April, Beach wrote Roosevelt again. In a subsequent memorandum to Ickes, Roosevelt once more shifted position:

May 4, 1936—Memorandum for the Secretary of the Interior: I must say I am inclined to agree with Rex Beach in regard to actual mining prospecting on your glaciers in Alaska. It seems to me a refinement of conservation to prevent mining on a glacier. Any scars on the face of nature would be infinitesimal in comparison with the magnitude and grandeur of the National Monument, and, in any event, nature would obliterate mining scars up there in half a generation. To wait until the Bureau makes a complete geological study and report may mean waiting until everybody now alive is dead. The Bureau has no money or plans for such a survey anyway. Let us cut red tape and get the thing started. F.D.R.[14]

A few weeks later Beach learned from Delegate Dimond that Interior was having a change of heart also, providing Dimond would consent to a rewording of the bill. As redrafted by Interior, then, the bill was introduced in the Senate on June 16 as Senate 4784,[15] *five days* before Congress adjourned for the Democratic Convention in Philadelphia. With Beach, Dimond, and Senators Reynolds and Schwellenbach working in the cloak rooms, the bill was reported out of the House Committee on Public Lands. Beach then attended a hastily called special meeting of the Senate Committee on Public Lands and in ten minutes sold the bill, after first being assured by Dimond that it was the principle of the whole thing that was so important, apparently, the principle of preventing land from being locked to mining. Included at the meeting were Delegate Dimond and Governor Troy's (Alaska) son-in-law, an Alaskan newspaper editor. Five minutes after the spectators and Beach left the committee room, the bill was reported out. It passed the Senate on June 18, the House on June 19, and Congress adjourned the next day. On June 22, Roosevelt signed the Act into law.

Conservation organizations which had worked for two years for establishment of the Monument were indignant, and a joint committee from eight such groups issued a report in the *National Park Bulletin* of February 1937, the concluding paragraph of which read: "The undersigned committee, representing several national organizations interested in the preservation of natural conditions in areas of outstanding scenic and scientific worth, has been organized to consider the Glacier Bay situation. It has seemed to us that the first essential step is to put before the country a full statement of the facts. We believe that this will convince all fair-minded persons that the opening of the Monument to mining without preliminary investigation of its mineral resources was an unjustifiable act attained by unfair means; that it involves serious danger to the purposes for which the Monument was established and that it constitutes a precedent exceedingly dangerous to the future of our National Park system." Cooper himself said later:

The entire procedure was thus carried through in one week. No one likely to attempt opposition knew of the affair until it was a *fait accompli*.[16]

But Rex Beach did not feel that way about the result of his efforts, efforts which in good part had been expended for the benefit of one man, Joe Ibach. Writing three years later, Beach summed it up this way:

This was my first close contact with Democracy at work and it impressed me strongly. With all its strength and its weakness, it was such a contrast to other forms of government that I was thrilled at being an American.

Here may be the place to state that I got a novel out of Glacier Bay but no gold whatever out of its lodes. As a matter of fact, to evidence my faith in its possibilities, I spent considerable time and good money in an effort to get something started, but that is a story in itself. The last of Joe Ibach's silver-gray foxes has gone to London, he has quit fur farming and is working his claims. That's the hard way to build a country but he thinks he's going to make a mine before he gets through. Time, and other venturesome, stout-hearted men like him, will determine whether it was worth while to reopen the Monument, but in any event the lofty purposes that led to its creation will not be defeated. The glaciers will continue to rumble, the grass and the saplings will grow and earnest scientists who are charmed by such things can goggle at the phenomena to their heart's content, no matter how many miners burrow into the high hills.

After the Dimond bill was enacted, I became the target of harsh criticism on the part of those learned societies which had induced President Coolidge to remove that area from the public domain and reserve it to their uses, nevertheless I don't feel at all apologetic. It is absurd to assert, as those scientists did, that in helping Tony Dimond establish a precedent for which Alaskans have long fought, we threatened the integrity of the national park system.[17]

Apparently there were a good many people who felt Rex Beach's version of democracy did not quite meet the qualifica-

Willow catkins. 1964. Photograph by CHARLES V. JANDA.

tions, especially in view of the fact so many had contributed to the establishment of the reservation with mining excluded. Nor were all those who expressed themselves members of the learned (and lofty?) societies Beach so obviously disliked. On August 15, 1936, *The Saturday Evening Post* came out with the following editorial:

> Why Have Any Principles? More than eleven years ago President Coolidge, following a campaign participated in by nearly a hundred scientific and conservation societies, established by proclamation the Glacier Bay National Monument in Southeastern Alaska. The features which make the Glacier Bay region especially worthy of protection are its tidewater glaciers of the first rank in a setting of magnificent fiords and lofty peaks; its great expanse of shores recently vacated by melting ice, on which are coming in a new vegetation and a new animal population—visible demonstration of what happened over all of northern North America at the close of the Glacial Period; and its numerous well-preserved relics of interglacial forest.
>
> On January third of this year a bill was introduced in the House of Representatives which provided "that all laws of the United States which apply to public lands and which relate to entry upon and use and appropriation of such lands for mining purposes shall apply within the Glacier Bay National Monument, Alaska, notwithstanding the reservation contained in the proclamation of the President, dated February 25, 1925."
>
> Because of extensive public protest this bill was quickly dropped, but was revived in the last three or four days of the session and rushed to passage. Yet it is a long-established principle that national parks and monuments should be wholly free from mining, lumbering and other forms of commercial development and exploitation. The point is that, if an area is sufficiently unique from the scenic, aesthetic, historical or scientific viewpoint to make it a national park, it is of more value for that purpose than for any other. If an area is properly chosen for national-park use, then that is its highest possible use, and not some other. It is difficult to understand this invasion of national-park principles and standards, especially in view of President Roosevelt's declaration at the recent dedication of the Shenandoah National Park that more such reservations are needed. Let us be consistent about these matters. If areas are more important for mining, lumbering, grazing and agriculture, then let us keep them for that use. But there is something childish in setting aside these superb reservations as national parks for all time, and then letting down the standards.
>
> What is even more important is the precedent set. If mining development is to be permitted in one park or monument, why not in all? Countless similar attacks have been made upon other national parks and monuments, and if all had succeeded there would be no parks and monuments left. Why set standards and declare for definite principles only to break them down again?

Rex Beach's first close contact with democracy at work may have proved thrilling, but as an example of selfish interests at work in the smoke-filled back rooms, the scene was a classic.

The letter of March 18, 1936, as drafted by Interior, was strong. But the memorandum of May 4 to Ickes was completely uninformed. No one, for example—except possibly Rex Beach—had said anything about mining *on* glaciers, and the statement that "nature would obliterate mining scars up there in half a generation" was simply not true. At that point Roosevelt should have been advised differently, but the Park Service failed to rise to the occasion. Perhaps Interior did an about-face in return for a promise of enlarged boundaries. Such plans were being discussed in a letter of June 25, 1937, from Charles West, Acting Secretary of the Interior, to Roosevelt:

> Washington, June 25, 1937. Memorandum for the President: In conformance with your memorandum of April 21 concerning the possibility of making Admiralty Island a wildlife sanctuary until such time as it may be turned into a national park, I have asked the Secretary of Agriculture to appoint a representative who, with a representative of the Department of the Interior, will study the problem in Alaska.
>
> I have suggested this method of procedure because I am advised by the National Park Service that Admiralty Island is believed to be of doubtful national park quality; that the Forest Service and the Alaska Game Commission have effected a wildlife management plan of apparent merit for Admiralty Island; and, that a desirable extension of Glacier Bay National Monument would provide comparable wildlife sanctuary in a region of great scenic beauty and scientific interest.
>
> The proposed joint study should be completed by the middle of the summer.[18]

Further mention of the proposed enlargement of Glacier Bay National Monument appears in correspondence between Ickes and Roosevelt; on January 24, 1939, Irving Brant, then editor of the *St. Louis Star*, wrote to Ickes as follows:

> I talked with the manager of Crown-Zellerbach pulp operation last summer, sounding him out as to the company's present interest in Alaska, and he said that the idea of building pulp mills up there had been abandoned as unfeasible; that if any use was made of Alaska timber in the future it would be rafted to Puget Sound. That can hardly occur before Vancouver Island is stripped to pulp timber. Practically speaking, it eliminates Alaska from commercial consideration for many decades.
>
> The people of Alaska have an implacable hostility to the grizzly bear, chiefly because it eats one salmon where human beings eat 100,000, and because it makes occasional raids around fox farms. The brown bear of Alaska can be protected on Admiralty Island, because it has range, food and cover permanently adequate. But if fox farms are allowed on the island, or if casual local lumbering develops, the slaughter now going on will turn into a ruthless war of extermination, as it is on the mainland in the neighborhood of all settlements. There is plenty of room on the mainland and on other islands for a hundred times as many fox farms as there are in Alaska, and for all the lumbering that ever will be needed, even if Alaska becomes a pulp mill center.
>
> I think that the Glacier Bay National Monument ought to be enlarged, but I noticed in talking with one of the Forest Service staff about the recent withdrawal of Forest Service

Johns Hopkins Inlet. 1965

Muir Inlet. 1964
Eider duck (?), Reid Inlet. 1965

opposition to the enlargement that he persisted in speaking of it as a proposal to transform it into a national park. The thought behind that suggestion, I think, coming from that source is that if Glacier Bay were made a national park it would make it practically impossible to establish Admiralty Island as a national park. Admiralty Island contains something less than 2,000 square miles. Canada has established one national park in the far north, as a sanctuary for the wood bison, containing 20,000 square miles.[19]

With Agriculture now on the scene, the summing up was not long in coming, from Ebert K. Burlew, Acting Secretary of the Interior, and Henry A. Wallace, Secretary of Agriculture, to Roosevelt:

Washington, March 6, 1939. Through: The Bureau of the Budget, The Attorney General, Division of Federal Register. My Dear Mr. President: We submit for your consideration a form of proclamation to enlarge the boundaries of Glacier Bay National Monument, Alaska, in accordance with the provisions of the Act of June 8, 1906.

The proposed proclamation would enlarge Glacier Bay National Monument by approximately 904,960 acres, composed of public domain and national forest lands. The proposed extension of the boundaries of the monument is based upon comprehensive studies carried out since the monument was established in 1924 [1925], and it is designed to round out the area geologically and biologically, as well as from the standpoint of its administration.

During the period of contracted ice fields which preceded the land glacial advance about a century and a half ago, the forest in this section of Alaska extended from timber line to the water's edge. The tree species were chiefly hemlock and Sitka spruce, the same as the mature forests of today. This forest, which was at least 400 years old, finally was overwhelmed and buried by ice and gravel during the last glacial advance and is now being uncovered by the retreat of the glaciers and by the erosive action of streams and waves.

In its retreat the ice is exposing two general types of land surface: (a) rock exposure, and (b) depositional accumulations. In some places gravel deposits have been built up by lateral drainage from the glaciers, forming extensive sheets of gravel in the low country and glacial terraces between the ice and the abutting mountains.

The vegetation of the area recently laid bare by the final retreat of the glaciers may be roughly marked off into three communities: (a) the pioneer community most recently vacated by the ice, characterized by a growth of certain mosses, perennial herbs and willows; (b) willow-alder thickets occupying the slopes around the middle portion of the area to be added to the monument, and (c) a conifer forest along the shores of the bays and the ocean, characterized by a growth of hemlock and Sitka spruce. Because of the rapidity of vegetational change, these communities lack sharpness of definition.

The Fairweather Range of mountains included in the proposed extension of the monument contains magnificent scenery and features of outstanding geologic importance. The entire area to be added to the monument presents an exceptional opportunity for the study of glacial action and postglacial ecology . . .

The proposed proclamation is drafted subject to all valid existing rights. Therefore, any private rights within the area will not be affected if the boundaries are extended.

The issuance of the proclamation is respectfully recommended.[20]

Executive proclamation 2330 followed in just six weeks, increasing the size of the Monument from 1820 square miles to 3850 square miles, which figure for some reason did not include water.[21]

It is certainly unfortunate the comprehensive studies mentioned by Burlew and Wallace, and according to them carried out from establishment of the Monument in 1925, were not presented to Roosevelt three years earlier. Nevertheless, Roosevelt and Ickes, in one grand sweep, made everybody happy. They pleased the Forest Service by not pushing Admiralty Island as a national park, they kept the Delegate from Alaska happy (and Rex Beach) by opening the Monument to mining, they pleased Interior by adding to Interior's empire about nine hundred square miles of land which had formerly been Forest Service domain. But the legislation of 1936, by opening the Monument to mining, had effectively precluded the establishment of Glacier Bay as a *national park* for years to come. If there was dissent from the Park Service, it was inaudible.

In theory everybody was happy except the homesteaders who were living on the Gustavus foreland and had been since about 1917. But it was fifteen years before a Gustavus part-time resident got around to really objecting. Then, in 1954, Charles Parker initiated a one-man letter-writing campaign to Alaskan editors.[22] Parker's letters were long on generalized statement and grandiose reasoning, but very short on fact. Gustavus was not quite the agricultural paradise he imagined, and there were other good reasons why it had never become the great agricultural community, not the least of which was the reluctance of local markets to purchase Gustavus produce. But the story of Gustavus is a story unto itself, and this is no place for it. Parker's campaign had the desired effect and on March 31, 1955, Presidential proclamation 3089 removed certain areas of Gustavus (and Excursion Inlet) from the National Monument.

After the establishment of the Monument in 1925, fourteen years passed before the National Park Service made a serious effort to see what Glacier Bay offered. In 1939, Earl A. Trager, then Chief of the Naturalist Division, and Frank T. Been, then Superintendent of Mount McKinley National Park, visited the Monument for twenty-six days and subsequently made a comprehensive report on the possibilities of making the area and its story available to the visiting public. Inspections occurred at intervals for the next ten years, leading up to the establishment of the first permanent position in the Monument, that of Supervisory Park Ranger in 1951, operating out of Sitka.

But throughout the 1940's and 1950's, there was apparently very little concerted effort on the part of National Park Service administration to push Glacier Bay toward national park status, although the qualifications were obviously there—qualifications which were duly noted by almost all Park Service personnel who visited the area in those years.

Dryas drumondii in seed, Adams Inlet. 1966

In 1958, Superintendent L. J. Mitchell arrived in Juneau, and shortly thereafter recognized that Glacier Bay National Monument should have had national park status long before. In Mitchell's own words, he "did not want to see the Monument go another thirty-five years as it had," meaning another thirty-five years without park status. In 1963, Mitchell started gathering information to support his beliefs, and spent one year putting together material relative to the feasibility of redesignating Glacier Bay as a national park.

Apparently this document had the desired effect, for in August 1965, the Advisory Board on National Parks, accompanied by the Assistant Secretary of the Interior and the Director of the National Park Service, visited Glacier Bay for eight hours. Statistically speaking, it is obscure to me just why the sun shone on this group for the full eight hours, but it did, perhaps fortunately. And then, during the first week of October 1966, the Advisory Board met in Washington, and among other resolutions endorsed a proposal to reclassify Glacier Bay National Monument as a national park. The Board further urged that legislation to establish a national park at Glacier Bay contain a provision repealing the Act of June 22, 1936 because "... mining is incompatible with the purposes of a national park...." Finally, the Board asked that such legislation be introduced and enacted during 1967, the Alaskan centennial.

Thirty years, almost, since the enlargement of the boundaries. But government moves slowly as do the glaciers. The difference is that glaciers have much more time through which to move. It is now up to the people to urge the President and Congress to bestow park status on the largest unit under the jurisdiction of the Park Service—2,764,000 acres or 4319 square miles of magnificent land, a unit former Superintendent L. J. Mitchell considers "absolutely the greatest thing we have in the National Park system today."

* * *

Late in September 1966, I had the unique opportunity of twelve days in Glacier Bay with the new Superintendent of the Monument, Robert Howe, both of us with the American Geographical Society field party surveying the terminal positions of the glaciers. This was Robert Howe's first complete tour of the inlets in Glacier Bay, and I am not sure which experience was the more rewarding—his own as he saw for the first time some of the land he was now administering, or mine as I watched the unbelievable enthusiasm of this National Park Service official as we tramped the moraines in the fog and the rain, as we moved through the ice in upper Muir Inlet, as we sat late into the night with the other members of the party, aboard USNPS *Nunatak*, and discussed Glacier Bay and the story of the land.

[1]Additional details in the history of the establishment of Glacier Bay National Monument can be found in Cooper (1956, V), from which I took much of my information.

[2]Charles C. Adams, Robert F. Griggs, and Barrington Moore. Griggs made famous The Valley of Ten Thousand Smokes following the great eruption of Katmai in 1912, and was essentially responsible for the establishment of Katmai National Monument.

[3]Cooper (1956, V); 4.

[4]*Juneau Daily Empire*, April 28, 1924.

[5]Beach letter to Roosevelt December 23, 1935; Beach letter to Cammerer January 3, 1936.

[6]Cooper (1956, V); 23.

[7]HR 9275, January 3, 1936.

[8]Roosevelt (1957, V); 472.

[9]Beach (1940, VI); 250.

[10]Roosevelt (1957, V); 487.

[11]Ibid., 518. Also Beach (1940, VI); 250.

[12]Cooper (1956, V); 26.

[13]Roosevelt (1957, V); 496.

[14]Ibid., 517-18.

[15]The bill was introduced by Senator Schwellenbach of Washington. Cooper (1956, V) adds that Beach made another call on Roosevelt the day before introduction of the bill, and that word then passed from the White House to Secretary of the Interior not to oppose the bill. As Cooper indicates, there is no official confirmation of the last two points.

[16]Cooper (1956, V); 29-30.

[17]Beach (1940, VI); 257, 259-61.

[18]Roosevelt (1957, V); 80.

[19]Ibid., 295-6.

[20]Ibid., 305-6.

[21]Issued April 18, 1939.

[22]Black (unpublished ms., V). One Parker letter is quoted in full by Black.

Great Blue Heron, Bartlett Cove. 1966

William O. Field, Muir Inlet. 1966

From the surveys of 1890 and 1892, section of map by H. F. Reid. USGS Sixteenth Annual Report, 1896.

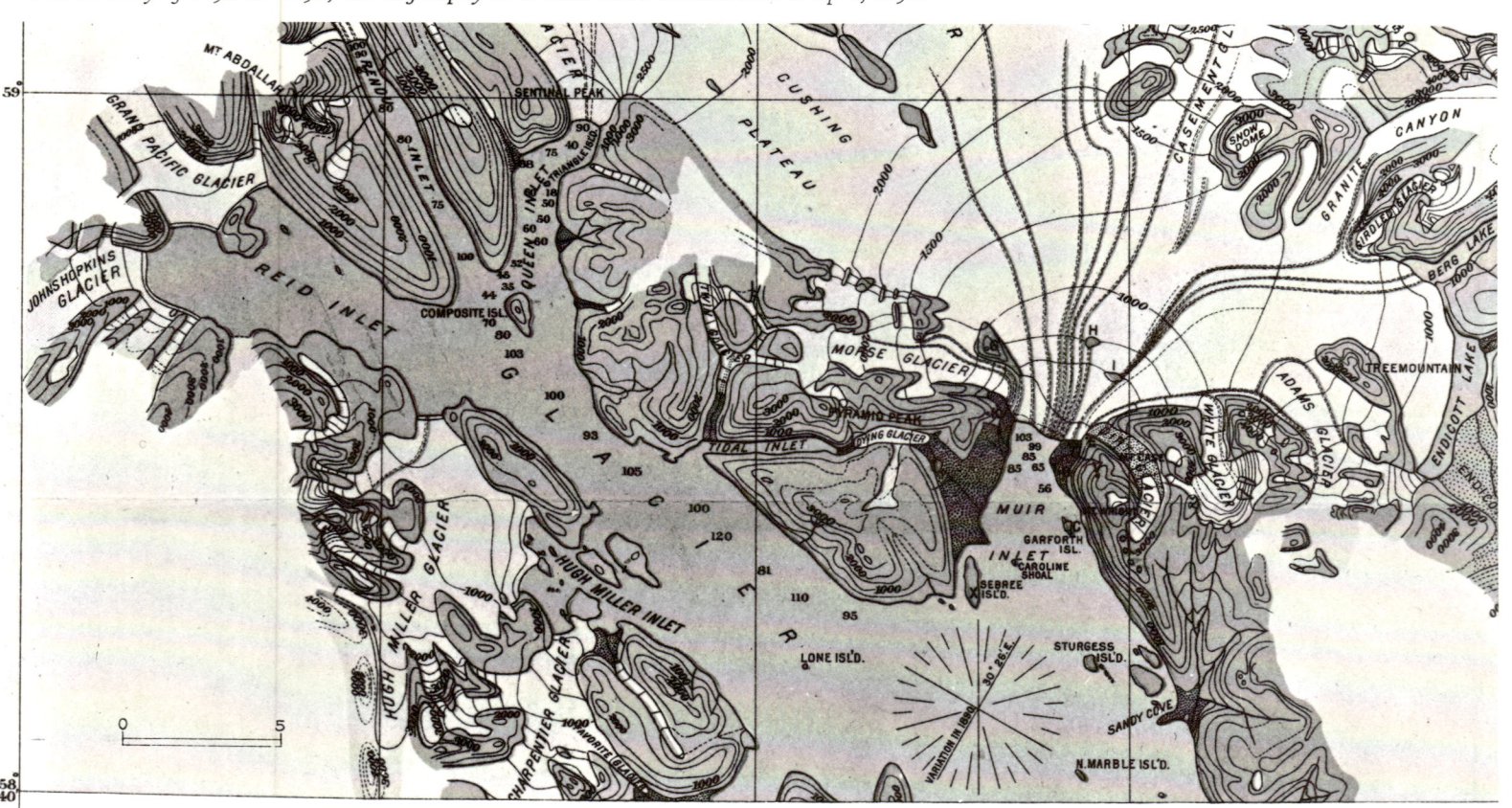

VI *Home at Glacier Bay*

These impressions are expanded from the field diaries of 1962-1966. The diary was written across much of the 4400 square miles of the Monument, many times from a tent in the rain, other times from a small boat pushing through the ice, from blizzard camps in the Fairweather Range, from summits, moraines, wilderness cabins, from the deep silence of the coastal forest, and just every so often, from a rock under a hot sun with warm feet and warm hands.

1962

29 April, south of Cape Fairweather: I cannot stop thinking of that coast from Cape Spencer to Icy Point. I think I have never seen a more savage meeting of rock and sea, and from the air in a violent rain squall there were some uneasy moments. Tonight at Cape Fairweather the surf is immense. High winds. Waves trailing luminous spindrift. Somewhere behind me, to the east, are the peaks.

30 April, southwest edge, Fairweather Glacier: We broke out of the alder two hours ago. Brutal alder. Brutal traveling through alder with eighty-pound packs. The tent is on the rocks of the moraine. This country is larger than we had anticipated, and Mount Fairweather does not look any closer.

4 May, top of the last ice fall, Fairweather Glacier: Four days since the alder, and we are still a day out of the proposed base camp area. This country is *much* larger than we had anticipated. The peaks are all around us tonight, Fairweather and the satellites. It is cold up here, and we have already passed to another world. The beach and the forest are years away.

11 May, head of Fairweather Glacier: I just came in from photographing Mount Salisbury and the moon. My fingers got very cold trying to work the camera, while the others were already in their sleeping bags, and warm—except Maki. He will remember that scene with me. It must have been the clouds; the shape of them and the movement across the summit. There was unbelievable space and silence above and behind Salisbury.

1 June, after the ascent, high camp, Lituya Mtn.: Clouds drifting on the summit when we were up there, but I had a glimpse to the east. It was Glacier Bay, and the fjords looked wild. The descent was amazing. Mushkin traversing through shrouded, muted space on the ice pinnacles of Lituya. A rare sight. No immense view, no peaks showing, no other part of Lituya showing. Whiteout. Shrouded space. *Nothing* but Muskin and the pinnacles.

Mushkin and Nielsen on the descent of Lituya Mountain. 1962

15 June, base camp, alone: Snowing harder. Complete whiteout. I cannot even see the stakes holding up the tent. This evening I am contemplating with some interest the matter of reference points. In other words, suppose I have another five days of complete whiteout? What substitute will the mind make for the normal visual reference points that will, in that case, have been missing for seven days? In the meantime, it continues to snow and I continue to see nothing.

9:00 P.M. At last. I can see some vague shapes over there somewhere. Mountains. I am emerging. Crouched in the doorway of the tent I am watching those shapes become mountains. The mountains are back at last.

11:00 P.M.: I am standing in the snow. The scene is one of outrageous desolation. Sullen sky, the peaks dark and cold, great storm clouds hanging close over the sea. And now out of the vast silence comes one of the loneliest sounds in all nature, the cry of geese. On the way to the Yukon through the outrageous desolation.

Lituya Mountain from Fairweather Glacier. 1962

1963

5 May, at 9500 feet approaching the Fairweather Mountains: It is 7:45 A.M. As usual I find myself jammed into a Piper Cub in early May. Boxes on my lap almost to my chin. High over the glaciers, ice and rock. And there ahead is Salisbury—Mount Salisbury in the early morning light. With the camera setting on the boxes at eye level, I am trying to photograph a mountain scene of terrifying primal clarity. Through the filthy window of this small plane. Why the hell doesn't Bennett wash the goddamned windows? Salisbury. Brilliant against the space above and beyond. If the window does not give me glare, if the wing was barely out of the ground glass, if the plane was steady for that moment—why the hell don't I take photographs where the conditions are not *always* wrong? Damn shouting, screaming noisy airplane, now bouncing high over the Fairweathers in the cold stark light of early morning.

24 May, upper icefall, Fairweather Glacier: We are resting alongside the icefall. Three of us. Sometimes large country can close in suddenly and trap even the competent traveler. This is large country and ten minutes ago it almost nailed us. On a short, steep snow slope, Maki broke through my left step to his knee—with eighty-five pounds on his back. Unable to release the waist strap, his leg was wrenched as the monster twisted him slowly downhill, slowly upside down.

I reached Maki in time to help with that awful weight—and there was no broken leg. Had there been a broken leg, this country would have tripled in size instantly. It is big enough already. But then, don't travel such country unless you are prepared to accept the possible.

26 May, heather bench, lower Fairweather Glacier: It seems we have been on the move for a long time from the head of the Fairweather Glacier, but even tomorrow will not get off the ice. Two curious ptarmigan are observing us closely as we sit here five hundred feet above the glacier surrounded by the most brilliant heather I have ever seen. At least, it looks that way because we have been living up on the snow. Coming down out of the high peaks, where there has been no vegetation, the first growing thing is the first ever seen, and the feel and smell—especially the smell—is an entirely new experience. So it has been with the heather.

We are just between two worlds here, the snow and ice we have almost, but not quite left, and the first vegetation of any consequence. In a day or two we will be down in the forest, finding out what trees are, and the glacier will be hard to remember.

30 May, airborne over Lituya Bay: Below me must surely be a paradise. At least it looks so in the evening light. Except that I can see where the 1958 wave damaged the shorelines. That night in 1958 Lituya Bay was no paradise.

Mount Fairweather from Fairweather Glacier. 1962

Muir Inlet from the south. 1964

1964

27 May, approaching Reid Inlet: We have been steaming northwest from Bartlett Cove for three hours, and according to the map we should be close to Reid Inlet. I have been on deck most of the way, and I notice a subtle but rapid change in the vegetation as we proceed. The heavy spruce-hemlock forest of the southern part of the Bay has given way to willow and alder thickets, and now only a ground cover which I learn is dryas mat. Since we are still twenty-five miles from the Grand Pacific terminus, I suppose even the ground cover will gradually disappear farther north.

28 May, Reid Inlet: This is the first morning here. After six snow expeditions in the last seven years, I find the camping relaxed and warm. I understand the red cabin was built by Joe Ibach, a prospector. It is small, and the three of us are living in the tent. I am impressed with the sound of the glacier, two miles from us. I have never heard a calving ice front, yet how many times have I walked on ice and snow? I can see now that we will be living with that sound, and the twenty-foot tides.

Early this morning I walked on the beach to the rocks. I thought I was alone, but I was observed by a silent bald eagle, three hundred feet up. There was no comment from either party and he left shortly.

Fifteen hundred feet above the cabins at 10:00 P.M. Looking north up Tarr Inlet. I find myself slightly unnerved at what I see. I guess I know the snow peaks, but this is something else.
30 May, Reid Inlet: In a cold wind I stood on a rock one-eighth mile away and had my first close look at the terminus of a tidewater glacier. I was not unprepared for the size, for I have certainly been in big country before. Nevertheless, the height impresses, and the power of that enormous mass pushing into the water. But the sound. If only I could write the sound.

5 June, Reid Inlet: I have become increasingly aware of a small bird with a collar on its neck. It runs over the tide flats and rock beaches, and when it stands still to see if I am following as it wishes, it tends to perform half a deep knee bend, as if it had hiccupped. It has knobby knees and is very insistent. According to the book it is a semi-palmated Plover, but it has knobby knees which is more important.

Tarr Inlet from the south. 1964

6 June, Lamplugh Glacier: I find I am learning something about the floating ice; how hard not to hit it, and I seem to be willing to hit bigger pieces than I was eight days ago. Nor can I forget the temperature of the water. Thirty-eight degrees means very little chance for any of us if we should swamp. There is no question that floating ice, water temperature, and twenty-foot tides require every bit as much attention as crevasses on a glacier and avalanches from above. Twenty foot tides, yet we can carry the boat easily when necessary. If we come back next year, we must have a larger boat.

8 June, Russell Island: Ice walls, floating ice, frigid water, twenty-foot tides, knobby knees, and now on this rocky beach two oyster catchers raising a stupid noise at our arrival. I watched them through the glasses, and discovered they tiptoe across the pebbles and rocks in a slightly crouching position, as if trying to be less visible and very quiet. While they are screaming. And then they reach a rock large enough to hide behind and crouch out of sight. Nothing is visible except the brilliant red and very long beak at one end of the rock, and the brilliant red, beady eye looking over the top. This is an absurd performance. Had they gone to the other end of the beach and stayed quiet, we would never have known they were there. But then, I am remembering this bird was here before I was.

Sitting here on Russell Island looking across at the magnificent panorama of the northern Fairweathers, I have just decided the oyster catcher is an absurd bird and will bear watching.

Johns Hopkins Glacier. 1964. Photograph by CHARLES V. JANDA.

19 June, Reid Inlet: An eagle soaring high over the small peninsula, harassed by gulls, terns, and oyster catchers protecting their eggs. Scream and cry, birds, but don't get too close to him.

20 June, steaming for Muir Inlet: Trees again and into the mist of Muir Inlet, and looming out of the mist the shape and luminosity of enormous icebergs. Enormous, silent, crowding in on us, the entire inlet choked with ice and the gloom of fog. Seals all around us. I am now willing to believe the land is coming out from under the ice. I must go walk on the new land. And if the Muir Glacier is calving all this, I must see it.

Goose Cove: Ashore, and the steamer *Nunatak* disappearing through the great white shapes. With the rowboat we continue north through the ice, against the tide—a mistake with so small a motor. Beside us a baby seal, pacing the boat and calling. I would like to touch him. I have never seen a more beautiful animal. He still calls.

22 June, Nunatak Cove: Across the cove there are two very large stumps. Haselton says they are six thousand years old, *in situ*. The Pyramids. They grew before the Pyramids were built. They are known as interstadial stumps, but the name is certainly unimportant.

I waded across the mud flats toward the two stumps, and on the way photographed geese tracks in the same mud. Then face to face with six thousand years of age.

23 June, Nunatak Cove: We walked for miles today over what Haselton calls The Plains of Abraham, north to McBride Glacier. This is new land, out from the ice since 1948. Here and there a bit of willow, an alder, one tiny spruce. Mostly nothing but gravel and rocks. But I saw something back there more remarkable to me than the alder and the moss and the tiny spruce. It was only one mile from the glacier, that spot. There was a stream and then a small pond, and in the pond was a horsetail stem, bent at right angles on the surface of the water. And resting his weary head on that stem, swaying ever so slightly in the current as he watched me, was a frog, a one- and one-half-inch long frog. I did not know his species and again I did not care. I do know the harsh landscape wasn't bothering him, nor did he think it worthless, or else of course he would not have been there. He had no intention of answering me how he came there, and even less intention of answering the very silly why, a question I would not have asked anyway. He was stoical as frogs are, and he was very much *there*, as frogs are inclined to be.

When I saw him, back there, I don't think I realized how much that frog meant to me. Now sitting here in the tent after dinner, I know.

24 June, Nunatak Cove: On a cold, gloomy day the water of upper Muir Inlet is five hundred feet below me choked with great and small icebergs, almost all of them from Muir Glacier. I regret we couldn't see the Muir from the col above McBride, for indeed it must be a sight. Below me and to the south as far as I can see and to the north and north-west hundreds of square miles of floating ice, brooding stark austere landscape, low rain clouds, dark, a screaming tern wheeling over me protecting her solitary almost unseeable egg, and on the way back to the tent—a baby oyster catcher.

Sitting in the rain above the mud of Nunatak Cove, I was two feet from the young one as a nervous but quiet mother edged toward me until she was six feet away. When I had moved off a sufficient distance, mother called baby, and it paddled unsteadily beneath her. Crisis over. You can return now, father, and when you and mother finish with your ritual dance and all the accompanying screeches of apparent joy, mother can go back to sitting on child. In the rain.

29 June, Nunatak Cove: Weather hellish. Days and days of rain. Everything is damp.

4 July, Goose Cove: Rained all night. But we are leaving for Sandy Cove regardless (almost) of the weather. Thirty miles to the south. In our twelve-foot rowboat. It is *not* raining (impossible, no?) at ten minutes before high tide as we leave, skies clearing, ice axe and oar up front for pushing ice, hardly room to sit, and goodbye Goose Cove and colony of eight oyster catchers screaming and screaming ravens and crows and gulls, and one quiet eagle.

Now pushing ice almost immediately, feeling our way through, bumping, finding short stretches of open water, calculating which bergs might roll, if they roll are they small enough, if the boat swamps save only the film and us and nothing else, bailing can, rocks, crampons, Diana leaning over the bow pushing the ice away, motor on, motor off and now rowing and can hear (they are not silent after all) the very musical icebergs creaking and sighing, no wind, three food boxes, two duffel bags, packsack, three gas cans, gas tank, sunshine on the Nunatak—the first in six days, Goose Cove receding, nearing Forest Creek, ice still heavy and we are running with the tide, sun at last, pushing, bumping, sideswiping, a rain squall south off Adams Inlet, Idaho Ridge across the Inlet now partly brilliant...

ye gods . . .

HUMPBACK WHALE . . .

Closer to shore than we are and three-fourths of a mile away. How to change course from parallel to perpendicular to shore is to point the bow immediately shoreward. With the motor off, his blow sounded like a muffled cannon roar, then he rolled under the bergs. He is close to shore, blowing, surely he will run out with the tide (?). *Of course* he will run with the tide (?).

Now beyond Forest Creek, ice still heavy, sunshine, yes the whale *is* moving out with the tide, nearing Adams Inlet, ice, ice, ice, into the rain squall, across Adams Inlet, no more whale, cliffs with one spruce halfway up in the sun, ice much thinner, Goose Cove distant, Riggs Glacier far beyond, the Nunatak appears a shadow, around the corner, out of the ice, John Muir's cabin site, running with the tide for Sandy Cove, new scenery, great cliffs to the water's edge, an occasional berg with cormorants sitting idiotically, another rain squall, North Sandy Cove and tufted puffins. Puffins by the hundred.

14 July, Bartlett Cove: Haselton was right. Ken Youmans does know a great deal about this damn wet, rainy, damp country called Glacier Bay. I found it remarkable to come out of the wilderness into the wilderness of Bartlett Cove and have placed at my disposal a reference library with card catalogue, all on Glacier Bay. Thus started my bibliography on the Glacier Bay National Monument. And in Youmans' apartment he and I talked for hours about the land and the few, the very few, characters who have lived on it (within the present boundaries) since the Tlingits. I learned something about the Ibachs of Reid Inlet, for Ken knew them well. I learned of Huscroft of Lituya Bay and Harbeson of Dundas Bay, and Vancouver and Lapérouse. I saw aerial photographs, charts, maps, books, journals, and Youmans' own remarkable scrapbook wherein he documents much of the land he has seen in the Monument. So it was Youmans who got me started on the historical research, and as we steamed out of Bartlett Cove this morning he waved goodbye with a big cigar in his mouth. He certainly knows this country. He ought to. He has lived permanently at Bartlett Cove since 1956, and the three summers prior to that in a tent as Bartlett Cove became a community.

Canada Goose, Nunatak Cove. 1964

1965

15 January, Berkeley: That damn wet, rainy, damp country called Glacier Bay seems less and less wet as I sit here in front of the fire thinking about the frog. And I think often of Reid Inlet. I hope the little red cabin is surviving the winter. This year we must see Muir Glacier. The early descriptions of it are preposterous. Exaggerated. I cannot fully understand why they went to such lengths to describe it.

29 April, en route Lituya Bay with Ken Loken: The wild coastline again, Cape Spencer to Icy Point. But from Icy Point north looks like easy walking, and across the front of the La Perouse Glacier is a good beach at low tide. I should have no trouble getting around the ice front.

Ken Loken, one of Alaska's great bush pilots, knows every rock on this coastline, almost. He is quite sure I can cross all the streams from Lituya Bay south thirty-five miles to Icy Point. My solitary beach walk should be successful then, unless a brown bear decides otherwise. Nor do I look forward to the ninety pounds which will be hanging behind me.

30 April, Lituya Bay: My camp here at Coal Creek looks across to Cenotaph Island. Lapérouse's country. In brilliant sunshine all day. The peaks are magnificent. Fairweather. Crillon. On landing yesterday and stepping ashore from the pontoon, I was unutterably delighted to be back in the wild. And now if the weather will hold.

As I get into the sleeping bag there are a few ominous clouds about.

1 May, Lituya Bay: I am sitting here in the small—much too small—tent, in the rain. In the pouring rain. It is 10:00 A.M. At least I had a hot breakfast over a fire before the skies opened. I notice water around the tent beginning to rise a bit. Possibly the drainage here is not quite as good as I thought.

It is now 8:00 P.M. It is still raining, but rain is not the word. I thought I had seen it rain last year at Goose Cove. Negative. It only sprinkled. *This* is the monsoon. I saw almost the monsoon on the Fairweather Glacier in 1962. I was alone then also. I was in an orange two-man tent. I am now in a gray two-man tent. No difference. I am beginning to think I will learn a wilderness lesson in the next few hours . . . Lesson: When traveling alone in rain country, do not try to save too much weight by carrying a small tent.

At any rate, I am here, and the month of May is always the best month for the coast. Statistically. The monsoon is definitely outside the door. It will probably stop by late tonight. Yet, it does not look that way at all. It looks as if this is the long monsoon. I can feel it. I notice the water around the tent has risen about a half inch since this morning.

Lituya Mountain. 1963

Mount Salisbury and the moon. 1962

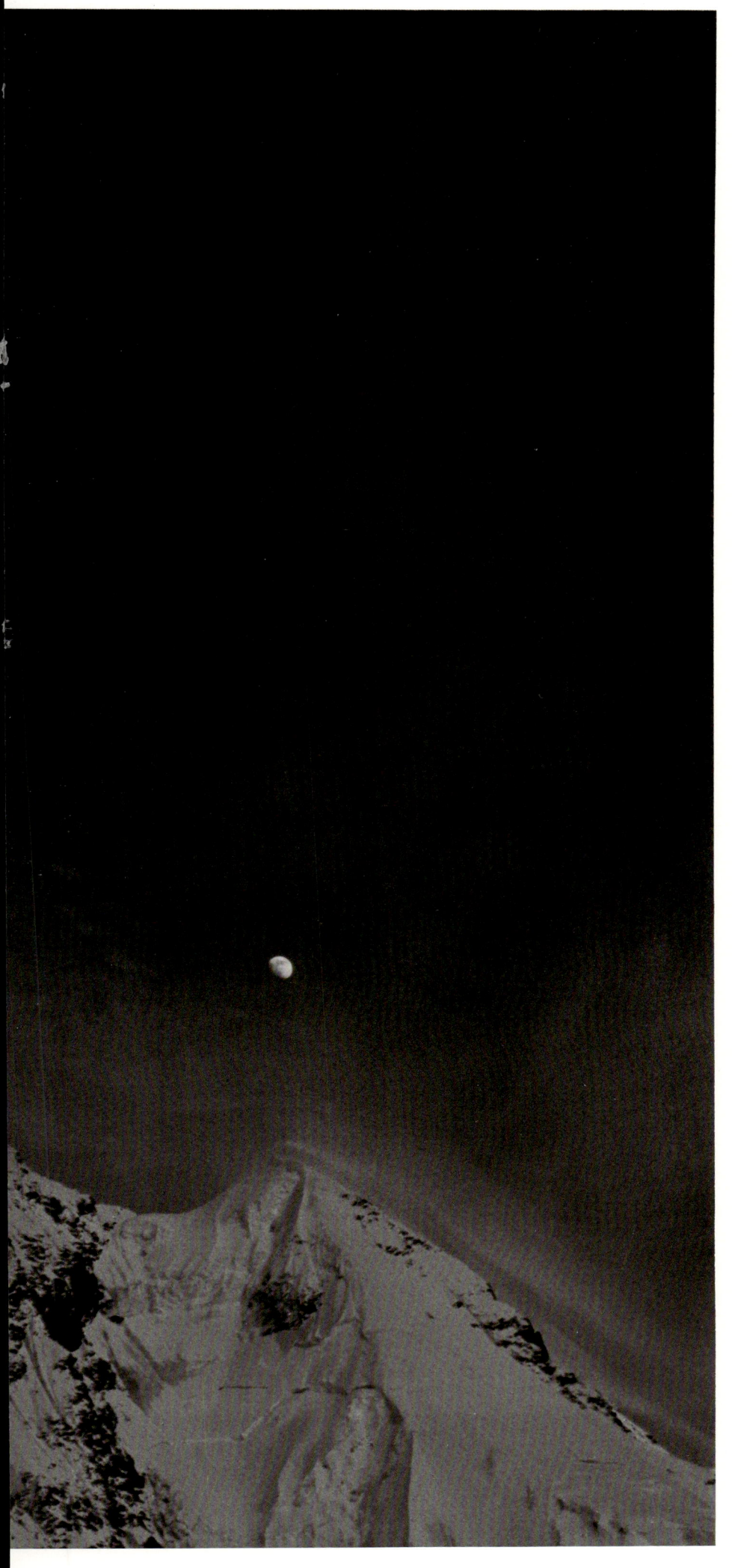

Midnight: I notice there is now a great deal of water *under* the tent as well as around it. The floor is billowing as if there were air underneath. I wish it were air. And a moment ago the left guyline pulled out and deposited the whole side of the tent on the sleeping bag and in my face. The wind out there is really very high. Which means I may lose the entire tent in a few minutes, unless I can get the line anchored again. Which means I must get dressed, including oilskins and very wet boots. In a gray two-man tent with one side collapsed. Without touching the other side, in dark screeching wind and rain. I think it will be a hard lesson.

1:00 A.M.: I am standing outside the tent deciding. I pulled too hard on the tie string of my rubber jacket and it ripped open fourteen inches. Considerable water will enter a slit that long. I don't know why I am deciding. There is nothing to decide. The tent is going to be washed away unless I move it. Immediately. In the dark screeching wind and rain.

4:00 A.M.: It is beginning to get light. The monsoon is still with me and the water is still rising around the tent. The foam rubber mattress is soaked, the down sleeping bag damp through, all clothes damp. I think I have lost. The tent must be moved again, and on the next move all will get wetter, including the cameras. It is no longer the monsoon. It is the deluge, and below me across the waters of Lituya Bay, through the dim light, horizontal rain, and fog, I can see the mast lights of what must be the entire halibut fleet. I am no longer alone. They have come in from the sea—across the bar and into the Bay. But out there beyond La Chaussee Spit, what must the open sea be like early this morning? It must be insane. The wind here is increasing.

10:00 A.M.: I have moved the tent a second time. I am in the forest, under the swaying trees and the occasional falling limbs. The sleeping bag is now soaked through. Which is why it just took me ten minutes to wriggle into it. One does not slide easily into soaked rip-stop nylon.

In wilderness, when you get behind you often cannot catch up. I am behind. The deluge is still with me and the wind is yet higher. In fact, I can see through the glasses that some of the boats have thrown shore lines. In Lituya Bay? Where according to Lapérouse not a ripple marred the face of the waters? Yes. Shore lines in Lituya Bay. I think I am too far behind. If the cameras go the way of the rest of the gear, I am finished. I think I shall stand on shore in the screeching wind and rain, hail the fleet, and re-group aboard a halibut troller. You win, deluge.

Mount Salisbury. 1963

30 May, Strawberry Island: All of Bartlett Cove saw us off this morning in our sixteen-foot boat. Three of us with gear and food for three weeks. The logistics are solved. The extra four feet makes the difference.

I have just looked through the ground glass at Carl Swanson's bird house. Swanson fox-farmed here in the 1930's. The building to which the bird house is attached is leaning considerably. The roof is falling in and all will collapse in a year or two, I presume. In fact, both roofs are falling in. But I am glad Swanson bothered to build a bird house out here on isolated Strawberry Island. Through the ground glass it looked beautiful, and from a distance so did the man house.

31 May, en route Reid Inlet: From Berg Bay this morning, where John Muir camped eighty-six years ago, we moved off for Reid Inlet. It has been raining steadily and we are all somewhat cold. Sitting for hours in an open boat in the weather is no way to keep warm. But one learns about the land. Glacier Bay is under mist and the peaks are not revealed to us. Nevertheless the land forms are with us hour after hour. The magnificent land forms pushing down into the water on all sides of us and disappearing into the clouds. Land forms scraped and rounded by the glaciers. Birds constantly flying out of the mist. Mammoth flocks of ducks rising from the water in confusion. Two thousand ducks taking to the air at once. Cormorant you are the fifth cormorant I have watched since Berg Bay, and each one of you has circled the boat exactly two times. Cormorant, why do you circle this boat two times? Pigeon guillemot, I am watching you also with the glasses. I see how you kick your feet like hell as you leave the water. Fatty with red feet. Hundreds of fatties with red feet.

Hour after hour. The trees are thinning out, but not the mist. Moving north through the fog and the rain and the cold. Beyond the mist two more headlands, then Reid Inlet. The wind is rising now and our freeboard is not ample. And then appearing from behind the last obstacle—if one knows where to look—the red cabin finished in 1940 by Joe and Muz Ibach. The cabin on the small piece of land which, on the back of a fuzzy photograph Joe Ibach called 'HOME AT GLACIER BAY.' Hello red cabin. All of us are relieved you are still here. Including Cicely who has never met you before. Who cares that we are cold and stiff, that we have been sitting in the cold rain for five hours, that we are hungry and the food boxes wet? Who cares. It was as if the red cabin would not be here, somehow, but it is here still standing and we are back at Reid Inlet.

Carl Swanson's cabin, Strawberry Island. 1965

Glaucous-winged Gull nest, South Marble Island. 1965

2 June, Reid Inlet: Late afternoon. The light! Look at the light on the glacier. The boat. Drag the boat off the beach and go, instantly. The race to the terminus of the Reid Glacier and up on the rocks at the east side. In stillness in front of the now silent glacier. Light on the ice cliff. Luminous. Great silence.

6 June, at Margerie Glacier: I am sitting here at the tent watching an iceberg trying to dislodge the bowline. The boat is two hundred feet offshore. If the iceberg wins we might be in poor shape, even though we brought extra food.

The same food that fell overboard as we arrived earlier. The box was set on the bow for a moment, just after landing, and then the glacier calved. It was big, and as I turned to look the swell from the preceding explosion hit the boat and all our food went over the side. Surrounded by floating grapefruits I shouted and cursed at the Grand Pacific, but it kept right on calving. It paid no attention to me. This country doesn't pay attention to anybody. Vice versa, or else.

We are camped alongside the Margerie Glacier, which is two hundred feet away. The Grand Pacific is very noisy and so is the Margerie. From the promontory between the two I can see for miles and miles to the south, almost all of the fjord under ice when John Muir was in Glacier Bay. And up here, ground cover is sparse. This is the end of the line by water. No farther north unless one travels up over the Grand Pacific on snowshoes. Canada over there, not very far from the terminus.

7 June, behind Russell Island: Returning from the Grand Pacific Glacier. Lunch in the hot sun. Rare hot sun. Tide incoming. No worries about the boat, avalanches, icebergs, wind. Rare moments when one does not have to pay attention. Just be here, nothing more. With the wild landscape, not sublime landscape even under hot sun. Still brooding always brooding landscape. With the glasses looking across for miles to the peaks, to Russell Island, to the spruce colonizing on the mainland east of Russell Island, the ravens and eagles on the beach ... eagles on the beach? Why eagles on the beach? Beyond, a half-mile from us, coming toward us directly ... BROWN BEAR.

Enormous. The great carnivore. Here he is, close, the incredible power as he moves ... I have seen you, brown bear, before you know of us. And then I watch you as your head goes up and swings side to side. Now you know of us and the reaction is superb. To the right instantly and at twenty-five miles an hour away for the hills. I am glad you so decided, brown bear.

9 June, Reid Inlet: The Ibachs of Reid Inlet. This is what is different about the little red wilderness cabin. Muz and Joe built a small monument here, though of course they would never have seen it that way—a small monument to an immense piece of land.

When I discovered that fuzzy old photograph of the red cabin near completion in 1940, the one on which Joe printed 'Home At Glacier Bay,' I objected to the unsharpness, a predictable reaction from a photographer. I also noticed the horizon was tilted. But I am looking at that photograph now, and now I know better. It should be fuzzy and the horizon should be tilted. It is a fine photograph and what counts is what is written on the other side.

11 June, upper Muir Inlet: Last year we came north through the ice of Muir Inlet in a seventy-foot boat, but now we are in a sixteen-foot boat in the heaviest ice I have yet seen anywhere in Glacier Bay. Mountains of floating ice all around us, fog and rain, miles and miles of ice. I have the same feeling I did last year, only much more so. I keep thinking about the land coming out from under—land that has been covered, at least this far north in the Monument, for perhaps two thousand years. But surrounded by mountains of almost-silent floating ice in the fog and rain, I cannot quite account for the strange intensity of thought. I think the intensity and the recognition go back. I think it has something to do with a man wrapped in animal hide and fur, crouched at the edge of a glacier twenty thousand years ago.

14 June, in camp, Wachusett Inlet: This is a strange, wonderful, desolate inlet. Heavy alder at the entrance which thins out quickly and then gravel. Hundreds of acres of gravel deposits, brown and gray, and two dying glaciers—the Burroughs and the Plateau. Almost the entire inlet under ice in 1930, an inlet now ten miles long. And if the ice is reducing in thickness by forty feet a year, the exquisite forms I photographed just two hours ago at the terminus of the Plateau Glacier will be gone next year and there will be more land out from under. Change, phenomenal change year after year, century after century.

26 June, summit of peak 4710, above Reid Glacier: There is no word between us now as the fog rolls up the Brady Glacier. Silent cold fog rolling in from the sea forty miles to the south. Two thousand feet below us is Heather Nunatak, isolated by light and then fog. Heather Nunatak disappears and the fog rolls on to the confluence with the Reid Glacier. The northern Fairweathers are aflame but here on the summit of this small peak it grows colder as the sun leaves us. We must stir now. We shall rope up and descend into the fog and the wind, the long snowshoe trip down the Reid, the rough moraines in the dark, the boat, gingerly through the ice, the return to the little red cabin.

4 July, Muir Point: Three days of rain, heavy rain. Pinned down where John Muir built his cabin seventy-five years ago this month. It was open country then, but now—alder. Choked with alder. Fifteen feet high. Impenetrable.

5 July, Wachusett Inlet: Tomorrow we shall try to walk overland to the Muir Glacier. By boat it is hopeless. The ice remains as it was three weeks ago. Packed. Not navigable to the terminus of the Muir.

6 July, Stump Cove: We have reached this cove via the beach, and shall now move overland toward the Muir Remnant, the dead ice that used to feed the great glacier.

I must confess this has for me the nature of a pilgrimage. I have read everything ever published on the Muir, and have looked at hundreds of the old photographs. But I simply must see it first hand. All the old exaggerated reports, the attempts at description—description that did not come off, and what was it really like in the 1890's to stand under the Muir terminus and hear the constant thunder? If we do not find the Muir today, perhaps next year?

The Muir Remnant is easy walking, miles of bare ice, no crevasses to speak of. Rain squalls and I am waving my fist at the weather. Will it *never* let us alone. Wind, more rain squalls—on and on across the bare ice. And the Muir Glacier? Where is the Muir Glacier? It has to be around somewhere. Impossible to have taken the wrong direction. Just keep going until we reach the water on the other side of White Thunder Ridge. But which exactly is White Thunder Ridge? I know we are all feeling a little sheepish. All the great pathfinders in this small group of four but we cannot find the Muir Glacier. Maki ahead but waiting now and wants me to go ahead. What difference? We are across the divide and I shall head for that small pass.

We are still walking on the Muir Remnant and the small pass is directly ahead of me. As I step off the ice and move over fifty feet of rock, the entire terminus of the Muir Glacier unfolds, two thousand feet below and two miles distant. Precisely at this moment there is *the* sound, the indescribable sound, the booming primeval thunder as somewhere across the face of the great glacier an immense piece of ice calves.

And now I understand. I understand all the old attempts at description. I understand why they were written and why they failed. The scene before me is staggering and I find no other word.

I remember standing in the Cathedral in the Desert of the Glen Canyon of the Colorado, three months ago. No sane person would have believed any such place could have existed, and I still do not fully believe it myself. In my ground glass, as the camera tilted toward the upper vault, was form and light beyond belief. As if that was not enough, a canyon wren chose that moment to speak. Have you heard a canyon wren speak? Don't, unless you are prepared. I was not prepared.

When I came over the last rise a few moments ago I was not prepared. Neither for the sight nor the sound.

I think back to 1860 or thereabouts, when the Muir Glacier separated at Tlingit Point from the main trunk. A hundred years later still at tidewater and still thundering. From the face of the glacier and five miles beyond—ice. Massive chaos of creaking, floating ice with not a square inch of water showing. Now I understand.

Muir Glacier terminus (one-mile section) from 800 feet, with floating ice. 1965

7 July, Forest Creek: Still riding the wave of yesterday's experience. And I realize that as a result of yesterday the fragments of two years are falling into place. The Muir Glacier and the scene directly in front of it. Irreducible to form on the ground glass, irreducible to words. Yesterday I reached bedrock. It took four years but I made it yesterday.

I write in scorching heat at the dry harsh brilliant site of an ancient forest. The stumps are small and there are not many left. The stumps are probably about two thousand years old. Mentally I travel to Bartlett Cove and the deep, silent, cool spruce and hemlock forest. Carpeted with moss. The harsh scene here was not always thus. Two thousand years ago the forest was here. Then the gravels came down, and the glaciers, and for centuries the ice lay over the land. Three hundred years from now the forest will be here again in all probability. But right now I sit in scorching heat breathing a dry, harsh landscape.

9 July, Wachusett Inlet: At 4:00 A.M. we begin to break camp, for today we say goodbye. At sunrise we move out of Wachusett Inlet into Muir Inlet. Four of us in our sixteen-foot boat, silent and watchful as we drift south on glass through brilliant ice under cloudless sky. We leave the ice age on the land and move south with the alder, the willow, the cottonwood, and still further south the spruce forests. In the eight hours it will take us to reach Bartlett Cove, we shall see one hundred seventy-one years of ecology, from the day George Vancouver anchored at Port Althorp. For almost two centuries the land has been emerging, new-born no longer nameless landscape.

And the mammoth flocks of ducks, the cormorants sitting idiotically, puffins, oyster catchers screaming—ceaseless movement of birds as we drift south out of the ice age.

Spruce, Bartlett Cove. 1964

1966

3 May, Crillon Lake: I am sitting here in the pouring rain in my green three-man tent with blue tent fly. In the woods near the shore of Crillon Lake. Just beyond the door is a brown bear trail. I am back, but find myself a bit sad for this is the beginning of the last field season on what has become for me the grand Project. There are no more 'next years.' I must finish the photography, the research, the writing, all of it. But it will be a great season. Unless it rains all the time. I wouldn't doubt it.

8 May, Crillon Lake outlet: I have just finished crouching over a smoky fire for my fourth hot meal in six days. I can see there are going to be a good many more cold dinners before I leave the coast. Three days moving through the deep woods on bear trails, three days of silence and moss and trees, a long time for such a short distance to the beach.

The other side of the stream from me as I drowned the smoky fire—a pair of wolves standing on the bank watching. Nervous, alert, exquisite.

10 May, La Perouse Glacier: Yesterday was of sun and wind and brown bear tracks all the way south. Today the gloom again. Cold wind and it will rain by tonight. The plan to walk the beach in front of the La Perouse has proven less than feasible. There is no beach. The La Perouse has advanced into the surf and the ground shakes as it calves into the sea. Hundreds of icebergs on the beach, wind and spray, the La Perouse Glacier pushing into the sea, savage meeting of ice and surf.

12 May, heading north: After struggling for one hour to get the fire going I managed the seventh hot meal in ten days. And then I returned to the beach and the booming surf. Yellow light and brown bear tracks. In fact, I have just noticed a rather large bear track covering mine of two hours ago. Or was his there first? I am not sure but I am studying the evidence. If his came second, it means he passed one hundred feet away while I was crouched over that frustrating fire. If so, why didn't he come back and say hello? I am still studying the evidence, but have reached no decision. Nevertheless I am going to decide his track was already there and I walked in it without noticing. Such a decision will enable me to sleep better tonight. Wonderful, the mind.

3 June, Bartlett Cove: Dr. and Mrs. William S. Cooper arrive for the dedication of Glacier Bay Lodge—the fiftieth anniversary of his first trip into the Bay. Also the fiftieth anniversary of the establishment of the National Park Service. Nothing but anniversaries this year. Well after all, the Park Service deserves a celebration too, for they manage this land. I'll wager they won't celebrate on canned wine, though. Even at Bartlett Cove. Indeed it is fortunate the Park Service is here in Glacier Bay. It is not so much that they manage this land in the usual sense. They can manage it by leaving it alone, one of the hardest lessons the species must learn. The Park Service has a large job here, however. As I see it, they must interpret the land to those who want to know. And they must protect the land against the predator. Of course, when I say predator, I do not mean wolf or bear or cow bird. I mean man, the most vindictive predator that ever lived. A good many men in America today still believe land is useless unless it can be put to practical use. In this respect, then, a good many men in America today are fools. But we are learning, if slowly. Yes, it is a good thing the National Park Service is at Bartlett Cove.

5 June, Blue Mouse Cove: Today Glacier Bay treated the Coopers to all the sun available. Great changes on the land since 1916 when he first came in here. Tonight, after anchoring at Blue Mouse, we have gone ashore—Dr. Cooper, Superintendent Robert Howe, and myself. Cooper is over there crawling around in the bushes on his hands and knees, pointing out plant specimens for Bob Howe. Just as he crawled around in 1916 and the subsequent expeditions. Except that he will celebrate his eighty-second birthday in August.

We shall return to the boat now. Cooper has stopped crawling around because it is getting dark. It *should* be getting dark. It is 11:00 P.M.

Above Reid Glacier. 1965

Gravel fan, Adams Inlet. 1966

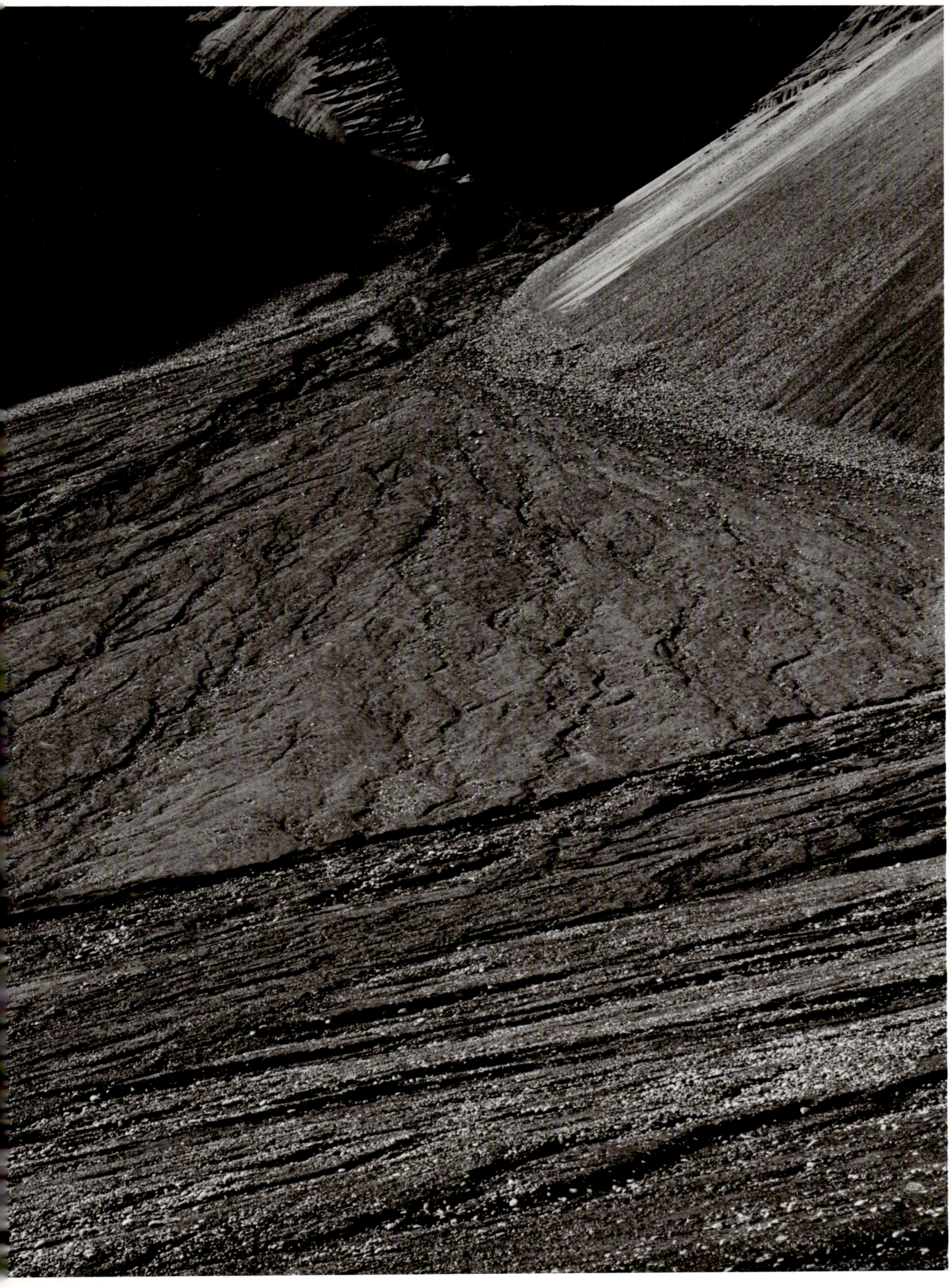

Tarr Inlet from the south. 1966

7 June, Reid Inlet: We are fifteen hundred feet above the cabins and looking north to Tarr Inlet. Two years ago I photographed this remarkable scene in color, and have now returned for the black and white. Over those two years I realized this is the vantage point from which I see everything that is Glacier Bay: The ice on the land, the peaks, the massive headlands, icebergs, the space and the light and the great, brooding quality of the land. Two years ago there was silence, and tonight there is silence. But the sound lingers on when one has heard. Down the centuries the booming primeval thunder. Below us lies all of Glacier Bay. Below us lies the great land.

* * *

11 June, Johns Hopkins Inlet: The call of a baby seal deep in Hopkins Inlet. Again, two years ago the call of the young seal in Goose Cove. But this one leaves its mother to come to us. This one wants to come aboard. And so I lift over the side one of the world's most beautiful animals. My fingers are oily from touching its fur. It rests in Diana's arms and is enamored of her woolly sweater. But if this child seal has retained its composure, no one else aboard has done so.

Deep in Johns Hopkins Inlet in a fourteen-foot boat. Impenetrable until 1929 because of floating ice, now navigable, as a rule, only late in the season. Seven glaciers move down the sides, and at the head of the inlet stands the Johns Hopkins Glacier, impossibly crevassed as it curves out of the high Fairweathers. The wildest of all the inlets in Glacier Bay.

Granite, Johns Hopkins Inlet. 1966

8 September, Adams Inlet: Moonscape, strange dry hot landscape— alone in the silence, not even birds here because they have gone south. Sitting in the heat studying the form and the light and there is a small noise. It is the noise of one rock rolling down the side of that gravel dune over there. One rock. No more.

Within the last thirty years, all of this land I walk on today has come out from under the ice. And in no other inlet can such land forms be seen. Where there were once a few—Geikie Inlet for example—the alder has obliterated the scene. The alder will obliterate this scene in another thirty years, but for now I sit on the moonscape, in the heat and the silence, and thank Chuck Janda for telling me to get in here.

My only regret with Adams Inlet is that I got here too late in the season—by only a few days—to see the dryas mat in seed. The puff balls of silver that come each fall. But suddenly, breaking out of the gravel hills and dunes, I see I have been fooled. Days and days of rain had soaked and matted the seed puffs, but today in the sun and the wind they have dried out. With the sun low on the horizon, returning to the tent through hundreds of acres of silver puffs, now yellow, now finally orange as the sun drops behind the Fairweather Range fifty miles away. Now crimson sky, now deep purple sky, now September darkness.

Sand Dune, Adams Inlet. 1966

10 September, Bartlett Cove: Eight years ago on the Juneau Icefields, I first heard of Glacier Bay and William O. Field. Perhaps one day, I thought then, I would get into the Bay and spend some time with Field. Eight years it took, but on my return from Adams Inlet he is here for his eighth visit to map the terminal positions of the glaciers. On August 14, 1926, Bill Field and his companions went ashore at the head of Geikie Inlet, packed up the Geikie Glacier, and in a few days stood on a col overlooking the enormous Brady Glacier. In front of them were all the great peaks of the southern Fairweathers, and from that day began Field's remarkable association with the glaciers of the Bay. The point in all the visits of the future was to observe systematically, in one man's lifetime, the changes in the glaciers as they receded and, in certain cases, advanced. Bill Field of the American Geographical Society, who has mapped these glaciers for forty years and knows more about their positions than any other man.

Tomorrow we steam north for the glaciers of Glacier Bay. For Bill Field the fortieth anniversary of his first visit. For me, the last days of the grand Project.

15 September, Rendu Inlet: In the mist and the pouring rain we stand here at the terminus of the Rendu Glacier. As with each inlet of Glacier Bay this one has its own personality. And for the first time since 1935 the Rendu advances. It has advanced 2500 feet since 1964. In 1964 the front was sloping, covered with dirt, stagnant. Now the terminus looms out of the mist in a sheer ice cliff—at tidewater again, noisy, pushing forward once more after thirty years of rest.

Last June I watched Cooper get excited as he crawled around in his bushes. *His* bushes, which is only fitting for he has known them longest. Now I watch Field running around gesticulating at one of *his* glaciers, for one of his glaciers is advancing when it shouldn't really be doing so. One of the big ones has suddenly come to life.

17 September, Johns Hopkins Inlet: And now Tyeen Glacier. Tyeen, which comes down from a high cirque and for years lies conservatively up there, a long distance above tidewater. But periodically it moves out of its small valley and rushes down the cliffs to the water. It did so in 1948, then withdrew. Now it is down again, tumbling, raging over the sheer rock face to the fjord. Tyeen is once again at tidewater. Tyeen Glacier has advanced 5000 feet in one year and calves again into Johns Hopkins Inlet.

20 September, Muir Glacier: For one hundred years the Muir thundered at tidewater. Now we stand only a few hundred yards from the terminus on a beach that came out from under two years ago. The Muir is no longer noisy. There are occasional small ice falls, but most of the right side of the terminus has grounded and there is very little ice floating in front of the glacier. The end of the line. I recall last year. The formless chaos of packed ice floating for miles beyond the terminus, the sound of constant thunder in the air, booming primeval thunder. It is quiet here now—once in awhile the swell from a small ice fall, against a beach that is new-born land.

But the thunder lingers on when one has heard. And maybe the glacier will come back. It has come back before.

Tyeen Glacier. 1966. National Park Service photograph by CHARLES V. JANDA.

Place Names

Note: Author of name and field date, where available, follows semi-colon. Source is in parentheses. Where date alone follows semi-colon, reference is to U.S. Board on Geographic Names decision list.

Abbe, Mt.—after Cleveland Abbe Jr., physiographer and climatologist; W. S. Cooper after expedition of 1935 (Cooper)
Abdallah, Mt.—H. F. Reid 1892 (Baker)
Adams Glacier—after C. A. Adams, with Reid 1890; H. F. Reid 1890 (Reid)
Adams Inlet—after C. A. Adams
Anchorage Cove—descriptive; Dall 1883 (Dall)
Ancon Rock—after sidewheel steamer *Ancon* (wrecked 1889), in Glacier Bay mid-1880's; Captain James Carroll, after the *Ancon* ran against the rock in 1886 (DeArmond)
Astrolabe Bay—after frigate *Astrolabe*, Lapérouse 1786
Barnard, Mt.—after E. C. Barnard, Commissioner for the U.S. International Boundary Commission
Bartlett Cove—originally Bartlett Bay, after the owner of the fishery there, a merchant of Port Townsend; the *Idaho's* pilot, W. E. George 1883 (Baker gives the date as about 1881, which is too early. See also Scidmore, *Alaska*)
Beardslee Islands—after Commander Lester Anthony Beardslee; U.S. naval officers 1880 (Baker)
Berg Bay—descriptive; called Berg Inlet in U.S. Coast Pilot 1883 (Baker), but apparently first shown as Berg Bay by Beardslee, U.S. Hydrographic Notice No. 97, 1880
Bertha, Mt.—after S.S. *Bertha*, Alaska Commercial Co. steamer (service 1888-1915)
Blackthorn Peak—descriptive; named Black Thorn by H. F. Reid (official 1896, Baker)
Boussole Bay—after the frigate *Boussole*, Lapérouse's ship 1786
Brady Glacier—after Rev. (later Governor) John G. Brady, Sitka missionary/teacher from 1878; Coast Survey 1883 (Baker)
Bruce Hills—after Miner Bruce, author of *Alaska*, who spent six weeks with Dick Willoughby in Glacier Bay 1889; W. O. Field 1947 (Field)
Burroughs Glacier—after John Burroughs, Harriman Alaska Expedition in Glacier Bay 1889; W. O. Field 1947 (Field)
Caroline Shoal—origin not known. First appears on British Admiralty chart 2431, corrected to Feb. 1890 (Baker)
Carolus, Point—Dall 1879 (Baker)
Carroll Glacier—after Captain James Carroll who first took a steamer (the *Queen*) into the northern part of Glacier Bay in 1892; H. F. Reid 1892 (Baker)
Case, Mt.—after Case School of Applied Science; H. F. Reid 1890 (Baker)
Casement Glacier—after R. L. Casement, with Reid 1890; H. F. Reid 1890 (Baker)
Cenotaph Island—for cenotaph erected; Lapérouse 1786 (Isle du Cénotaphe, Lapérouse)
Cenotaph Point—location of cenotaph; Dall 1874 (Coast Pilot 1883)
Charpentier Glacier—see following: H. F. Reid 1892 (Baker)
Charpentier Inlet—after Jean de Charpentier, Swiss glaciologist; W. S. Cooper following the expedition of 1935 (Cooper)
La Chaussee Spit—descriptive; Lapérouse 1786 (la Chaussée, Lapérouse)
Composite Island—descriptive; H. F. Reid 1892 (Baker)
Cooper, Mt.—(unofficial) after W. S. Cooper, ecologist, primarily responsible for the campaign for Glacier Bay National Monument
Cormorant Rock—descriptive; Lapérouse 1786 (Roche de Cormorans, Lapérouse)
Crillon, Mt.—after the French General Louis des Balbes de Berton de Crillon; Lapérouse 1786 (Farquhar)

Cross Sound—Captain James Cook who discovered it on Holy Cross day, May 3, 1778 (Cook)

Dagelet, Mt.—after MM. Lepaute Dagelet, astronomer Lapérouse expedition; U.S. Coast Survey 1874 (Coast Pilot 1883)

De Langle Mt.—after viscount de Langle, commander of the *Astrolabe,* Lapérouse expedition

Dirt Glacier—descriptive; H. F. Reid 1890 (Cushing, Reid)

Dixon Harbor—presumably after Captain George Dixon, circumnavigation 1785-1788; published by the Coast Survey 1889 (Baker)

Drake Island—origin of name not known. First appears on British Admiralty chart 2431, corrected to 1890 (Baker)

Dundas Bay—after the Point Dundas of Vancouver; Superintendent of the Coast Survey, presumably 1879 (Coast Pilot 1883). First applied to the bay on Russian chart, Sarichef Atlas (Davidson)

Dundas, Point—Vancouver 1794 (Vancouver)

Escures, Mt.—after MM. d'Escures, first lieutenant of the *Boussole,* Lapérouse expedition. Lost with twenty other men July 13, 1786, Lituya Bay, when two of the three small boats he was commanding were swamped in the entrance rips

Fairweather, Cape—by Captain James Cook 1778 (Cape Fair Weather, Cook)

Fairweather, Mt.—descriptive of the weather at the time; Captain Cook 1778 (Mount Fair Weather, Cook)

Favorite, Mt.—after the steamer *Favorite* of the Northwest Trading Co., first steamer in Glacier Bay, 1880, Commander L. A. Beardslee aboard; (the Favorite Glacier, which no longer exists, was named by H. F. Reid in 1892)

Francis Island—apparently so named by the British Admiralty in 1890 (Baker)

Garforth Island—apparently so named by the British Admiralty in or about 1890 (Baker)

Geikie Glacier—after Sir Archibald Geikie, Scotch geologist; John Muir who discovered it in 1879 (named later, Muir)

Geikie Inlet—H. F. Reid, probably 1892 (Scidmore)

Gilbert Island—after Grove Karl Gilbert, geologist; W. S. Cooper following the expedition of 1935 (Cooper)

Gilman Glacier—after Daniel C. Gilman, first president of Johns Hopkins University; W. S. Cooper following the expedition of 1935 (Cooper)

Glacier Bay—descriptive; Commander L. A. Beardslee aboard the steamer *Favorite* 1880 (Beardslee)

Glacier Pass—descriptive; W. O. Field 1947 (Field)

Goose Cove—because geese were first seen here by W. S. Cooper in 1929; W. O. Field 1947 (Field)

Grand Pacific Glacier—John Muir some time after the expedition of 1879. In 1892, Reid retained that name for the largest of what had become (by that time) three glaciers (Scidmore). The natives apparently knew it as the "Great Glacier" (Beardslee, Dall), but I have been unable to find the phonetical rendition

Gustavus, Point—Dall 1879 (Coast Pilot 1883)

Harbor Point—descriptive; Dall 1874 (Coast Pilot 1883)

Hoonah Glacier—after Hoonah tribe of Tlingit Indians; W. S. Cooper following the expedition of 1935 (Cooper)

Hunter Cove—after Captain Hunter of the S.S. *City of Topeka* which brought H. F. Reid's party to Muir Inlet in 1892; W. O. Field 1947 (Field)

Icy Strait—Strait of Ice (Lohtianoi) of the Russians, including Cross Sound, now the eastern continuation of the Sound (Baker)

Icy Point—descriptive; Tebenkov 1849, Chart VIII (Lohtianoi Point, Tebenkov)

Idaho Ridge—after the excursion steamer *Idaho* (wrecked 1889), first commercial steamer to enter Glacier Bay, July 1883, Captain James Carroll commanding, pilot W. E. George and Elizah Ruhamah Scidmore aboard; W. O. Field 1947 (Field)

Johns Hopkins Glacier—after Johns Hopkins University; H. F. Reid 1892, by which time it had separated from the Grand Pacific (Scidmore, Reid)

Johns Hopkins Inlet—see previous. Called Johns Hopkins Fiord by W. S. Cooper following the expedition of 1935 (Cooper)

Johnson Cove—after John A. Johnson, fox farmer on Willoughby Island about 1930-1940

Justice Creek—after the hanging incident of 1899, which occurred in this general area; L. J. Mitchell 1962 (Mitchell)

Kashoto Glacier—after Kashoto, chief of the Hoonahs, visited at Hoonah by John Muir and his party on the way to Glacier Bay, 1879; W. S. Cooper and W. O. Field following the expedition of 1935 (Cooper)

Klotz Hills—after Otto J. Klotz of the Topographical Survey of the Dominion of Canada; W. O. Field 1947 (Field)

Lamplugh Glacier—after G. W. Lamplugh, geologist, second man to study Muir Glacier (1884); probably by Lawrence Martin after seeing the glacier in 1911

La Perouse, Mount—after Lapérouse; Dall 1875 (Coast Pilot 1883)

Lituya Bay—a native (Tlingit) word phoneticized H'lit-tu-yúh (Dall), meaning "the lake within the point" (Emmons). The earliest mention I can find (Ltua) appears in the journal of the *Three Saints* (Ismaïloff and Bochoroff) for July 3, 1788, manuscript translation to English by Ivan Petroff. Lisianski (1805) showed it Ltooa Bay, Tebenkov as Ltua, Grewingk as Altua Basin, Russian Hydrographic chart 1378 as Altua Bay or Port Frantsuzof, Galiano as Lina Bay, Lapérouse as Port des Français, and some whalers knew it as Frenchman's Bay. Davidson (1867) reports it as Sturya Bay as taken from Shiltz's (Shields?) report to Baranoff of 1796

Lituya Mountain—name published by Tebenkov 1849 (Baker)

Lone Island—descriptive; H. F. Reid 1892 (Baker)

Marble Islands, North and South—descriptive; pilot W. E. George, probably from the *Idaho* in 1883 (Coast Pilot 1883)

Marchainville, Mt.—after MM. de la Borde Marchainville, commander of the *Astrolabe's* pinnace, one of the two boats lost with all hands in Lituya Bay, Lapérouse expedition 1786

Margerie Glacier—after M. de Margerie, French morphologist with 12th International Geological Congress in Glacier Bay 1913; Lawrence Martin 1913 (Romer)

Maynard Glacier—after Lt. Commander Washburn Maynard of U.S.S. *Pinta,* who picked up H. F. Reid in 1892 in Icy Strait; W. S. Cooper after expedition of 1935 (Cooper). Both Maynard and Charpentier Glaciers were originally parts of the Hugh Miller Glacier as seen by Muir in 1879

McBride Glacier—after H. McBride, with Reid 1890; H. F. Reid 1890 (Reid)

McConnell Ridge—after R. G. McConnell, with 12th International Geological Congress in Glacier Bay 1913; W. O. Field 1947 (Field)

Merriam, Mt.—after C. Hart Merriam of Harriman Alaska Expedition, Editor of Harriman Alaska Expedition reports, former Chief of Biological Survey, U.S. Dept. of Agri.

Hugh Miller Glacier—after the geologist Hugh Miller; John Muir, who first saw it in 1879, but named later (Muir)

Hugh Miller Inlet—after the geologist Hugh Miller; H. F. Reid 1892 (Baker)

Miller Peak—after Ben C. Miller, first NPS official in charge of Glacier Bay National Monument; 1957

Minnesota Ridge—after Univ. of Minnesota for W. S. Cooper's affiliation with that institution; W. O. Field 1947 (Field)

Morse Glacier—after J. F. Morse, with Reid 1890; H. F. Reid 1890 (Reid)

[157

Muir, Camp—(unofficial) after John Muir; H. F. Reid 1890 (Reid)

Muir Glacier—after John Muir; Captain James Carroll in July 1883 aboard the mail-steamer *Idaho*, navigating from a tracing of Beardslee's chart 225 of 1880 (Scidmore)

Muir Inlet—see Muir Glacier (also Scidmore)

Muir Point—1948

Murphy Cove—after William Murphy of the U.S.S. *Jamestown* and schooner *Active*, drowned at the Cove January 9, 1890 (*Sitka Alaskan*, March 21, 1891; DeArmond files)

Nunatak Cove—descriptive; Twenhofel 1946 (USGS Bulletin 947-B)

Netland Island—after L. Netland, surveyor Alaskan Bdry. 1907

Nunatak, The—descriptive; originally called Nunatak Knob by W. O. Field; Twenhofel 1946 (USGS Bulletin 947-B)

Palma Bay—by Malaspina 1791 (Baia de la Palma, chart No. 3, Atlas to Galiano's voyage, 1802)

Paps, The—descriptive; used by Lapérouse three times in his written instructions to MM. d'Escures, but not capitalized. The name does not appear on de Monneron and Bernizet's drawing of Lituya Bay. Apparently first published on Coast Survey chart 742, 1875 (Lapérouse)

Passage Rock—descriptive; Dall 1874 (Coast Pilot 1883)

Plateau Glacier—descriptive; W. S. Cooper 1921 (Cooper)

Ptarmigan Creek—descriptive; prospectors during or before 1930's (?)

Puffin Island—descriptive; 1949

Pyramid Peak—descriptive; H. F. Reid 1890 (Reid)

Queen Inlet—after the steamer *Queen* (Pacific Coast Steamship Co., called *Queen of the Pacific* until 1890), in Glacier Bay 1890's, usually under the command of Captain Carroll (see Carroll Glacier); H. F. Reid 1892, aboard (Baker, Scidmore)

Red Mt.—descriptive; H. F. Reid 1890 (Baker)

Reid Glacier—after Harry Fielding Reid, geologist; Harriman Alaska Expedition 1899 (Gilbert, Harriman Alaska Ser. 3)

Rendu Glacier—after M. Le Chanoine Rendu, French glaciologist; H. F. Reid 1892 (Scidmore)

Riggs Glacier—after Thomas Riggs, U.S. Boundary Commissioner, former Governor of Alaska; W. O. Field 1941 (Field)

Romer Glacier—after Eugenjusz Romer, geographer with 12th International Geological Congress in Glacier Bay 1913

Rush Pt.—descriptive for tidal flow past this point; H. F. Reid 1892 (Reid). On Reid's map of 1892 (USGS 16th annual) he shows Rush Pt. on the western extremity of what is now Lester Island. Rush Pt. is now shown on the western shore of Glacier Bay, opposite the original location

Russell Island—after Israel Cook Russell, USGS (formerly Photographic Island)

Salisbury, Mt.—after Rollin D. Salisbury, eminent student of pleistocene and recent glaciology, University of Chicago; W. S. Cooper 1935 (Cooper)

Sandy Cove—descriptive; H. F. Reid 1892 (Baker)

Sawmill Bay—sawmill site 1907-1937; Coast & Geodetic Survey ca. 1910 (Shotter)

Scidmore Glacier—after Elizah Ruhamah Scidmore, author of books and articles on Alaska, first in Glacier Bay aboard the *Idaho* 1883; W. S. Cooper after expedition of 1935 (Cooper)

Sealers Island—because there was a native seal blind on the island 1926; W. O. Field 1947 (Field)

Sebree Island—after Commander Uriel Sebree, U.S.N., about 1890 (Baker)

Sentinel Peak—descriptive; H. F. Reid 1892 (Baker)

Sitakaday Narrows—native name for Ice Bay, according to Muir who spelled it Sitadakay. Scidmore has it Sittghaee or Great Cold Lake, and George Hall (former Park Historian at Sitka National Monument), in *Stories of Glacier Bay collected at Hoonah*, MS July 1960, recorded it as Sed-eeta-gee-ah or Bay From Where the Ice Receded

Sitt-ghaee Peak—direct translation of Tlingit 'Ice Bay'; W. O. Field 1947 (Field)

Snow Dome—descriptive; John Muir after the trip of 1880 (Baker, official 1882?)

Spencer, Cape—after Lord Spencer; Vancouver 1794 (Vancouver)

Spokane Cove—after S.S. *Spokane*, Pacific Coast S.S. Co.; W. O. Field 1941 (Field)

Steelhead Creek—descriptive (so called in *Daily Alaska Empire*, Nov. 16, 1959)

Strawberry Island—descriptive; W. S. Cooper 1929 (Cooper). Formerly Scidmore Island as named by Captain Carroll in 1883 with Eliza Scidmore on the bridge of the *Idaho* (Scidmore)

Sturgess Island—first published on British Admiralty chart 2431, 1890 (Baker)

Tarr Inlet—after Ralph Stockman Tarr, glaciologist; Lawrence Martin 1913 (Romer, Martin)

Taylor Bay—after C. H. Taylor of Chicago; Supt. of the U.S. Coast Survey 1874 (Coast Pilot 1883). Taylor supported the proposed expedition to climb Mt. St. Elias with C. E. S. Wood in 1877, and explored briefly Taylor Bay with Wood after the expedition had collapsed near Cross Sound. The two men went back to Sitka, and Wood returned to explore Glacier Bay. See Wood Lake

Tidal Inlet—because of tidal observations in that inlet in 1890; H. F. Reid 1890 (Reid)

Tlingit Pt.—after Tlingit Nation of Indians; W. S. Cooper following the 1935 expedition (Cooper)

Toyatte Glacier—after Toyatte, a Stickeen nobleman and captain of John Muir's native guides and crew for the trip of 1879. Toyatte was shot and killed in a native quarrel shortly after the party returned to Ft. Wrangell (Muir, S. Hall Young); W. S. Cooper and W. O. Field following the expedition of 1935 (Cooper)

Tree Mountain—descriptive; John Muir after the expedition of 1890 (Baker—official 1892?)

Triangle Island—descriptive; H. F. Reid 1892 (Reid)

Tyeen Glacier—after Tyeen, captain of John Muir's native guides and crew for the trip of 1880 (Muir); W. S. Cooper and W. O. Field following the expedition of 1935 (Cooper)

Van Horn Ridge—after F. R. Van Horn, with 12th International Geological Congress in Glacier Bay 1913; W. O. Field 1947 (Field)

Wachusett Inlet—after U.S.S. *Wachusett*, station Sitka early 1880's

Whidbey Passage—after Lt. Joseph Whidbey, R.N., one of Vancouver's principal assistants during explorations and surveys (1792-1795) in the region

White Glacier—descriptive; H. F. Reid 1890 (Reid)

White Thunder Ridge—descriptive for noise from Muir Glacier; Douglas M. Brown who first visited and climbed the ridge in Aug. 1946 (Brown)

Willoughby Island—after Richard G. Willoughby, Alaskan pioneer; U.S. Navy 1880 (Coast Pilot 1883, Beardslee). Willoughby was living on Lemesurier Island at the time he accompanied Beardslee in the charting of Glacier Bay, 1880

Wood Lake—after Lt. Charles Erskine Scott Wood, the first white man known (1877) in Glacier Bay, shifted from the extinct Wood Glacier

Wright, Mt.—after Rev. George Frederick Wright, author, who spent a month at Muir Glacier in 1886; H. F. Reid 1890 (Baker)

Young, Mt.—after Rev. S. Hall Young, John Muir's companion in Glacier Bay 1879 and 1880

Bibliography

I. Earth Sciences

Baldwin, S. P. Recent changes in the Muir Glacier. Amer. Geol. 11, June 1893.

Barendsen, G. W., E. S. Deevey, and L. J. Gralenski. Yale natural radiocarbon measurements III. Science 126, November 1957. (Interstadial stumps)

Bengtson, K. Recent history of the Brady Glacier, Glacier Bay National Monument; IASH Commission of Snow and Ice, Pub. No. 58 extract, Symposium of Obergurgl, Gentbrugge, Belgium 1962.

Burchard, E. F. Marble resources of southeastern Alaska. USGS bull. 682, 1920.

Cooper, W. S. The problem of Glacier Bay, Alaska; a study of glacier variations. Geog. Rev. 27, January 1937.

Cushing, H. P. Notes on the Muir Glacier region and its geology. Am. Geol. 8, October 1891.

———. Notes on the geology in the vicinity of Muir Glacier. Nat. Geog. 4, 1892.

———. The movement of Muir Glacier. Amer. Geol. 11, April 1893 (letter).

———. Notes on the areal geology of Glacier Bay, Alaska. New York Acad. of Sci., trans. 15, 1895-6.

Dall, W. H. Alaskan tertiary deposits. Am. Jour. Sci. 24, 1882.

Davis, T. N. and N. K. Sanders. The Alaska earthquake of July 10, 1958: Intensity distribution and field investigation of northern epicentral region. Bull. Seism. Soc. Am. 50, April 1960.

Emerson, B. K. and C. Palache. *In* B. K. Emerson, and others. Geology and Paleontology; Harriman Alaska Ser. 4, 1904.

Field, W. O. Glacier studies in Alaska 1941. Geog. Rev. 32, January 1942.

———. Glacier recession in Muir Inlet, Glacier Bay, Alaska. Geog. Rev. 37, July 1947.

———. The variations of Alaskan glaciers 1935-1947. Union Géodésique et Géophysique Internationale, Assemblée Générale d'Oslo, 1948.

———. Report on the North American glaciers. Union Géodésique et Géophysique Internationale, Assemblée Générale de Bruxelles, 1951.

———. Observations of glacier variations in Glacier Bay, southeastern Alaska, 1958 and 1961, Glacier Bay National Monument. Am. Geog. Soc., prelim. rep., June 1964.

Flint, R. F. Glacier thinning during deglaciation, part II. Am. Jour. Sci. 240, February 1942.

Geographical Journal 69, April 1927. The Fairweather Range, southeastern Alaska; retreat of glaciers.

Gilbert, G. K. Glaciers and glaciation. Harriman Alaska Ser. 3, 1904.

———. See C. L. Andrews (VI).

Goldthwait, R. P. Seismic soundings on South Crillon and Klooch Glaciers. Geog. Jour. 87, June 1936.

———. Dating the little ice age in Glacier Bay, Alaska; Rept. Int'l. Geol. Congr., 21st session, Norden, part 27, 1960.

———. I. C. McKellar and Caspar Cronk. Fluctuations of Crillon Glacier system, southeast Alaska. Bull. Intl. Assn. Sci. Hyd. 8, No. 1, 1963.

———. Evidence from Alaskan glaciers of major climatic changes. Royal Met. Soc., December 1966 (to be published).

———. See Goldthwait, et al (II).

Haselton, G. Glacial geology of Muir Inlet, southeastern Alaska. IPS 18, Ohio State Univ., November 1965.

Hicks, S. D. and W. Shofnos. The determination of land emergence from sea level observations in southeast Alaska. Jour. Geophys. Res. 70, July 15, 1965.

Kennedy, G. C. and M. S. Walton, Jr. Geology and associated mineral deposits of some ultrabasic rock bodies in southeastern Alaska. USGS bull. 947-D, 1946. (Lituya Bay-Crillon)

Klotz, O. J. Notes on glaciers of southeastern Alaska and adjoining territory. Geog. Jour. 14, November 1899.

———. Recession of Alaskan glaciers. Geog. Jour. 30, October 1907.

Lamplugh, G. W. On ice-grooved rock surfaces near Victoria, Vancouver Island, with notes on the glacial phenomena of the neighboring region, and on the Muir Glacier of Alaska. Proc. of the Yorkshire Geol. and Polytech. Soc. 9, 1885.

———. Notes on the Muir Glacier of Alaska. Nature 33, January 28, 1886.

Lindsay, J. F. Observations on the level of a self-draining lake on the Casement Glacier, Alaska. Jour. Glac. 6, No. 45, 1966.

Mannerfelt, C. Resultaten från de sista årens glaciärmätningar i Alaska. Ymer, Arg. 57, 1937. (Glacier measurements in Alaska during recent years—Glacier Bay region.)

Martin, L. Gletscheruntersuchungen längs der Küst von Alaska. Petermanns geographische Mitteilungen, August and September 1912 (La Perouse Glacier).

Mathes, F. E. Variations of glaciers in the continental U.S. and Alaska 1933-38. Gauthier-Villars, Paris, 1939.

MacKevett, E. M. et al. Mineral Resources of Glacier Bay National Monument, Alaska. USGS open file rep. in prep., 1967.

Meehan, T. Some evidences of great modern geologic changes in Alaska, part II. Proc. Acad. Nat. Sci., Phila., June-October 1883.

———. Notes on glaciers in Alaska, part III (part I under Meehan, II). Proc. Acad. Nat. Sci., Phila., November-December 1883.

Mercer, J. H. The response of fjord glaciers to changes in the firn limit. Jour. Glac. 3, March 1961.

Mertie, J. B., Jr. Notes on the geography and geology of Lituya Bay. USGS bull. 836-B, 1931.

Miller, D. J. Giant waves in Lituya Bay, Alaska. USGS prof. paper 354-C, 1960.

———. The Alaska earthquake of July 10, 1958: Giant wave in Lituya Bay. Bull. Seism. Soc. Am. 50, April 1960.

———. Geology of the Lituya district, Gulf of Alaska tertiary province, Alaska. USGS open file (map), 1961.

Miller, D. J. and F. S. MacNeil. *Lituyapecten* from Alaska and California and stratigraphic occurrence of *Lituyapecten* in Alaska. USGS prof. paper 354-K, J, 1961.

Miller, M. M. Alaskan glacier studies, 1946. AAJ 6, 1947.

———. Taku glacier evaluation study. U.S. Dept. of Comm., Bur. Pub. Records, January 1953.

———. Inventory of terminal position changes in Alaskan coastal glaciers since the 1750's. Proc. Am. Philos. Soc. 108, June 1964.

Muir, J. Notes on the Pacific Coast glaciers; Harriman Alaska Ser. 1, 1902.

Pierce, C. Is sea level falling or the land rising in southeastern Alaska? Surveying and Mapping 21, March 1961.

Preston, R. S., E. Person and E. S. Deevey. Yale natural radiocarbon measurements II. Science 122, November 1955.

Price, R. J. Land forms produced by the wastage of the Casement Glacier, southeast Alaska. IPS 9, Ohio State Univ., February 1964.

———. The changing proglacial environment of the Casement Glacier, Glacier Bay, Alaska. Inst. of Brit. Geog., Trans. and Papers No. 36, 1965.

Reed, J. C. Some mineral deposits of Glacier Bay and vicinity. Econ. Geol. 33, January-February 1938.

Reid, H. F. Report of an expedition to Muir Glacier, Alaska. U.S. Coast & Geod. Surv. ann. rep., part II, 1891.

———. Observations at Tidal Inlet, July 9 and 10, 1892; handwritten comments. U.S. Coast & Geod. Surv. open file, Washington, D.C.

———. Studies of Muir Glacier, Alaska. Nat. Geog. 4, March 1892.

———. Variations of glaciers. Jour. Geol., 1895-1916.

———. Glacier Bay and its glaciers. USGS 16th ann. rep., 1894-1895, 1896.

Romer, E. Some contributions to the physiography of Glacier Bay, Alaska, 1913. Manuscript at World Data Ctr. A: Glaciology. Am. Geog. Soc., New York.

———. A few contributions to the physiography of Glacier Bay, Alaska. Przeglad geograficzny, T.9, 1929.

———. A few remarks on the tree and névé lines in the Canadian and Alaskan cordillera. Przeglad geograficzny, T.9, 1929.

Rossman, D. L. Ilmenite-bearing beach sands near Lituya Bay, Alaska. USGS rep., open file Ser. No. 420, 1957.

———. Geology and ore deposits in the Reid Inlet area, with notes on a mineralized area near Lituya Bay. USGS bull. 1058-B, 1959.

———. Geology of the eastern part of the Mt. Fairweather quadrangle, Glacier Bay, Alaska. USGS bull. 1121-K, 1963.

———. Geology and petrology of two stocks of layered gabbro in the Fairweather Range, Alaska. USGS bull. 1121-F, 1963.

Rubin, M., and C. Alexander. USGS radiocarbon dates IV. Science 127, June 1958 (Crillon Lake).

Russell, I. C. Origin of the gravel deposits beneath Muir Glacier. Am. Geol. 9, March 1892.

Seitz, J. F. Geology of Geikie Inlet area, Glacier Bay, Alaska. USGS bull. 1058-C, 1959.

Smith, P. Occurrences of molybdenum minerals in Alaska. USGS bull. 926-C, 1942 (Brady Glacier).

Stevenson, J. J. Some notes on southeast Alaska and its people. Scot. Geog. Mag. 9, 1893.

Stone, K. H. Alaskan ice-dammed lakes. Annals of the Assn. of Am. Geog. 53, September 1963.

Tarr, L. S. and L. Martin. The earthquakes at Yakutat Bay, Alaska, in September 1899. USGS prof. paper 69, 1912.

———. Alaskan glacier studies. Nat. Geog. Soc., 1914.

Taylor, L. D. Ice structures, Burroughs Glacier, southeast Alaska. IPS 3, Ohio State Univ., 1962.

———. Structure and fabric on the Burroughs Glacier, southeast Alaska. Jour. Glac. 4, October 1963.

Tocher, D. The Alaska earthquake of July 10, 1958: Movement on the Fairweather fault and field investigation of southern epicentral region. Bull. Seism. Soc. Am. 50, April 1960.

Twenhofel, W. S., G. D. Robinson, and H. R. Gault. Molybdenite investigations in southeastern Alaska. USGS bull. 947-B, 1946 (Muir Inlet).

Twenhofel, W. S., J. C. Reed, and G. O. Gates. Some mineral investigations in southeastern Alaska. USGS bull. 963-A, 1949 (Muir Inlet).

———. Recent shore-line changes along the Pacific Coast of Alaska. Am. Jour. Sci. 250, July 1952 (Lituya Bay and Glacier Bay).

U.S. Bureau of Mines. Molybdenum deposits, Muir Inlet, Alaska. War Min. Rep. 40, January 1943.

———. Muir Inlet or Nunatak molybdenum deposits, Glacier Bay, southeastern Alaska. War. Min. Rep. 300, June 1943.

U.S. Geological Survey. Landscapes of Alaska. USGS with USNPS; ed. H. Williams, Univ. of Cal. Press, Berkeley, 1958.

Washburn, H. B. The Harvard-Dartmouth Alaskan expeditions, 1933-1934. Geog. Jour. 87, June 1936.

Washburn, H. B. and R. P. Goldthwait. Movement of South Crillon Glacier. Geol. Soc. Am. bull. 48, November 1937.

Welch, R. A. The form and origin of landforms produced during the wastage of Casement Glacier, Alaska. Thesis for degree of M. A., Univ. of Okla., Norman, Oklahoma, 1964.

———. Ecological observations in the Muir Inlet area, Glacier Bay National Monument, Alaska. IPS 15, Ohio State Univ., 1965.

Williams, G. H. Notes on some eruptive rocks from Alaska. Nat. Geog. 4, supp. II, March 1892.

Wright, C. W. Lode mining in southeastern Alaska. *In* Report of investigation of mineral resources of Alaska in 1906. USGS bull. 314, 1907 (Lituya Bay).

Wright, F. E. and C. W. Wright. The Glacier Bay National Monument in southeastern Alaska: Its glaciers and geology. Unpublished manuscript, USGS open file (field work of 1906 and 1931).

———. Abstract of 1906 survey. *In* Reid (see Variations of glaciers XII).

Wright, G. F. The Muir Glacier. Am. Jour. Sci. 33, Ser. 3, January 1887 (with flora by A. Gray).

———. The ice age in North America and its bearings upon the antiquity of man. D. Appleton & Co., New York, 1890.

———. Mr. Cushing and the Muir Glacier. Am. Geol. 8, November 1891 (letter).

II. Life Sciences

Alexander, A. M. See J. Grinnell.

Bailey, A. M. Notes on the birds of southeast Alaska. Auk 44, January, April, and July 1927.

Cash, E. Some discomycetes new to Alaska. Jour. Wash. Acad. Sci. 44, 1954.

Cooke, W. B. Some fungi from Alaska. Northwest Sci. 29, 1955.

Cooper, W. S. The recent ecological history of Glacier Bay, Alaska. Ecology 4, April, July, and October 1923.

———. The seed-plants and ferns of the Glacier Bay National Monument, Alaska. Torrey Bot. Cl. bull. 57, May 1930.

———. A third expedition to Glacier Bay, Alaska. Ecology 12, January 1931.

———. The layering habit in Sitka spruce and the two western hemlocks. Bot. Gaz. 91, June 1931.

———. A fourth expedition to Glacier Bay, Alaska. Ecology 20, April 1939.

———. Additions to the flora of the Glacier Bay National Monument, Alaska, 1935-36. Torrey Bot. Cl. bull. 66, October 1939.

———. An isolated colony of plants on a glacier-clad mountain. Torrey Bot. Cl. bull. 69, June 1942.

Crocker, R. L. and J. Major. Soil development in relation to vegetation and surface age at Glacier Bay, Alaska. Jour. Ecol. 43, July 1955.

Goldthwait, R. P., et al. Soil development and ecological succession in a deglaciated area of Muir Inlet, southeast Alaska. IPS 20, Ohio State Univ., 1966.

Gray, A. See G. F. Wright (I).

Grinnell, J., et al. Birds and mammals of the 1907 Alexander expedition to southeastern Alaska. Univ. of Cal. pubs. in Zoology 5, February 18, 1909.

Herrick, F. H. Microscopical examination of wood from the buried forest, Muir Inlet; supp. III. Nat. Geog. 4, March 1892.

Heusser, C. J. Late pleistocene environments of north Pacific North America. Am. Geog. Soc. spec. pub. 35, New York, 1960.

Hibben, Mrs. F. C. Pacific eider nesting at Glacier Bay. Condor 44, July 1942.

Holmes, S. J. Amnipod crustaceans of the expedition. *In* M. J. Rathbun, and others; Crustaceans. Harriman Alaska Ser. 10, 1904.

Jewett, S. G. Bird notes from southeast Alaska. Murrelet 23, September-December 1942.

Keeler, C. Days among Alaska birds. Harriman Alaska Ser. 2, 1901.

Lawrence, D. B. Recent glacier history of Glacier Bay, and development of vegetation on deglaciated terrain with special reference to the importance of alder in the succession. Amer. Phil. Soc. Yr. Bk. 1950, 1951.

———. Development of vegetation and soil in southeastern Alaska with special reference to accumulation of nitrogen. ONR proj. NR 160-183, Dept. of Bot., Univ. of Minn., 1953.

———. Glaciers and vegetation in southeastern Alaska. Am. Sci. 46, June 1958.

Meehan, T. Catalogue of the plants collected in July 1883, during an excursion along the Pacific Coast in southeastern Alaska, part I (parts II and III under Meehan, I). Proc. Acad. Nat. Sci., Phila., January-April 1884.

Nutting, C. C. Hydroids of the expedition. Harriman Alaska Ser. 13, 1905.

Rowlee, W. W. List of plants collected near Muir Glacier. App. I, Nat. Geog. 4, March 1892.

Saunders, D. A. The algae. *In* J. Cardot, and others. Cryptogamic botany. Harriman Alaska Ser. 5, 1904.

Searle, H. Isopod crustaceans of the northwest coast of North America. *In* M. J. Rathbun, and others, Crustaceans. Harriman Alaska Ser. 10, 1904.

Shaw, C. G., and R. Sprague. Additions to Alaskan fungi. Res. studies of the State Coll. of Washington, 22 (3), 1954.

Sprague, R. Some leafspot fungi on Western Gramineae, VII. Mycologia 46 (1), 1954.

———. Some fungi on Alaskan species of *Carex*. Res. studies of the State Coll. of Wash. 22 (3), 1954.

———. Some leafspot fungi of Western Gramineae, VIII. Mycologia 47, March-April 1955.

———. A check list of the fungi of Glacier Bay, Alaska. Res. studies of the State Coll. of Wash. 23, September 1955.

———. A check list of the diseases of grasses and cereals in Alaska. Plant Disease Reporter, supp. No. 232, May 30, 1955.

———. Some leafspot fungi on Western Gramineae, X. Mycologia 48, September-October 1956.

Sprague, R. and D. B. Lawrence. The fungi of deglaciated Alaskan terrain of known age, parts I and II. Res. studies of Wash. State Univ. 27, September and December 1959.

———. The fungi of deglaciated Alaskan terrain of known age, part III. Res. Studies of Wash. State Univ. 28, March 1960.

III. Anthropology

Ackerman, R. E. Archeological survey, Glacier Bay National Monument, southeastern Alaska, parts I, II, III. Lab. of Anthr., Wash. State Univ., Pullman, Washington, 1964, 1965, 1967.

Alaska Magazine 1, March 1927. How the white men came to Lituya and what happened to Yeahlth-Kan who visited them: The Tlingit tradition of La Perouse's visit.

Emmons, G. T. The basketry of the Tlingit. Mem. of the Am. Mus. of Nat. Hist. 3, July 1903.

———. Native account of the meeting between La Perouse and the Tlingit. Am. Anthr. 13, April-June 1911.

Goldschmidt, W. R. and T. H. Haas. Possessory rights of the natives of southeastern Alaska. Rep. to the Comm. of Indian Aff., Washington, D.C., 1946 (mimeo).

Hall, G. Report of a visit to Hoonah, Alaska, July 1960, for the purpose of acquiring data on the Tlingit Indian legends of Glacier Bay. Manuscript, USNPS files, Juneau, Alaska.

Krause, A. The Tlingit Indians. Am. Ethn. Soc., Univ. of Wash. Press, Seattle, 1956.

Laguna, F. D. The story of a Tlingit community. Smithsonian Inst., Bur. Ethn. bull. 172, Washington, D.C., 1960.

———, et al. Archeology of the Yakutat Bay area, Alaska. Smithsonian Inst., Bur. Ethn. bull. 192, Washington, D.C., 1964.

Swanton, J. R. Social conditions, beliefs, and linguistic relationship of the Tlingit Indians. 26th ann. rep., Bur. Am. Ethn., Washington, D.C., 1908.

———. Tlingit myths and texts; Bur. Am. Ethn. bull. 39, Washington, D.C., 1909.

Wood, C. E. S. Among the Thlinkits in Alaska. Century Mag., July 1882.

IV. Journals, Reports, Charts

Alaska Mining Record, Juneau. 9, No. 9, 1896 pg. 5 (Lituya Bay gold mining). 9, No. 49, 1897 pg. 4 (Lituya Bay). March 4, 1895 (Berry Mining Dist., Glacier Bay).

Beardslee, L. A., Reports of. Sen. Ex. Doc. 71, 1882.

Cook, J. A voyage to the Pacific Ocean 1776-1780. London, 1784, 3 vols. and folio.

Dall, W. H. Alaska and its resources. Lee and Shepard, Boston, 1870.

———. Report on Mount St. Elias, Mount Fairweather, and some of the adjacent mountains. In U.S. Coast Surv. Rep. 1875. 44th Cong., 1st sess., Hse. ex. doc. 81, 1878.

———. Pacific Coast pilot, Alaska, part 1. U.S. Coast & Geod. Surv., 1883.

Davidson, G. Report of Assistant George Davidson relative to the coast, features, and resources of Alaska territory, 1867. 40th Cong., 2nd sess., Hse. ex. doc. 177 (Lituya Bay).

———. Coast Pilot of Alaska, part 1. U.S. Coast Surv., Washington, D.C., 1869.

———. Explanation of an Indian map. Mazama, April 1901.

———. Glaciers of Alaska that are shown on Russian charts or mentioned in older narratives. Geog. Soc. of the Pac., Trans. and Proc. 3, Ser. 2, San Francisco, June 1904.

Ecology 6, April 1925. Note on the establishment of Glacier Bay National Monument.

Golder, F. A. Bering's Voyages. Res. Ser., Am. Geog. Soc., New York, 1922, 2 vols.

International Boundary Commission Report, Tongass Passage to Mt. St. Elias, Dept. of State, 1952.

Ismaïloff (and Bocharoff). See Shelekhoff.

Lapérouse, J. F. A voyage 'round the world 1785-1788; trans. fr. the French. London, 1799, 3 vols. and folio.

Lebedev, D. M. Voyage of A. Tchirikov on packet boat *St. Paul* to American shores. Acad. of Sci., Moscow, 1951 (in Russian).

Reid, H. F. Notebooks and journals of expeditions of 1890 and 1892. Manuscript and transcript at World Data Ctr. A: Glaciology. Am. Geog. Soc., New York.

Scidmore, E. R. The first district of Alaska from Prince Frederick Sound to Yakutat Bay. In Rep. on Pop. and Res. of Alaska at the 11th census, 1890, Washington, D.C., 1893.

Shelekhoff, G. Voyages of, II. Cruise of the ship *Three Saints* from Kadiak to Ltua Bay. Pac. Manuscripts K-4, Russian America, Bancroft Library, Univ. of Calif.

Tebenkov, M. Atlas of the northwest shores of America and hydrographical notes to the atlas. St. Petersburg, 1852.

Trager, E. A. The Glacier Bay expedition of 1939. Manuscript report after the boundary enlargement of 1939. USNPS files, Juneau, Alaska.

Vancouver, G. A voyage of discovery to the North Pacific ocean and round the world. London, 1799, 3 vols. and folio.

V. History, Bibliography, Place Names

Arctic Bibliography, U.S. Government Printing Office, Washington, D.C.

Baker, Marcus. Geographic Dictionary of Alaska, second edition. USGS, Washington, D.C., 1906.

Bancroft, H. H. History of Alaska. San Francisco, 1886.

Black, B. History of Glacier Bay National Monument. Unpublished manuscript, USNPS files, Juneau, Alaska.

Cooper, W. S. A contribution to the history of Glacier Bay National Monument. Dept. of Bot., Univ. of Minn., 1956.

Farquhar, F. P. and M. P. Ashley. A list of publications relating to the mountains of Alaska, AAC, New York, 1934.

Lewis & Dryden. Marine history of the Pacific Northwest, ed. E. W. Wright, Portland, 1895 (reprinted 1961).

National Park Bibliography, II. Dept. of the Interior, 1941.

Roosevelt, Franklin D. and Conservation, 1911-1945, ed. E. B. Nixon. National Archives and Records Service, F.D.R. Library, Hyde Park, New York, 1957, 2 vols.

Wickersham, J. A bibliography of Alaskan literature, 1724-1924. Cordova Daily Times, 1927.

VI. Popular Accounts, Editorials

Alaska Magazine 1, March 1927. The Alaskan adventures of Jean Francois Galoup de La Perouse.

Alaska Sportsman. July 1936. The Glacier Bear; J. Krause. February 1938. Lituya, the bewitcher; J. Williams. February 1949. Gold at Lituya Bay; C. P. McBeth (1896 season). October 1958. Night of terror; H. Ulrich (giant wave of 1958). August 1964. Lituya's elusive gold; A. Mallory (1930's). May 1966. May 1893 (steamer *Seaolin* in Lituya Bay). September 1966. This month in Alaska's history; B. DeArmond (the wreck of the *Ancon*).

Alaska-Yukon Magazine, August 1908. Muir Glacier.

Andrews, C. L. Muir Glacier. Nat. Geog. 14, December 1903 (with note on Muir Glacier by G. K. Gilbert).

———. The retreat of Muir Glacier. Mountaineer 24, 1931.

Badè, W. F. The life and letters of John Muir. Houghton, Mifflin & Co., Cambridge, 1924, 2 vols.

Badlam, A. The wonders of Alaska. The Bancroft Co., San Francisco, 1890.

Baldwin, S. P. Muir Glacier, Alaska. Sci. Am. 66, April 9, 1892.

Beach, R. Personal exposures. Harper & Bros., New York, 1940.

Beardslee, L. A. Log of the *Favorite* 3 (August 20, 1880, in Glacier Bay). Letter to Forest and Stream; Forest and Stream 15, January 27, 1881 (signed 'Piseco').

Brown, D. M. More glaciers advance. Appalachia 19, June 1953.

Bruce, M. Alaska, its history and resources, gold fields, routes

and scenery. G. P. Putnam's Sons, New York, 1899.
Burroughs, J. Narrative of the expedition. Harriman Alaska Ser. 1, 1901.
———. Far and near. Houghton, Mifflin & Co., Cambridge, 1904.
Chickering, J. W., Jr. The Muir Glacier, Alaska. Sci. Am. Supp. 26, December 8, 1888.
Collis, S. M. A woman's trip to Alaska. Cassell Pub. Co., New York, 1890.
Deane, W. F. Muir Inlet ice factories. U.S. Coast and Geod. Surv. Jour., No. 1, January 1948.
Gannett, H. The Harriman Alaska expedition. Nat. Geog. 10, December 1899.
Gilbert, G. K. See C. L. Andrews (above).
Hallock, C. Our new Alaska. Forest and Stream Pub. Co., New York, 1886.
———. Our cache near the Pole. Broadway Pub. Co., New York, 1908.
Juneau Daily Empire, April 28, 1924. Editorial against establishment of the National Monument.
Kincaid, T. Harriman Alaska Expedition. Mazama 2, No. 2, 1901.
Lawrence, D. B. Some glaciers of southeast Alaska. Mazama 31, December 1949.
London, J. The unexpected. McClure's Mag., August 1906.
Martin, L. Glaciers and international boundaries. Sci. Am. Supp. 76, August 30, 1913.
———. Excursions in northern British Columbia and Yukon Terr. and along the N. Pac. coast, Guide Book 10. Geol. Surv., Ottawa, 1913.
Morse, F. The recession of the glaciers of Glacier Bay, Alaska. Nat. Geog. 19, January 1908.
Muir, J. Alaska. Am. Geol. 2, May 1893.
———. Discovery of Glacier Bay. Century Mag., n.s. 28, June 1895.
———. The Alaska trip. Century Mag. 54, August 1897.
———. An adventure with a dog and a glacier. Century Mag. 54, September 1897.
———. Stickeen. Houghton, Mifflin & Co., Cambridge, 1909.
———. Travels in Alaska. Houghton, Mifflin & Co., Cambridge, 1915.
Pacific Discovery. September-October 1959. Earthquake in Lituya Bay; B. Powell. January-February 1960. Voyage to Vanikoro; Discombe and Anthonioz (Lapérouse).
Saturday Evening Post, August 15, 1936. Editorial against opening the National Monument to mining.
Scidmore, E. R. Alaska, its southern coast and the Sitkan archipelago. D. Lathrop & Co., Boston, 1885.
———. The Muir Glacier in Alaska. Harper's Weekly 36, July 23, 1892.
———. Goat-hunting at Glacier Bay, Alaska. Californian Illus. Mag. 5, April 1894.
———. The discovery of Glacier Bay, Alaska. Nat. Geog. 7, April 1896.
———. Appleton's guide book to Alaska and the northwest coast. D. Appleton & Co., New York, 1899.
Williams, J. Alaskan adventure. The Telegraph Press, Harrisburg, Pennsylvania, 1952.
Woolen, W. W. The inside passage to Alaska, 1792-1920. Arthur H. Clark Co., Cleveland, 1924.
Young, S. H. Alaska days with John Muir. F. H. Revell Co., New York, 1915.
———. Alaska days with John Muir. The Outlook, May 26, June 23 and July 28, 1915.
———. Hall Young of Alaska, the Mushing Parson. Fleming H. Revell Co., New York, Chicago, 1927.

VII. Mountaineering

Bohn, D. Portrait of an expedition. AAJ 13, 1963.
Carpé, A. An attempt on Mt. Fairweather. Appalachia 16, December 1926.
———. The conquest of Mt. Fairweather. Alpine Jour. 43, 1931.
———. The climb of Mount Fairweather. Mountaineer 24, 1931.
———. Mt. Fairweather conquered. AAJ 1, 1931 (letter).
———. The ascent of Mt. Fairweather. Harvard Mountaineering 3, 1931-2.
Child, W. S. Crillon 1933. AAJ 2, 1934.
Field, W. O. The Fairweather Range, mountaineering and glacier studies. Appalachia 16, December 1926.
Geog. Rev., October 1931. (Note on the Fairweather climb.)
Ladd, W. S. The Fairweather Mountains. AAJ 1, 1929.
———. The Fairweather climb. AAJ 1, 1932.
Miller, M. M. Mt. Bertha. Mountaineer 33, 1940.
———. Mt. Bertha, Fairweather Range, 1940. Harvard Mountaineering 6, 1943.
Moore, T. Mt. Fairweather is conquered at last. The Sportsman 10, October 1931.
Paumgarten, H. An attempt on Mt. Crillon. Alpine Jour. 45, May 1933.
Scheiblehner, L. East face of La Perouse, Fairweather Range. AAJ 12, 1960.
Seitz, J. F. Ascent of Mount La Perouse. AAJ 8, 1953.
Sherman, P. and F. Broda. Fairweather, the centennial summit. CAJ 42, 1959.
Washburn, H. B. Bradford on Mt. Fairweather. Putnam's Sons, New York, 1930.
———. Backpacking to Fairweather. Sportsman Magazine, April 1931.
———. The attack on Crillon. Appalachia 20, June 1934.
———. The conquest of Mt. Crillon. Nat. Geog., March 1935.
———. The ascent of Mt. Bertha. AAJ 4, 1941.
———. (Note on Mt. Fairweather attempt), Appalachia 18, December 1930.
———. Mt. Crillon, 1934. Harvard Mountaineering 4, 1936.

VIII. Photographic Sources

Harriman Alaska Expedition, souvenir album, May-August 1899, 2 vols., Univ. of Wash. Library, Seattle, Washington. Photographs by Edward Curtis and Grove Karl Gilbert.
Museum of Science, Science Park, Boston. Aerial and high mountain photographs by Bradford Washburn.
Photo Shop Studio, Sitka, Alaska. 1928 expedition to Glacier Bay. Photographs by James H. Gilpatrick.
University of Oregon Library. C. L. Andrews collection. *In* Special collections. Photographs by C. L. Andrews, in Glacier Bay 1903 and 1913.
U.S. Geological Survey, Photographic Library, Federal Center, Denver. Aerial photographs and photographs from the Wright brothers unpublished ms., Glacier Bay 1906 and 1931.
U.S. National Park Service, Park Headquarters, Glacier Bay National Monument, Bartlett Cove, Alaska. General collection, contemporary.
Washington State Historical Museum Library, Tacoma. Some historical, including Edward Curtis, in Glacier Bay 1899.
World Data Center A: Glaciology, American Geographical Society, New York. Comprehensive historical, beginning 1883.

Index

Note: Glacier Bay has been abbreviated here as GB.

Adams, C.A.: in GB 1890, 64
Alder: in nitrogen fixation, 49
Ancon, steamer: in GB 1884, 59, 61
Artists: in GB, 78fn32
Asónques: in GB 1877, 43

Baker, Marcus: in Lituya Bay 1874, 32
Bartlett Bay (Cove): naming 1883, 57; 1899 earthquake, 73
Bates, Robert: on Huscroft of Lituya Bay, 33, 34
Bay of great glaciers: mentioned to G. Davidson, 43; John Muir's arrival in, 45
Beach, Rex: on Joe Ibach, 87; mining campaign, 89; and democracy, 99, 101. *See also* GBNM, mining campaign
Beardslee, L. A.: in GB 1880, 50, 52; first chart of GB, 52
Beardslee Islands: naming 1880, 52
Berg Bay: John Muir's camp 1879, 45
Bering, Vitus: naming of Mount St. Elias 1741, 25
Boussole, frigate: in Lituya Bay 1786, 27
Brady, John G.: in GB 1878, 54fn32
Burroughs, John: in GB 1899, 71, 73
Buschmann, August: in GB (Bartlett Bay) 1899, 73, 78fn42

Cabin group: at Reid Inlet, landscaping of, 89
Canadian port: in Tarr Inlet, 87, 92fn15
Carolus, Pt.: in 1794, 54fn3. *See also* Whidbey, Lt.
Carpé, Allen: on Huscroft of Lituya Bay, 34
Carroll, Capt. James: in GB 1883, 57, 59; discussion of, 59; in GB 1890, 64, 66; photograph, 68; in GB 1900, 75; in GB 1907, 75; story about, 78fn11
Carroll Glacier: naming 1892, 71
Casement, R. L.: in GB 1890, 64
Cenotaph Island: Lapérouse at, 1786, 27; naming 1786, 29; placing of cenotaph 1786, 29
Climbing: *See* Pyramid Peak
Cocheen: of the Hoonahs, in GB 1877, 43
Cook, Capt. James: aboard H.M.S. *Resolution* 1778, 26
Coon-nah-nah-thklé: with C. E. S. Wood, in GB 1877, 45; temporary camp, 54fn14
Cooper, W. S.: in GB, four expeditions, 82; photograph, 84; in GB 1921, 1935, 84; summary of observations, 85; in GB 1966, 145; mentioned, 87. *See also* GBNM: establishment; mining campaign
Cozian: in GB 1880, 54fn32
Cross Sound: naming 1778, 26; mentioned, 38
Curtis, Edward: in GB 1899, 71, 73
Cushing, H. P.: in GB 1890, 64

Dall, W. H.: in Lituya Bay 1874, 32
Davidson, G.: at Chilkat 1869, 43
Dennin, Michael: Nelson party, in Lituya Bay 1898, 32, 33
Discovery, H.M.S.: at Port Althorp 1794, 38
Dundas Bay: Lt. Whidbey in, 1794, 38; John Muir in, 1880, 49; cannery, 73; history of, 78fn42
Dundas, Pt.: naming 1794, 38

Earthquake: of 1899 in GB, 73, 75
Ecology: succession, 41; changes in landscape, 49, 50; succession in Muir Inlet, 50; succession in GB, 50; general, 82, 84, 85
Excursion Inlet: Section removed from Monument, 104

Fairweather, Cape: naming 1778, 26

Fairweather, Mount: naming 1778, 26
Fairweather Range: first sighted 1741, 25
Favorite, steamer: in GB 1880, 50, 52
Field, William O.: photograph, 108; American Geographical Society map, 109; in GB 1966, 154

Geikie Glacier: discovery 1879, 47
Geology: G. W. Lamplugh, 61; H. F. Reid, 80; modern era, 85, 87; references, 92fn14
George, W. E.: pilot, in GB 1883, 57
George W. Elder, steamer: in GB 1890, 64; in GB 1899, 71
Giant wave: of 1936, 34; of 1853, 35; of 1958, 35
Glacier Bay: length, 1794 to present, 40; discovery, 40; first exploration, 43, 45; John Muir's arrival 1879, 45; descriptive, 47, 57, 59, 61, 64, 66, 71, 73, 75; first chart, 52; naming 1880, 52; place names in, 52
Glacier Bay National Monument: Advisory Board resolution, 106
— boundary change, 104; enlargement, 101, 104
— establishment: W. S. Cooper, 94, 96; Ecological Soc. Am., 94; R. F. Griggs, 94; *Juneau Daily Empire* editorial, 94, 96; temporary withdrawal of 1924, 94; proc. of 1925, 96
— largest unit in Park system, 106
— mining campaign: correspondence, 96-97, 99; National Park Service, 97; act of June 1936, 99; *Saturday Evening Post* editorial, 101; mining bill, 106fn15
— National Park Service officials in: E. A. Trager and F. T. Been, 104; Advisory Board, R. Howe, L. J. Mitchell, 106
Glaciology: recession, 49, 50; G. F. Wright, 61, 64; H. F. Reid, 71, 80; F. E. and C. W. Wright, 80; modern era, 85, 87; references, 92fn14
Goldthwait, R. P.: Inst. of Polar Studies in GB, 85, 87
Grand Pacific Glacier: discovery 1879, 47; retreat of, 50
Griggs, R. F., 94, 106fn2
Gustavus lands: removal from Monument, 104

Hallock, C.: in GB 1884, 59, 61
Hanging of 1899: Lituya Bay, 33, 36fn17; sequel, 36fn19
Harbeson, S.: in Dundas Bay, 78fn42
Harriman Alaska Expedition: in GB 1899, 71, 73
Haselton, G.: geology, 85; in GB 1964, 124, 127
Historical reproductions: Fairweather Range by J. E. Stuart, 20; Tlingit, from Lapérouse, 29; Lapérouse, loss of boats 1786, 30-31; Jim Huscroft, 34; Vancouver map 1794, 40; sea otter from Vancouver, 41; Russell Island 1879 by John Muir, 48; Glacier Bay by A. Langsford, 56; Muir Glacier 1893, 62-63; John Muir's cabin 1890, 67; Capt. Carroll, 68; Crevasse in Muir Glacier, 68; Steamer *Queen* at Muir Glacier, 69; W. S. Cooper, 84; Capt. Tom Smith, 84; *Yakobi* at Reid Inlet, 85; Joe and Muz Ibach, 96; Reid Glacier 1929, 97; H. F. Reid map, 108; William O. Field, 108
Hoonah: John Muir visit 1879, 45
Hoonahs: in GB, 43; C. E. S. Wood in GB with, 43; John Muir in GB with, 47, 49
Horsman, W.: in Dundas Bay, 78fn42
Howe, R.: National Park Service, in GB 1966, 106
Hugh Miller Glacier: discovery 1879, 47
Huscroft, J.: story, 33-34, 35; photograph, 34; B. Washburn plaque, 34
Hypsithermal period: in GB, 84

Ibach, Joe and Muz: description, 87; at Lemesurier Island, 87; at Reid Inlet, 87, 89; photograph, 96
Ibach, H.: in Dundas Bay, 78fn42

Idaho, steamer: first commercial steamer in GB, 1883, 57; in GB 1884, 59; history, 78fn2
Il-khak: of Yakutat Bay, Koloshi chief, 32
Interstadial stumps, 57, 66, 82, 84, 85
Ismaïloff (and Bocharoff): in Lituya Bay 1788, 32; burial of copper plate, 32

Jamestown, U.S.S.: at Sitka 1880, 52
Johns Hopkins Inlet: first penetrated 1929, 82
Juneau Daily Empire: editorial against Monument, 94, 96

Kadichan: with John Muir, 45, 47
Kah-Lituya: legend of (Tlingit), 35
Kahsteen: legend of (Tlingit), 41
Klohkutz: Chilkat chief, and G. Davidson, 43
Kooshta-kah: land otter man, 45; legend of (Tlingit), 54fn18

Lamplugh, G. W.: in GB 1884, 61
Land emergence, 85
Lapérouse: in Lituya Bay 1786, 27; narrative, 27-29; loss of boats, 29; engravings, 29, 30-31
Lawrence, D. B.: ecology, 85
LeMesurier: with Lt. Whidbey 1794, 40
Lituya Bay: Yeahlth's arrival, legend of (Tlingit), 26, 27; Tlingits entering, 28; 1958 earthquake, 35; visits to, 36fn14. *See also* Giant wave; Huscroft, J.; Ismaïloff (Bocharoff); Kah-Lituya; Prospecting; Tlingits; Trial; Yosemite; *Yukon*, steamer
Loomis, H.: with John Muir 1890, 64

McBride, H.: in GB 1890, 64
Mapping: Lt. Whidbey, Cross Sound 1794, 38, 40; H. F. Reid, GB 1890, 64, 69, and 1892, 71
Maps: Vancouver 1794, 40; H. F. Reid 1890-92, 108; American Geographical Society, termini-positions 1794-present, 109; M. Sunwoo, end papers
Martin, L., 82, 87
Mining: claims at Reid Inlet, 87, 89
Mitchell, L. J.: National Park Service, 106
Moore, B.: first to suggest Monument, 94
Morse, J. F. in GB 1890, 64
Muir, John: trip of 1879, 45, 47, 54fn21; first view of GB, 47; 1880 trip, 47-48, 49, 50; Muir Glacier sled trip, 66; building of cabin 1890, 66; ascent of Snow Dome, 66
Muir, Camp: naming 1890, 64
Muir Glacier: retreat of, 50; naming 1883, 57; first tourists landed, 59; descriptive, 57, 59, 61; 1899 earthquake, 73; following earthquake, 75
Muir Inlet: naming 1883, 57; ice advance, 84; ice recession, 84. *See also* Earthquake; Ecology; Geology; Glaciology

National Park Service: largest unit in Park system, 106
— officials in G.B.: E. Trager, F. T. Been, 104; Advisory Board, R. Howe, L. J. Mitchell, 106
Nelson, E. W. and H.: in Lituya Bay 1898-99, 32, 33

Pacific Coast Steamship Co., 59, 78fn12
Parker, A. L. and L. F.: mines in GB, 92fn19
Pleasant Island: John Muir at, 1879, 45
Port Althorp: H.M.S. *Discovery* anchored at, 1794, 38
Port des Français (Lituya Bay): naming 1786, 27
Prospecting: on Lituya Bay coast, 33; at Reid Inlet, 87
Pyramid Peak: first roped ascent in Monument 1890, 68

Queen Inlet: naming 1892, 71
Queen, steamer: description, 59; in GB 1890, 64, 66, 68; photograph, 69; in GB 1892, first ship north of Tlingit Pt., 71; in GB 1900, 75; travel folder, 78fn12; 1892 soundings, H. F. Reid map, 108

Recession: Grand Pacific Glacier, 50; Muir Glacier, 50; in Muir Inlet, 84; in Glacier Bay, 84
Reid, H. F.: in GB 1890, 64; first map 1890, 64; mapping 1890, 64, 69; mapping 1892, 71; first complete map, 71; in GB 1931, 80; section 1890-92 map, 108
Resolution, H.M.S.: off Cross Sound 1778, 26
Richardson, T. J.: artist, in GB 1891, 69, 71
Russell, I. C.: description of the Yukon, 50; mentioned, 64
Russell Island: climbing of, John Muir, 47; in 1879, 54fn24; mentioned, 43

St. Elias, Mount: naming 1741, 25
St. Elias's silver bear: in GB 1877, 43, 54fn13
St. Paul, packet boat: off northwest coast 1741, 25. *See also* Tchirikov, A.
Scidmore, E. R.: in GB 1883, 57, 59; in GB 1884, 59; in GB 1891, 69; identification, 78fn3
Shaw-whad-seet: legend of (Tlingit), 41
Sitadakay (Bay from where the ice receded), 47
Smith, Capt. Tom: in GB 1916, 1929, 1935, 82; photograph, 84; letter to W. S. Cooper, 87; on the Ibachs, 89
Spencer, Cape: Lt. Whidbey at, 1794, 38
Spokane, steamer: travel folder, 61; in GB 1907, 75
Stickeen: trip of 1880, 48; on the Brady Glacier, 48-49

Taik-nukh-Takhtu-yakh: chief, Lituya Bay 1788, 32
Taylor, C. H.: with C. E. S. Wood 1877, 43
Taylor, L. D.: glaciology, 85
Taylor Bay: discovery 1794, 38; deserted Indian village 1794, 38; exploration 1877, 43; exploration 1880, 48; deserted Indian village in 1880, 48; Hoonahs in, 49
Tchirikov, A.: commanding *St. Paul* 1741, 25; loss of boats, 25, 26
Terminal moraine: at Bartlett Cove, 85
Terminus: of trunk glacier 1835, 1855, 49; in 1855, 1860, 1879, 1880-92, 50
Three Saints, galleon: in Lituya Bay 1788, 32
Tlingit legend: Yeahlth, 26, 27; giant wave, 35; Kah-Lituya, 35; GB, 41; Kahsteen, 41; Shaw-whad-seet, 41, 54fn6; Kooshta-kah, 45, 54fn18
Tlingits: in Lituya Bay, 36fn13, 18
Topeka, City of, steamer: in GB 1901, 75
Toyatte: with John Muir 1879, 45, 47; shooting of, 48
Trial: citizens court, Lituya Bay 1899, 33

Vancouver, Capt. George: surveys of 1794, 38, 40; mentioned, 26

Wachusett Inlet: gravels, 80, 82
Washburn, B.: plaque, Huscroft of Lituya Bay, 34
Whidbey, Lt.: mapping from the long boats 1794, 38; Indian visitation, Dundas Bay, 38; Indian visitation, Pt. Carolus, 40; discovery of GB, 1794, 40; terminus of 1794, 54fn3; comparison of ice thickness, 80
White, Nina and Jimmy: in Dundas Bay, 78fn42
Willoughby, R.: in GB 1880, 52; previous explorations in GB, 52; in GB 1883, 57; explorations and mines, 54fn32
Willoughby Island: L. A. Beardslee at, 1880, 52; creation of Berry Mining Dist. 1880, 54fn32
Wood, C. E. S.: in GB 1877, 43, 45
Wright, F. E. and C. W.: in GB and Lituya Bay 1906, 80
Wright, G. F.: rejection of Tlingit tradition, 41; in GB 1886, 61, 64

Yakobi, steamer: in GB 1929, 1935, 82; photograph, 85; in GB 1938, 89
Yeahlth: legend of (Tlingit), 26, 27, 36fn7
York, W.: with John Muir 1890, 66, 68
Yosemite: comparison with Lituya Bay, 32
Youmans, K.: in GB 1964, 127
Young, S. Hall: with John Muir 1879, 45, 47; with John Muir 1880, 47-48, 49
Yukon, steamer: in Lituya Bay 1874, 32

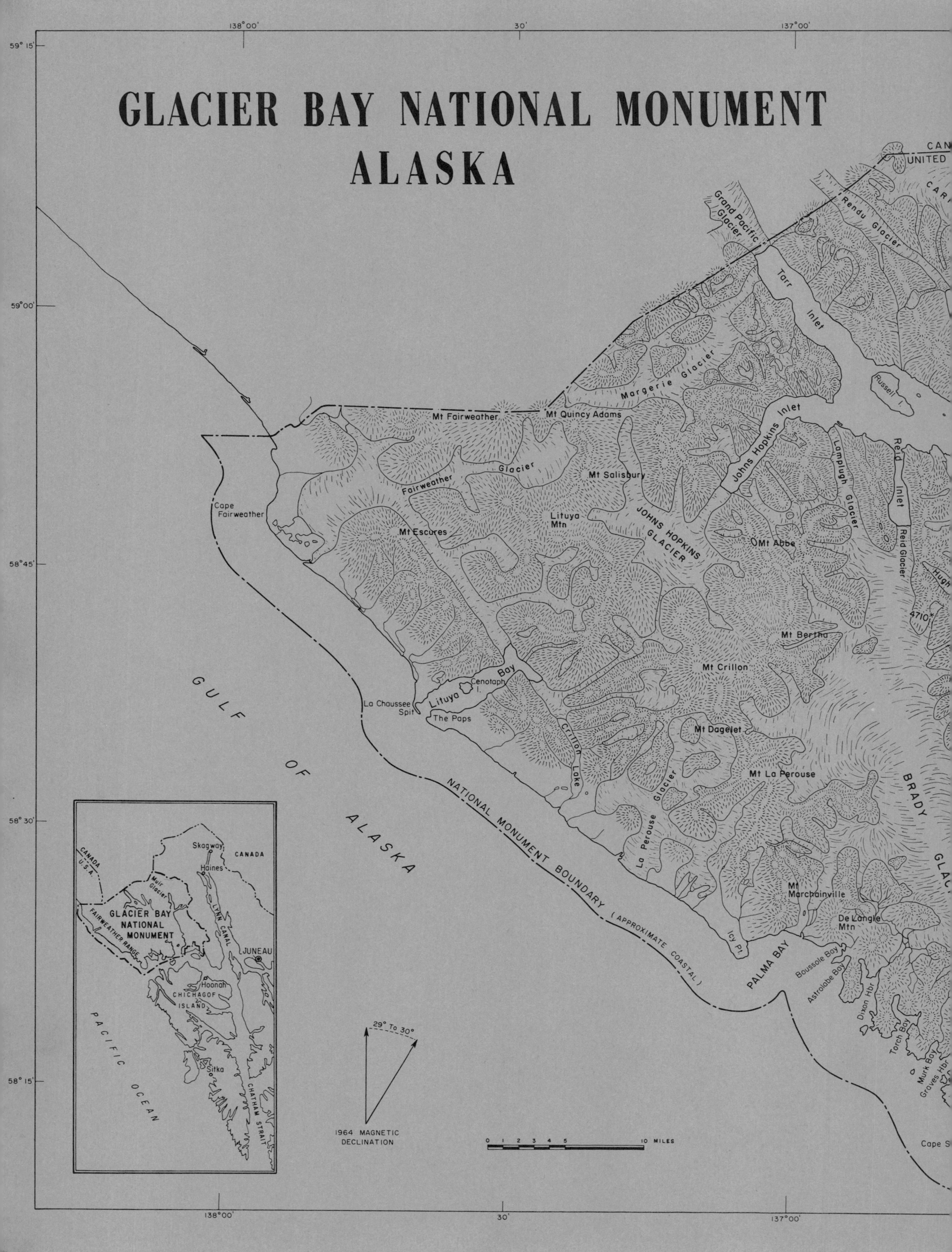